The
RESURRECTED
PIRATE

The Life, Death, and Subsequent Career
of the Notorious George Lowther

CRAIG S. CHAPMAN

Schiffer
Military History

4880 Lower Valley Road
Atglen, PA 19310

Designed by Jack Chappell
Cover design by Jack Chappell
Type set in Carta Marina/Blackbeard/Esperanza/Garamond

ISBN: 978-0-7643-6907-0
Ebook: 978-1-5073-0513-3
Printed in India

Published by Schiffer Publishing, Ltd.
4880 Lower Valley Road
Atglen, PA 19310
Phone: (610) 593-1777; Fax: (610) 593-2002
Email: Info@schifferbooks.com
Web: www.schifferbooks.com

For our complete selection of fine books on this and related subjects,
please visit our website at www.schifferbooks.com. You may also write
for a free catalog.
    Schiffer Publishing's titles are available at special discounts for bulk
purchases for sales promotions or premiums. Special editions, including
personalized covers, corporate imprints, and excerpts, can be created in large
quantities for special needs. For more information, contact the publisher.
    We are always looking for people to write books on new and related
subjects. If you have an idea for a book, please contact us at proposals@
schifferbooks.com.

To Ziko, Dahlia, Abby, Liam, Ben, and Dan—history has much to teach.

The violence of the wicked will drag them away.

—Proverbs

Ignominy thirsts for respect.

—Victor Hugo, *Les Miserables*

CONTENTS

MAPS

ACKNOWLEDGMENTS

Although much has been written about pirates such as George Lowther, I knew this project would require digging past the superficial histories and down to contemporaneous records, where a truer account of his life might emerge. First, let me recognize three institutions that provided much of what I needed. The online resources of the University of North Carolina–Chapel Hill Library were particularly helpful in locating newspaper accounts from that era, crucial sources that often included testimonies about recent pirate attacks. The two most vital repositories of early-eighteenth-century records are the National Archives at Kew and the National Maritime Museum in Greenwich, both in the United Kingdom. I owe many thanks to archive researcher Len Barnett, who spent days poring through scribbled captains' logs, lieutenants' logs, muster rolls, paybooks, etc. Len made critical discoveries in these old records that opened a fuller picture of George Lowther's life. Research by Dr. Joseph Gibbs pointed me to important sources about the Royal African Company and the mutiny led by Lowther and Capt. John Massey. Boston tour operator Benjamin Edwards and the director of the Charleston Museum, Carl Borick, provided useful information about particular episodes in Lowther's sea depredations.

Several individuals assisted me with facts, observations, and critiques. Richard Blakemore and Duncan Harrington piloted me through details of British maritime practices and court documents (written in Latin). I also leaned on piracy experts Benerson Little and Cindy Vallar to ensure that my version of events was consistent with pirate activity in the early 1700s. Once the factual account was settled, I relied on critiques from my literary friends, Thomas Burns and Paul Crockett. Their feedback enhanced my narrative into something more palatable for readers. I also owe thanks to Greg Johnson for his tireless support.

Most of all, I dearly value the encouragement (not to mention the forbearance) of my loving wife, Mary, who stood by me as I struggled to put this remarkable story together.

PROLOGUE

T his work is a dividend from my previous book, *Disaster on the Spanish Main: The Tragic British-American Expedition to the West Indies during the War of Jenkins' Ear*. While chronicling the imperial conflict between Britain and Spain in the Caribbean, I unexpectedly came across an unusual character who played a significant role in the later stages of the campaign: George Lowther. Admiral Vernon, who had captured Porto Bello at the beginning of the war, recruited Lowther to gather intelligence about Spain's colonial possessions. Identified mostly as "Lowther the pirate," he gained a seat at the table among the generals and admirals as they planned operations in Cuba and Panama in 1741–42. The label piqued my curiosity. A quick search revealed that George Lowther had indeed been a well-known and feared buccaneer during the heyday of Atlantic piracy, an original "pirate of the Caribbean." He was one of the initial seventeen pirates written up in Charles Johnson's seminal work, *A General History of the Pyrates*. He had launched a mutiny aboard a slave ship, then led a company of sea bandits that terrorized the West Indies and coast of North America for over two years. Yet, the most astonishing fact I discovered while reading his biography was that he had killed himself in 1723—sixteen years before he made contact with Admiral Vernon.

Reading further, I learned that Johnson was not the only historian who was mistaken about Lowther's supposed suicide: all pirate sources listed his death in 1723. Strangely, there was no secret about his later life. Admiral Vernon's papers, later edited and published by Bryan Ranft, frequently mentioned Lowther, as did other documents from the British expedition. The few historians who wrote about the War of Jenkins' Ear, such as Robert Beatson (1804), Herbert Richmond (1920), and Richard Harding (1991), freely cited Lowther's participation in British operations. The evidence was apparent, but the separate cultures of naval and piracy historians had obstructed communications in regard to George Lowther.

Few things excite historians more than an opportunity to correct the historical record with newly discovered facts, or in this case, overlooked facts. I took the plunge and studied Lowther in greater depth.

Researching a pirate biography poses challenges. Records are scarce: they left no captains' logs, ships' rosters, or autobiographies. Nevertheless, enterprising researchers can still find firsthand testimonies and original sources. Accessing contemporaneous newspaper accounts, archival records, naval logs, court documents, etc. allowed me to go beyond Johnson's colorful and well-traveled description of Lowther's depredations at sea.

The more I learned, the better his story became. Crucial details emerged that enabled me to reconstruct parts of his pre- and postpiracy life, offering a different context to his character. More-precise information gave me new insights into his habits and mindset as he roamed the Atlantic. His close association with the likes of Edward Low and Francis Spriggs, as well as his relatively long pirating career, made him a useful subject to reveal the conditions, pressures, and truths of the sea-robbing vocation. Lowther's actions as a pirate captain yielded interesting aspects to his nature, leadership, and decision-making. His story, told from his point of view, exposes the brutal yet seductive pirate way of life and the trauma it inflicted on its victims, as well as the perpetrators themselves.

Looking at Lowther's whole life, not just his sea-roving days, unveiled a picture of the man that was far more interesting and complicated than the brute Johnson described. He devoted his last years in a failed personal quest to undo the damage he had done to his name and, thereby, provided a dramatic and emotional element to his tale.

A story written from a seafarer's viewpoint will, of necessity, encounter marine terminology, almost a separate language onto itself. This book preserves the vocabulary and jargon of British tars from the age of sail, not just for accuracy but also to establish the atmosphere of being on the deck of Lowther's pirate sloop as he trolls the sea lanes and bears down on his prey. I am sensitive that readers may stumble over authentic, though obscure, terms such as "clapp'd on a wind" or "anchor a thwart their harse," but the quotes and expressions from the era make important contributions to the settings and senses of this history. An extensive glossary is included to guide readers through the picaresque vernacular.

A potential source of confusion for early-eighteenth-century histories stems from the calendars used by different nations. By 1700, Catholic countries and most of Protestant western Europe had adopted the Gregorian calendar, but not Great Britain. British histories, therefore, list dates of events as happening eleven days earlier than Spanish or French sources. Because the great majority of cited evidence comes from English-speaking sources, dates are given according to the Julian calendar.

This book illuminates previously hidden years of George Lowther's life, but there are parts still obscured, and some mysteries are likely sealed forever, such as how he escaped from Blanco Island. However, opportunities exist for further research. With more digging, his family origins and earlier service in the Royal Navy could be more fully developed. Some details about his years in Panama and his business activity in Jamaica may eventually come to light. George Lowther was an interesting person whose bizarre life still holds future revelations to entertain researchers and readers alike, something that would be a worthwhile dividend from this work.

· CHAPTER 1 ·

A LIFE AT SEA

BLANQUILLA ISLAND, OFF TIERRA FIRME
(MODERN VENEZUELA), OCTOBER 1723

He could hear them coming—coming for him. Spaniards this time. Armed with pistols, muskets, and swords, they crashed through the underbrush and slashed away at the loose foliage, cursing and swearing at the hot work and sweltering conditions. Teams of them roamed the bleak Caribbean isle, tracking signs in the sand and searching under every shrub—coming for him.

George Lowther, former Royal Navy seaman, one time mate on a slave ship, and, of late, pirate captain, had to keep moving like the proverbial prey in a fox hunt. He was chased by a rancorous band sent by a Spanish governor to bring him to justice. A few weeks earlier, a South Sea Company slave ship, *Eagle*, surprised him and his pirate crew while they were careening their sloop. The slave traders seized the sloop and most of his crew while he and the rest of his men fled into the brush. *Eagle* hauled off the pirate sloop to a Spanish port, stranding Lowther and a few of his loyal crew on a miserably small spot of land in a vast sea. Blanco Island, flat and sterile, offered no secure hiding places. The soil, soft enough for the iguanas to leave claw marks, would show his footprints and lead his pursuers straight to any haven he might use. No way to flee, either. He could go only a few miles in any direction before reaching the land's end where the angry sea slapped the island's rocky shoreline, forming an impenetrable barrier. Trapped like a rat in a terrier pen, Lowther had no way to avoid the patrols other than dodging into the thickest tangles of prickly pear cacti and lignum vitae trees. He could barely push through the coppice, because the branches, dense and stiff, could be used to stave in a man's skull without sustaining a dent. Scratched by thorns and raked by the brush, Lowther dove into the most-abrasive scrub to throw off and discourage his pursuers.

The search dragged on. Every so often, Lowther could hear the Spaniards' lusty shouts whenever they captured one of his crew. After beating and binding their hapless victim and mocking his piteous cries for mercy, the patrols dragged the doomed pirate back to their ship. From there the Spaniards would haul his shipmate back to Cumana, where a cruel and certain fate awaited him. Some of Lowther's crew, the weak and stupid, gave up and surrendered, hoping for leniency. They were spared the gallows only to be sentenced to a slave galley: a more protracted form of execution.

Lowther expected no mercy and had no desire to share the same fate as John Massey or Charles Harris, two of his past partners—better to keep moving from thicket to thicket. He could only hope that the patrols would tire of their pursuit before they cornered him, or he dropped from exhaustion. It was a slim hope, at best. Even if he avoided their snares, they could simply camp at the freshwater spring near the anchorage and wait for him to drag his desiccated body to them or die of thirst. Should he manage to evade capture, his future looked almost as bleak. He would be left marooned on a desolate island in the midst of the sea to thirst and hunger, and then to die, alone and unattended. The pirate's awful circumstances played on his mind too, reminding him that his own evil acts had brought him to this extremity. As one contemporary preacher wondered, "In how sad a Case is that Person then, who has a vast Load of Sin upon his Conscience?"[1]

Driven to desperation, where could the pirate find solace? Did he plead to the face of fortune that had so recently turned from him, or bargain with the devil for one last favor, though he had nothing left to offer? Or did he pray to the God he had forsaken years earlier, begging for one last chance at redemption?

Reflecting back to his God-fearing days, Lowther could feel only remorse and anguish at what had become of his life at sea, a life that had once shown honor and promise but was ending in horror and disgrace.

DEPTFORD DOCK, LONDON, ENGLAND, MARCH 5, 1715

Breathing in a lungful of the brackish scents of the Thames, Able Seaman George Lowther tossed his kit into a launch tied up at the dock and climbed aboard. The boat's crew pulled him and several other sailors out to HMS *Assistance*, a fifty-gun ship moored in the river. The moment the launch pulled alongside, Lowther lifted his kit to his shoulder and climbed up the ladder to the deck of the fourth-rate ship of the line that had recently come out of ordinary (*see Glossary*). He gave his name to the purser's mate to record in the log, then went below to stake out a place to string his hammock and lay claim to one of the sea chests in the cramped space before the mast. As an experienced mariner and one of the first to sign aboard, he could pick a better sleeping spot than the ordinary seamen who were just breaking into the trade. Lowther called London his home and likely came from Westminster. Regardless of his neighborhood upbringing, his time at sea had stamped him into the image of the many sailors who roamed the docks of Rotherhithe and Wapping dressed in woolen Monmouth caps, short coats, and canvas trousers stained with tar. He had learned his trade on ships tossed about on the sea, and could stand on the "horses" strung along a yardarm as confidently as he could scamper up the shrouds. Years of experience aboard ship had drilled naval jargon into his head, to the point that he could point out to a lubber the difference between a clew line, brace, lift, bowline, and stay, all of which looked like a thousand random ropes strung overhead to a novice mariner.[2]

No physical description of George Lowther has survived other than an oblique reference that he was a large "lusty man." Little is known about his origins. Given his rating as an able seaman, he had already spent time at sea, which suggests that he was born before 1695. A baptismal record exists from 1685 at St. Martin-in-the-Fields Parish in Westminster for a George Lowther, son of William and Rachel, but others with the same name appear in London during the period, frustrating a firm identification. Although the surname is ancient and many branches of the family counted themselves among the landed gentry, he appears to have come from humble beginnings.[3]

Men such as Lowther had many different reasons for going to sea, most born of necessity. Lack of opportunity, debts, and utter poverty forced large numbers of young men to seek some form of living aboard navy or merchant ships. During the recent war with France and Spain, even the reluctant found themselves forced into Her Majesty's service after a press gang yanked them off a merchant ship or out of a local tavern. On the other hand, Lowther may have been motivated to join the fleet to serve the Crown against its Bourbon enemies. Whatever his original circumstance, he had adapted to a seaman's life. Once he stowed his personal gear, he greeted his new shipmates and began attending to the needs of the ship.[4]

HMS *Assistance* had originally launched sixty-five years earlier, not long after King Charles I's beheading. After seeing action in several wars, the ship had gone in for its third refit to a fifty-gun configuration in 1713. Like most Royal Navy vessels, *Assistance* was "ship-rigged," with square sails hung from horizontal spars athwart the hull, as opposed to "fore-and-aft-rigged" vessels, which have their sails attached vertically to the masts in line with the hull. Its main armament consisted of twenty-two 18-pounder culverins on the lower gun deck and twenty-two 9-pounder demiculverins on the upper gun deck. The ship mounted another six 6-pounder sakers in the forecastle and quarterdeck. Coming out of the Limehouse drydock, *Assistance* measured 130 feet stem to stern and 35 feet at the beam, with a burthen of 710 tons. Seaman Lowther was one of 240 men in its crew.[5]

The ship might have been old, but its newly appointed commander was a young and promising naval officer, Capt. Edward Vernon. The twenty-nine-year-old had gone from a "king's letter-boy" to ship's captain during the War of the

Spanish Succession. In 1707 he had saved his ship, HMS *Rye*, when Adm. Cloudesley Shovell's fleet had run aground on the Scilly Islands, taking four of Her Majesty's ships and 1,500–2,000 sailors to the bottom, including the admiral. Vernon moved to the fifty-gun HMS *Jersey* after the disaster and took it to the Caribbean to join Capt. Charles Wager's squadron. His career suddenly stalled in 1712 when his Tory politics ran afoul of the incoming Whig government, and he was forced onto half pay. However, his reputation as a skilled seaman and competent leader helped restore him to a ship's command after a two-and-a-half-year hiatus.[6]

Vernon, son of a former secretary of state, represented a new breed of ship's captain. Unlike the commanders of previous generations who disdained the lower classes, he had come to value the health, morale, and well-being of his crew. He had served alongside them in naval battles as a junior officer and observed the difference in performance between a robust sailor and a sickly one. As historian Peter Kemp remarked, Vernon "laboured long and assiduously for the betterment of conditions on board ship." He made recommendations to improve air circulation below decks for health reasons and would famously alter the liquor ration to reduce drunkenness aboard ship. Sailors named the watered-down concoction "grog" after his nickname "Old Grog," a moniker he acquired because he often wore a grogram coat at sea. Stern but compassionate, Vernon had little difficulty recruiting his crews once his name began circulating among Royal Navy seamen. Instead of resorting to impressment, Vernon was able to send surplus mariners from *Assistance* to other ships to help them fill their complements.[7]

It was no coincidence that George Lowther joined Vernon's crew. The two had served together at some point and knew each other—more than that, they respected one another. Lowther admired the officer's seamanship and discipline, while Vernon thought highly of Lowther's skills and dependability. Royal Navy seamen were free to pick the ships they signed on to, and Lowther, familiar with Captain Vernon, volunteered for *Assistance*.[8]

A navy seaman's life was sometimes dangerous, often miserable, and always arduous. As one popular ballad put it, a sailor was in for "a damned hard life, full of toil and strife." Lowther and his shipmates spent a week hauling *Assistance* by hand between the dock to load supplies, then back into the river to lash up with a hulk to take on naval stores, and finally out to HMS *Shrewsbury* for secure anchorage while they prepared the ship for sea duty. On March 12 the able seamen climbed the masts and began rigging the ship. Caps and crosstrees were fixed to the mastheads, then the shrouds were drawn down to the sides of the ship to stabilize and support the vertical structures. Next, the myriad lines and blocks to handle the sails were tied off to the crosstrees and horizontal yards. While the experienced mariners, climbed to the tops and strung rigging aloft, the ordinary seamen secured the bowlines and buntlines on the deck or winched stores into the hold. The ship's sails arrived on March 24, and the crew went aloft to bend on, or fasten, the canvas sails to the yards and stays. Five days later, *Assistance* received its anchors and cables, enabling the ship to secure itself. Adm. Sir John Jennings, a commissioner of the Admiralty, came aboard *Assistance* on April 2 and raised his white ensign for the day, signifying the ship's entry into the fleet.[9]

April 4, 1715, marked a red-letter date for the crew of *Assistance*. At 11:00 a.m., the ship unlashed from *Shrewsbury*, unfurled its sails, then caught fresh southerly gales for a short trip down the Thames. Two and a half hours later, *Assistance* anchored at Longreach near Gravesend. The brief sail meant the ship had entered sea duty, a welcome event as the men transitioned from "rigging pay" to "sea pay." The change boosted their wages to the full monthly rate: for able seamen, twenty-four shillings per month (£1 4s). The crew took on their guns, powder, and shot before joining the North Sea Fleet at the Nore on April 24. *Assistance* did not have to wait long before an overseas mission called it out to sea.[10]

George I, king of Great Britain and elector of Hannover, having joined the coalition against Sweden in the Great Northern War, dispatched Adm. Sir John Norris and his fleet of nineteen ships of the line to the Baltic. Land forces from Denmark, Russia, and Prussia were besieging the Swedish stronghold of Stralsund in Pomerania. The Danish king requested British help in securing the passage of merchant ships past the coasts of Sweden and out of the Baltic Sea. *Assistance* raised anchor on May 19 and bore northeast in fair weather. With the ship under sail, the crew had busy days pulling on the braces to reorient the sails each time the wind changed direction, reefing and unreefing the topsails, setting or furling the gallants, etc. The work often called the able seamen to sidle along the yards 50 feet or more above the deck while tugging on canvas sails. During daylight hours, the crew mended, repaired, scrubbed, and tarred the wooden surfaces and rigging to keep the ship serviceable. At night the master scheduled watches in four-hour shifts, beginning at 8:00 p.m. The ship often stayed active at night, and the watches had to perform the same functions as the crew in daylight. However, with a crew complement of 240, the night shifts had enough men to manage the ship, and Lowther usually could spend his off-watch time catching some sleep, drinking his rum ration, or smoking his pipe. He would run up a charge for tobacco equal to a month's pay during his time on *Assistance*.[11]

Captain Vernon and his crew spent the summer and fall shepherding merchant convoys from the Kattegat to the Gulf of Finland and enforcing a British, Danish, Dutch, and Russian blockade of Stralsund. The only occasions the men had for firing the guns were the frequent salutes exchanged between the dignitaries of the several fleets. Even without a naval battle, the crew of *Assistance* labored constantly. The longboat made regular trips to shore for water and provisions. Whenever the ship repositioned, the crew had to sound the bottom with a leaded line to ensure the ship had sufficient clearance above the rock-strewn seafloor. This simple chore required some training and a degree of skill. Standing on the lee cathead (a beam protruding from either side of the forward bulkhead), a sure-footed sailor twirled the hand lead overhead, then cast it forward of the ship, playing out the line. Once the ship passed over and the line hung straight down, the sailor called out the depth from the line mark at the surface. The most difficult task occurred whenever a storm brewed up and Vernon sent the men aloft to strike the topmasts and yards to keep them from snapping in strong gales. Lashed by the rising winds and chilling rains, Lowther and his shipmates climbed the shrouds to the tops, where they unbent the gallants and topsails, then struck and lowered the yards. The loft men carefully removed the shrouds, stays, and upper rigging, not an easy job when the gusts threatened to tangle the lines. Next came the trickiest part of the work—unseating the topmasts from the bottom masts and lowering them to the deck. Once the tops had been properly struck, the crew secured the topmasts and stowed the sails and rigging below. The work resumed in reverse order the moment the weather abated.[12]

As the siege of Stralsund came to a close in December 1715, the Admiralty re-called the Baltic Squadron. HMS *Assistance* dropped anchor back in Britain on the first day of 1716, then underwent a refitting at Sheerness, giving Seaman Lowther and much of the crew a few days of leave to blow their shillings in port. By mid-March the ship went back on sea duty. The Great Northern War still dragged on, but the Admiralty decided not to return *Assistance* to the Baltic. Instead, Captain Vernon's ship anchored in the Downs near the seaport of Deal for routine service in home waters, which likely pleased the crew, who preferred it to the stress of wartime duties. While tending the ship off Deal, Lowther was blissfully unaware that a different sort of conflict had brewed up on the other side of the Atlantic—not between kingdoms and navies, but a clash pitting honest seafarers against men universally despised as villains.[13]

FRENCH SLOOP *ST. MARIE*, BAHIA HONDA, CUBA, 10:00 P.M., APRIL 3, 1716

Captain d'Escoubet and the crew of *St. Marie* peered across the starlit bay at an astonishing and ominous sight. Two periaguas, flat-bottomed Spanish canoes, had entered the bay's narrow entrance and were rowing toward them, each with a sloop in tow. As the periaguas approached, the terrified Frenchmen could see the men in them, naked except for the pistol bandoliers slung across their chests and the cutlasses brandished in their hands. Even more bewildering, these men were not natives but lily-white New Englanders, led by treasure seekers turned pirates, Sam Bellamy and Paulsgrave Williams. D'Escoubet's men grew more troubled as the periaguas tossed aside the towlines attached to the sloops then surged toward *St. Marie*. A nervous crewman called to them, asking where they were going.[14]

"Aboard! Where do you think?" A smattering of musket fire followed the flippant response. The two periaguas soon reached the French sloop. One captured a dory trying to escape while the men in the other climbed up to *St. Marie's* weather deck. A sudden boom from a gun threw the assailants and Frenchmen into confusion. Bellamy's overcharged men were on the verge of massacring the sloop's crew for firing the gun, when a sailor in one of the pirate sloops cried out, "It was an accident." That reassurance and d'Escoubet's quick surrender narrowly avoided a bloodbath.

Capt. Henry Jennings, an experienced sea rover operating under the governor of Jamaica's commission, drew alongside his new prize with the sloops *Barsheba* and *Mary*. He and his protégés (Charles Vane, James Carnegie, and Leigh Ashworth) came aboard the next morning to help supervise the rifling of *St. Marie*. Jennings and company had agreed to join with Bellamy and Williams only the previous evening and likely did not trust the upstart sea bandits. Inspecting the ship's manifest, Jennings learned that the French sloop had been selling contraband goods to the local population. That meant he would not have trouble with Spanish authorities for seizing it. However, Britain and France were now at peace, and the taking of *St. Marie* stepped beyond his privateering warrant into outright piracy. No matter, an entry on the manifest soon swept aside any misgivings: *St. Marie* was carrying 30,000 pesos de ochoa (pieces of eight).

When asked where the coins were, d'Escoubet told the pirates the money had been removed from the sloop for safekeeping and buried in an unknown location where they would not find it. Jennings and his cutthroats had an easy answer for the Frenchman's subterfuge. D'Escoubet later complained that the pirates "tormented the crew to that inhumane degree that they extorted after the vilest manner from them a discovery where they said the money lay." The total value of the sloop, its cargo, and the pesos came to a hefty 700,000 livres, equivalent to more than £30,000.

The news got better. A short time later, another periagua entered Bahia Honda and pulled alongside *St. Marie*, unaware that it was now a pirate's prize. Captured and tortured, the Frenchmen in the periagua revealed that a second French sloop, *Marianne*, was anchored in Mariel Bay, only 26 miles east—another plum ripe for plucking! Jennings sent his lieutenant, James Carnegie, in the sloop *Discovery* to bag the *Marianne*, accompanied by one of Bellamy's periaguas. That periagua returned a day or so later, this time with bad news. Capt. Benjamin Hornigold, a rival privateer of Jennings, had also graduated from sea rover to sea bandit and seized *Marianne* before Carnegie got to Mariel. Worse, Jennings's men observed Hornigold's sloop, *Benjamin*, pass Bahia Honda's entrance heading westward in company with *Marianne*.

Infuriated that he had been beaten to the punch, Jennings ordered his pirate fleet to pursue Hornigold and his crew, which likely included his protégé Edward Thache (a.k.a. Blackbeard). The crews of *Barsheba* and *Mary* quickly exited the bay and bore leeward while the prize crew aboard *St. Marie* and Bellamy's periagua prepared to depart. Some of Bellamy's men helped *St. Marie* get on its way until the sloop cleared the harbor entrance. At a command from Bellamy, the New Englanders jumped the prize crew and took control of *St. Marie*. Jennings's men looked on helplessly as the New England pirates yanked the bags of pesos out of the hold and tossed them into Bellamy's periagua, which soon fled eastward against the prevailing easterlies.

Farther west, Jennings, seeing that Hornigold had too great a lead to be caught, came about and worked his way back to *St. Marie*, only to discover that he had been robbed by Bellamy and Williams. Thrown into a towering rage, he took out his vengeance on the periagua they left behind by cutting it to pieces. He collected his prize and his fleet of sloops, then sailed to the burgeoning pirate enclave in the Bahamas instead of returning to Jamaica, having forfeited his commission from the governor.

The rare conjunction of Jennings, Vane, Hornigold, Thache, Bellamy, et al., some of history's most infamous buccaneers, marked a sea change in the long, sordid evolution of Atlantic basin piracy. The former privateers had cast away the pretense of legitimacy they had formerly operated under during the recently terminated war with Spain. Rules of engagement that had once constrained them were discarded as they shifted from officially sanctioned roving to licentious robbery. Their quick, easy hauls of small fortunes caught the attention of loose seafarers and covetous ships' captains who swapped legitimate commerce for thievery. Spanish, French, Dutch, and British merchants were now targets for any villain who cared to roam the sea for victims. The windfalls from this collection of corsairs in early 1716 helped spark an unprecedented outburst in piracy that would engulf the West Indies, the North American colonies, the coast of West Africa, and, eventually, George Lowther.

HMS *ASSISTANCE*, OFF DEAL, ENGLAND, SUMMER 1716

After giving the ship a few months of light duty, the Admiralty called out *Assistance* for a new mission that was diplomatic in nature. The Ottoman Empire had declared war on the Austrian Empire in April 1716, causing concern in London for their Habsburg ally. The king appointed Edward Wortley Montagu as ambassador to the Ottoman court and gave him the mission of settling the conflict. Grandson of the 1st Earl of Sandwich, Montagu had been a member of Parliament and a junior commissioner of the Treasury, though his greatest achievement had been wooing the beautiful and accomplished Mary Pierrepont away from the suitor her father preferred, Clotworthy Skeffington. Lady Mary Wortley Montagu would immortalize their diplomatic journey from Vienna to Adrianople and Constantinople through her published letters and adoption of the practice of smallpox inoculation. While in Constantinople, their son would become the first known Briton to be immunized by "ingrafting." The procedure began with a minor incision in the patient's skin, followed by rubbing a pox scab from a survivor into the small wound. The patient usually suffered a mild, localized case of smallpox that led to lifetime immunity from the dreaded disease.[15]

The Montagus sailed to Rotterdam on a yacht then traveled by coach to Vienna, but their baggage required a vessel of deeper draft. The Admiralty made HMS *Assistance* available for foreign service, and on August 16 the crew loaded forty-two parcels belonging to the ambassador onto the ship. Because *Assistance* was bound for the Orient, it drew a secondary mission to carry an envoy as far as Port Mahon in Minorca with a "Present from his Maj.^ty of Great Britain to the Dey of Tripoly." The ship and its crew left the Nore for the Mediterranean Sea in October 1716.[16]

Seaman Lowther and the rest of *Assistance*'s crew enjoyed a commoner's version of a grand tour of the Mediterranean at a leisurely pace, occasioned by the slow proceedings of the Montagus' travels and diplomatic negotiations. The passage still had its perils: one man was lost overboard off Gibraltar. Captain Vernon, ever meticulous, kept the men working tirelessly to maintain the ship: replacing a sprung maintop mast, scrubbing and caulking the hull, unbending and drying the sails, etc. The work aside, *Assistance* made several stops in Cadiz, Port Mahon, Villa Franca, Genoa, and Leghorn, allowing the crew welcome opportunities to roam the taverns and bawdy houses while the ship lay at anchor. The ambassador and Lady Mary finally arrived in Adrianople in March 1717, and *Assistance* dropped anchor at Constantinople on March 30.[17]

Under the wary eye of an Ottoman fortress, Captain Vernon supervised the unloading of the Montagus' baggage, including two chests of money, and the loading of the outgoing ambassador's personal effects onto *Assistance*. The trips back and forth to shore allowed Lowther and his fellow seamen to mingle with the Muslim population and take in the sounds, sights, and smells of a distinctly dissimilar society. Instead of church bells ringing, muezzins sung calls to prayer from the city's minarets. In the streets and markets, the Britons marveled at the mix of peoples from Persia, India, the Black Sea, and North Africa and the curious goods hawked by local merchants. The mariners tasted unfamiliar dishes, drawn by the aromas of cinnamon, strange fruits, and sizzling kebabs. The coffee houses may have reminded them of the brown cafés in Amsterdam, but strangely, like all public venues, they included no women. When the sailors did see females in the street, there were no drooping bodices or smiling faces. The women covered themselves and avoided any interaction. Their seeming confinement within their own culture led many Westerners to look upon Turkish women as objects of pity. It took the letters of Lady Mary to give British society the perspective from the other side of the veil. "The Turkish ladies," she wrote, "are perhaps freer than any ladies in the universe and are the only women in the world that lead a life of uninterrupted pleasure exempt from cares; their whole time being spent in visiting, bathing, or the agreeable amusement of spending money."[18]

The port of call in Constantinople came to an end when Sir Robert Sutton, Montagu's predecessor, boarded *Assistance* on May 16. The ship weighed anchor that evening. Captain Vernon had instructions from the Admiralty to transport Sir Robert to a new diplomatic posting, then to come home. The delicate state of relations with the Ottomans became apparent to Vernon when he was about to pass the Turkish fleet near Gallipoli. Vernon's lieutenant called on the Turkish admiral, known as the Captain Bashaw, to discuss protocols for exchanging salutes, only to be turned away. Miffed, Vernon sailed by without firing a customary salute. The ship delivered Ambassador Sutton to Toulon in July, then sailed on to Britain. Remembering his near brush with disaster ten years earlier, the captain shortened sail and sounded the depth to the seafloor as he approached the Scilly Islands near the channel entrance. *Assistance* safely arrived in the Thames by October 21 and moored at Woolwich, 8 miles below the Tower of London.[19]

With fewer threats abroad, the Royal Navy had begun scaling back its operational tempo. The Admiralty slimmed the number of ships in sea pay from eighty-seven in May to sixty-six by the end of October. HMS *Assistance* headed back to ordinary, and Captain Vernon was reduced to half pay. Once the ship docked, the paymasters came aboard to pay off the crew. George Lowther collected £35 4s 3p in "neat wages" after deductions for charitable contributions, tobacco, and "slop clothes" purchased while on board. Securing his wages in a purse, Lowther tossed his kit onto his shoulder and stepped down the gangplank to the dock. He soon disappeared into the streets, alleyways, and public houses of southeast London.[20]

Lowther would slip from the sight of history for the next three years. Schooled by his time under the diligent and punctilious Captain Vernon, he may have signed on to another navy ship or used his naval experience in the merchant marine. Literate, intelligent, and familiar with the organization and running of a ship, Lowther had the requisite skills to advance himself in the seafaring world. His prospects for an honorable life at sea looked favorable, but he would learn that the oceans' hazards included more than storms and shoals. When he finally resurfaced, Lowther would find himself in the company of a troubled man with a tormented soul and employed by a troubled company without one.

◆ CHAPTER 2 ◆

THE ROYAL AFRICAN COMPANY

THE SLAVE TRADE

Since 1441, when Antão Gonçalves and Nuno Tristão returned to Portugal with ten "blackamoors" seized off the coast of what is now Western Sahara, European nations had financed much of their expanding maritime empires through a pernicious trade in human beings. At first, the lure of gold and ivory drew Portuguese explorers to the Atlantic coasts of Africa, but the discovery of the Americas opened a vast market for slave labor to prop up nascent colonial economies in the New World. Eager European merchants and investors made their livelihoods selling textiles, gunpowder, and iron bars to African kings and tribal chiefs. In exchange, the native lords found a ready outlet for their captives and impoverished villagers rounded up by slave hunters. For the price of a lump of iron worth little more than ballast in their holds, traders could purchase adult Africans and sell them in West Indies markets for a handsome profit.[1]

The earnings looked enticing, though the misery that accompanied involuntary servitude flew in the face of Christian sensibilities. The scene of the first slave market in Portugal left many feeling uneasy at the plight of the people they had turned to chattel. "But what heart could be so hard as not to be pierced with piteous feeling to see that company? For some kept their heads low and their faces bathed in tears, looking one upon another; others stood groaning very dolorously." European lords and merchants overcame their misgivings through feeble justifications that they were bringing the Africans into a more civilized society and saving their souls. "When the Nakedness, Poverty, and Ignorance of these Species of Men are considered; it would incline one to think it a bettering their Condition, to transport them to the worst of Christian Slavery." This illusory reasoning was soon obviated by the attraction of wealth from the slaves' free labor in New World plantations and the lucrative transactions that carried them there. With the enforced bondage taking place out of sight on distant shores, Europeans found it easier to accept the monetary benefits and ignore the unpleasant byproducts of their commerce. Later observers would comment on the true conditions the enslaved Africans faced. "By Transfretation [transportation] they get the brown Bread, without the Gospel. . . . They are fed, it's true, but with the same Diet and Design we do Horses; and what is an aggravating Circumstance, they have a property in nothing, not even their Wives and Children."[2]

The growing demand for slaves in the West Indies drew English seafarers into the trade during the sixteenth century, but interest in Africa scaled up only after the restoration of Charles II. Wealthy and influential Englishmen obtained a royal charter and monopoly rights to establish a permanent English presence on the west coast of Africa. The charter company, later known as the Royal African Company, built stations from Fort James on the Gambia River to Whydah in the current state of Benin. The strategically placed factories protected merchants from French and Dutch competitors and served as staging posts for collecting and loading the Africans onto the ships. The company never prospered. Saddled with the costs of keeping up fixed facilities, it struggled with debt and lost market share to independent traders, especially after surrendering its monopoly rights in 1698. It sank further after a 10 percent duty on private traders expired in 1713. One traveler to the African coast observed, "The Company's Trade . . . every year grows worse; buying dearer . . . and selling cheaper." By 1720, the company's margins had been squeezed to just £7 for each slave sold and delivered. With declining numbers of slaves transacted, the company barely covered its operating costs and had to stop subsidizing the costly African factories, "leaving them to subsist by their own Management or starve."[3]

The financial picture looked dire until the May 1720 stockholders meeting, when James Brydges, the 1st Duke of Chandos, joined the company's board of directors. Chandos fended off collapse by infusing the tottering company with cash and vitality. By July, newspapers were giving notice of his influence: "The African Company are resolv'd, it seems to carry on their Trade with much greater Vigour than they have done hitherto." In one of his first initiatives, the duke organized a mission "to make a new Settlement on the River Gambia . . . and they are going to send over Workmen to build a Fort, and then a Company of Soldiers to garrison it, and so keep out the Pyrates from nestling in that River and interrupting their Commerce." Corsairs had wrought havoc on the African coast and heavily damaged the Gambia River station. The company set aside £3,525 to cover salaries and provisions for the restoration of Fort James, situated on the Gambia River. To protect the expedition from sea rovers, Chandos petitioned the Royal Navy to provide an escort to the African factories. The Admiralty answered favorably and committed two fifty-gun ships of the line to make the voyage. "The Swallow and Enterprize Men of War are appointed as Convoy to the 10 African Ships that are going out and are now getting ready at Portsmouth," the papers observed. "It is not doubted but that they will clear the Coast of those Robbers, or at least oblige them to keep further off."[4]

The Royal African Company proceeded to enlist young men for service in the distant and depressing Gambian station. The workmen and soldiers had to rebuild and protect the station to prop up the company's trade in gold, ivory, and slaves. The company's managers, the Court of Assistants, extended generous terms to those willing to endure soldiering in a place known more for disease and death than prosperity. Advertisements promoted the soldiers' pay, set at twenty shillings (one pound) per month, and the conditions of service. "The Company will pay for his Passage, and Accommodation with Provisions to Africa and back again . . . and to have Diet and Lodging provided there, at the Company's Charge." As further incentive, the company promised that "each Souldier shall have Two Months Pay advanced them before-hand, and 20 s. as a free gift." A similar solicitation went out for shipwrights, carpenters, coopers, and other artificers to perform repairs to the Gambian fort. Chandos picked Lt. Col. David Dunbar, deputy commander of the 35th Regiment of Foot, to supervise the enlistments and take command of Fort James. It was an unfortunate selection. Dunbar would later be described as "a bankrupt colonel . . . needy, greedy and arrogant."[5]

GAMBIA CASTLE, THAMES RIVER, LONDON, FALL 1720

George Lowther had come up in the world since leaving the navy. His experience and education made him a candidate for more responsibility within the maritime profession. After his time on HMS *Assistance*, Lowther had learned how to read nautical maps, chart courses, and use a quadrant to estimate a ship's latitude, skills necessary to navigate the ocean. With those qualifications, he squeezed his way from a naval tar berthed below deck to a quarterdeck position of second mate, or, as one contemporary put it, he had "hove-in hard at the harse-hole." Lowther landed a job on a slave ship, the *Gambia Castle*, a merchant vessel in service to the Royal African Company. The ship, under the command of Capt. Charles Russell, had been contracted to transport the carpenters and some of the soldiers destined for the company fort in the Gambia as part of Chandos's recovery convoy. Another ship, *Martha*, would carry the remainder of the expedition's troops and workmen. A third ship, *Otter*, had already sailed for Cork to pick up civilian passengers who would occupy a new settlement on the Gambia River near the fort.[6]

Lowther may have noticed the familiar lines of *Gambia Castle* as he stepped onto its deck. It had a burthen of 280 tons and carried eighteen guns but a crew of only twenty-eight. The imbalance of guns to crew—the ship had only enough men to load and fire half of one broadside—suggested the previous history of the vessel. The recently purchased and renamed ship was likely a former navy frigate that had outlived its usefulness, like HMS *Queenborough*, sold the year before. Descending into the dark and musty lower decks, Lowther made a closer inspection of the craft and discovered the reason why the navy had gotten rid of it: the frigate was in sore need of repair. Rotted timbers below the waterline caused leaks, and decayed beams and riders meant that the ship was not structurally sound. It needed time in drydock. Lowther may have suggested a period of maintenance to Captain Russell, but time did not permit a rebuild. Events would soon force the ship to take passengers aboard, notwithstanding the leaks.[7]

SOMERSET HOUSE, LONDON, NOVEMBER 2, 1720

After making his way from Africa House on Leadenhall Street to Somerset House on the Strand, James Blakeley, deputy secretary of the Royal African Company, linked up with two army captains, Robert Folliot and John Duncomb, at their garrison, the onetime home of Princess (later Queen) Elizabeth. The officers had recently been released from their duties with the 35th Regiment of Foot and seconded to the Royal African Company for the upcoming expedition. As the day neared its close, the three company officials walked across the street to the Savoy Prison, where many of the company's recruits were kept, to execute an annoying yet urgent task. Trouble had bubbled up. Recruits for the expedition had been complaining about their ill treatment, and word of their discontent had somehow gone all the way to the lords justices in Whitehall. Folliot and Duncomb's commander and newly appointed governor of the Gambian fort, David Dunbar, ordered the officers to meet with the recruits and squelch the griping.[8]

Since summer, Colonel Dunbar and his recruiting officers had combed the streets of London to haul in the requisite number of "volunteers." The recruiters had resorted to some questionable tactics. Unlucky fellows who thought they were joining one of the king's regiments discovered they had actually been enrolled with the Royal African Company. Others got sweet-talked at an alehouse about the honor of wearing the scarlet uniform, before they got whisked off to the Savoy. Meanwhile, Dunbar and his subordinates appeared to have pocketed most of the bounties and subsistence pay for the men they signed. To protect his investment, Colonel Dunbar instructed Thomas Morphey, the Savoy Prison's provost marshal, to lock up more than seventy recruits until their convoy to Africa was ready to sail. A couple of fortunate internees got bailed out by friends or loved ones who resorted to depositing suitable bribes into the provost marshal's hands. Others chose to complain. James Campbell wrote a letter to Colonel Dunbar asking for his enlistment bonus and to be freed from confinement, but the governor responded by ordering Morphey to clap Campbell in irons and throw him "in the Condemn'd Hole." Dunbar's stern measures failed to mollify the company's recruits or stifle their protests, necessitating the visit by Blakeley, Folliot, and Duncomb.[9]

The three officials gathered in the provost marshal's residence, adjoined to the prison, where they agreed to receive the complainants. The audience did not go well. One of the recruits, Joseph Williams, had the gall to ask Captain Folliot for the enlistment bonus he was due. Enraged at the soldier's insolence, Folliot drew his sword. Before he could strike a blow, a second recruit, John Smith, jumped on the captain and wrested away the sword, precipitating a riot. Other soldiers swarmed Captain Duncomb and disarmed him. Instead of smiting the malapert enlistees, the two officers found themselves dodging sword thrusts. The nimble officers "saved their Lives by leaping out of the Window." The terrified Blakeley tried to distract the rioters by emptying his purse on the floor. Luckily for the secretary, the commotion drew the guards from Somerset House, who burst into the chamber. Egged on by the two captains and Blakeley, the guards escalated the violence by "firing Ball among the Rioters." Private Williams had his hat shot off and his skull grazed by the indiscriminate fire. One of the guards with a bayonet speared Private John Whalebone in the chest. After firing more rounds into the confined space, the guards managed to drive the rioters back into the prison, where they finally secured them.[10]

The company officials and guards marched four of the riot's ringleaders, including Smith and Williams, to a justice of the peace that evening. However, the officers did not obtain the quick pound of the gavel they expected. Justice Jeffrey Saunders heard the charges levied against the rioters, then questioned the accused about their conduct. His questions gave the recruits a chance to air their grievances. Appalled by Dunbar's measures, Saunders detained everyone while he hurried over to the secretary of state's residence to advise him of the Royal African Company's management of its recruits. "Returning about One o'Clock in the Morning, [Saunders] committed the Secretary, the two Officers, and the four Soldiers to Newgate" Prison. Ten days later, Colonel Dunbar found himself standing before the Court of King's Bench charged with inhumane treatment of his own soldiers that "was hardly to be parallel'd among the Christian Slaves in Turkey." Seeking the court's mercy, Dunbar released the men from prison. Though most of the enlistees agreed to abide by their contracts with the Royal African Company, "several have taken the Opportunity to shew them a fair Pair of Heels." They were the smart ones. None of the others would enjoy favorable outcomes.[11]

Despite the gesture, Colonel Dunbar did not escape indictment and was forced to resign his post as governor of the Gambia River station. It would take him another nine years before he could land another remunerative position as the surveyor of the King's Woods and lieutenant governor of New Hampshire. Dunbar would bungle that assignment too. He tried, but failed, to break off the coast of Maine from Massachusetts to form his own colony. It was still a better fate than his successor would endure—the Savoy riot was but a harbinger of darker events that would envelop the men destined for the Gambia.[12]

Chandos and the company worked around this latest setback. On December 1, the lieutenant colonel of the 34th Regiment of Foot, Thomas Whitney, assumed the governorship in Gambia "in the room of Colonel Dunbar." Whitney's commission directed him "to take upon you the care and charge of rebuilding our forts and castles and reestablishing our settlement on that river and defending the same against all assaults or opposition." He would not be a governor in all respects. The company instructed Whitney not to "have any concern in the trade, or the accounts thereof to be kept with the Company, but only to take upon him that part of the service, which appertains to military matters." The £500 salary provided the necessary inducement for Whitney to inherit the mess left by Dunbar.[13]

LONDON WHARF, LATE DECEMBER 1720

Second Mate Lowther adapted well to his new role of directing the activities of other sailors. His knowledge and demeanor earned the respect of the able seamen, who applied themselves to the many tasks to be done to make the ship ready for the voyage. The men had to prepare spaces below deck to receive passengers after the Savoy riot forced the company to find alternate living arrangements for the soldiers and workers destined for the Gambia. Water, beer, and food barrels had to be stowed for the African passage. The men also loaded £3,000 of supplies and goods for the trade factory and £475 of "purchase money." Besides mending lines, replacing frayed cables, and other normal maintenance tasks, the crew had to make up for past neglect.[14]

Worries about the vessel's seaworthiness had led to an official inspection of *Gambia Castle* by the Admiralty that found several shortcomings. The Royal African Company replied to the poor inspection report by saying they hoped "she may rapidly be made fitt to proceed [on] the Voyage with the Convoy." However, given the importance of the mission to the Gambia and other factories on the African coast, they assured the Admiralty that if it could not be repaired in time, the convoy need not wait on *Gambia Castle*. Meanwhile Lowther and the crew did double duty readying the ship for departure by patching worm-eaten planks and reinforcing weakened beams.[15]

With the convoy preparing to sail for Africa, Governor Whitney scrambled to replace the subordinate officers on the expedition, especially the engineer officer. Fortunately for him, there was a readily available candidate, a distressed man who would play a crucial role in George Lowther's path to infamy.

Whipped by a chill wind coming off the Thames, Captain-Lieutenant John Massey of the British Army climbed onto the *Gambia Castle* and introduced himself to Captain Russell, First Mate James Dudley, and Lowther. The ship's officers had little time to socialize with the army officer, given the repair work they had to supervise. Massey, newly joined to the expedition, went below to greet "such of the Artificers and Soldiers as had been hired by the African Company, and stood to their Contracts." As he settled aboard and met his new troops, Captain Massey undoubtedly ruminated over the shambles of what had become of his career. The remote African outpost, which dealt mostly in slaves and ivory, was not the sort of place where an army officer could enhance his reputation. He still had his commission and his qualification as an engineer, but this latest assignment looked more like a banishment than an opportunity. For that, he could blame a woman and drink.[16]

Massey's army service had begun well and seemed to have quelled the feral tendencies of his youth. "A natural Wildness was observ'd in the Genius of [his] Person . . . (which was sometimes esteem'd a Degree of Lunacy, at other Times only a Heat and Vivacity of Temper)." The family, unable to manage the spirited young man, "resolv'd to let him push his Fortune, either by going to Sea, or as a Soldier." They purchased an ensign's commission for him in the army, and Massey soon found himself in Flanders fighting under the Duke of Marlborough in the thick of the War of the Spanish Succession. Braving fire, fear, and fatigue, he discovered the value of discipline that had eluded him at home. He performed capably at the brutal siege of Lille in 1708 and earned a lieutenancy. In the following years, he served at the sieges of Mons, Douai, and Bouchain. He came through the years of combat unscathed—not for lack of courage. "Tho' he pressed as forward in every Place as possibly might be, he did not receive one honourable Scar." During the dangerous and tedious sieges, the young officer paid attention to the tactics and formalities of eighteenth-century military operations. These deliberate campaigns, when properly conducted, "appear'd to him to be like beating down Men at Nine-pins." Such observations on the technical aspects of warfare would motivate him to learn more about the science of military engineering.[17]

Once Britain signed the Treaty of Utrecht, ending its role in the war, Massey returned to Britain with his disbanded regiment and went on half pay. The young officer, after beholding the horrors of war, took to heart those lessons that had escaped him in his youth. "He resolv'd to lead a Life entirely sober and regular, and accordingly went every Day to the Prayers, and every Sunday to hear Sermons." Though he was not among the officers who resurrected the 34th Regiment of Foot for the Pretender crisis in 1715, he was on the regiment's list of officers that year at the rank of captain. The 34th Foot, under the command of Col. Thomas Chudleigh and Lt. Col. Thomas Whitney, did not deploy to Scotland but remained in the south of England. At some point, Massey also qualified as a military engineer.[18]

Captain Massey's troubles began while still in southern England. "A lewd Woman of the Town whom he lov'd, made him in a short Time take but little Pleasure in a sober Life." Infatuated, Massey had hopes of marrying her when the regiment received sudden orders to deploy to Ireland in 1717. The lovelorn officer, stuck in Ireland, fell back on old habits and "gave too much way to the debaucheries generally practiced in that nation." His superiors must have perceived his relapse. Notably, he did not escort his regiment when the 34th Foot was redeployed to Spain in 1719 during the War of the Quadruple Alliance.[19]

The Duke of Chandos stepped in to restore Massey's career, perhaps as a favor to the family—it was no favor to Massey, more an excuse to remove him from further temptations. The duke used his influence to find constructive employment for the wayward officer with the Gambian expedition. He seemed a logical choice as a replacement officer. The captain had served alongside Colonel Whitney, the new governor, and could fill in as the engineer for the reconstruction of Fort James. Massey accepted the assignment and appeared to have put his heart into serving king, company, and his men to the best of his abilities. Sadly, his leadership qualities would fall short under the moral and ethical challenges that would confront him at Fort James.[20]

While Massey acquainted himself with his men and the ship, Russell, Dudley, and Lowther made last-minute preparations for getting underway. The mates used the soldiers to supplement the crew for simple work such as loading provisions in the hold, freeing the mariners for work requiring nautical skills. Topmasts and yards had to be secured and then rigged. Loft men bent on the sails and tied off the lines and tackle. Wooden surfaces had to be tarred and the chain pumps manned to pump out the water collecting in the bilge. The ship's carpenter and craftsmen bound for the Gambia did what they could to help seal the hull and buttress the timbers in the lower decks.

The arduous duty paid off. *Gambia Castle* slipped its mooring in January, along with the rest of the company ships. After an easy sail down the river, the ships turned south toward the channel for a linkup with their naval escort.

HMS *SWALLOW*, SPITHEAD, DECEMBER 28, 1720

From the deck of his ship, Capt. Chaloner Ogle watched a flotilla of merchant vessels from the Thames coast into Spithead and join his convoy already collecting in the harbor. "The Easterly Wind we have had for two Days past, hath brought hither from the Downs, the following Ships from the Royal African Company, bound to Guinea: the Gambo, Captain [Russell], the Martha, Captain Levet, the Widah, Captain Barlow, Cape Coast Sloop, Captain Wilson, Congo Sloop, Captain Collins, Widah Sloop, Captain Potter." Captain Ogle, skipper of HMS *Swallow*, had overall command of the ships heading to the West African coast. Colonel Whitney, governor of Fort James, would arrive in Portsmouth within a few days and sail with him aboard *Swallow*. The junior army officers, Massey, Lieut. John Shute, and Ens. James Alexander DeSoulies, were stuck on the smaller merchant vessels. Besides the relief expedition to the Gambia River, Ogle would escort other company ships to Sierra Leone. Captain Mungo Herdman, the commander of the second escort ship, had replaced HMS *Enterprize* with *Weymouth*, another fifty-gun ship of the line.[21]

An interesting character served as mate on *Weymouth*—a man named Alexander Selkirk. While still a boy, Selkirk had run off to sea and joined a privateering venture to the South Seas. After he complained about the seaworthiness of their ship, the captain marooned him on a Pacific island. Selkirk survived on his own for four years before getting rescued by another privateering ship commanded by Woodes Rogers. His survival story became the inspiration for Daniel Defoe's classic *The Life and Adventures of Robinson Crusoe*. Selkirk may have escaped death while marooned, but he would not survive his time on HMS *Weymouth*, dying from a tropical fever while off the Gold Coast in December.[22]

The convoy remained off Portsmouth while *Swallow* and *Weymouth* finished storing eight months of provisions for a protracted voyage along the West African coast. Ogle planned to keep the two warships together with all the commercial ships until they reached Cape Verde, the western tip of Africa. Beyond the cape the *Gambia Castle*, *Martha*, and their support sloops would split for the Gambia River while *Swallow, Weymouth*, and their charges bore away for Sierra Leone. Once free of their escort duty, the two Royal Navy ships would sweep down the coast, hunting for the troublesome pirates who had done so much harm to the Royal African Company's trade.[23]

By the beginning of February, Ogle's ships were loaded and the crews were ready. Everyone checked the flags to see when the prevailing westerlies might abate. It had taken the Duke of Chandos and the company the better part of a year to organize and prepare the mission designed to eliminate the pirate threat and reverse the slide in the company's fortunes. Thirteen months later, Capt. Chaloner Ogle would be basking in glory and riches, the Royal African Company would be out £10,000, Colonel Whitney along with most of the soldier-recruits would be dead, George Lowther would be roving the West Indies, and John Massey would be entrenched in the state of denial.

CHAPTER 3

VOYAGE TO THE GAMBIA

Conditions were right for sailing. Late winter marked the beginning of the best season to cruise west from Spithead. Cool, high-pressure systems over northern Europe swung the channel's prevailing winds more easterly until June, when steady westerlies blew in that could bottle Atlantic-bound ships in port for weeks. The rising tide surging around the north side of the Isle of Wight could help push the ships eastward out of the Solent. Once the tide crested at Dover, the tidal currents would reverse and give the convoy five hours of strong ebb flows toward the western channel exit. Captain Ogle signaled his sister ship, HMS *Weymouth*, and the smaller merchant ships to weigh anchor and steer south out of the roadstead toward the English Channel.[1]

The procession made an impressive spectacle. "This Morning sailed from Spithead his Majesty's Ships . . . the Swallow and Weymouth, with the following outward-bound belonging to the African Company, viz. Royal Africa, Martha, Widaw, Gambia-Castle, Cape-Coast Castle, Widaw Sloop, Gambia-Castle Sloop, Cape-Coast Sloop, Greyhound Sloop, Congo Sloop, and the Area Sloop, all for Guinea. The Men of War are got already as far as S. Helens [St. Helens], but will hardly be able to proceed, the Wind being so much Eastward of the South." As the ships lingered at nightfall in the Isle of Wight's lee, the sky put on its own impressive spectacle, an aerial display that John Atkins, the surgeon aboard HMS

Swallow, described as *Scintillae volantes* [flying sparks]. "In the Evening from six to nine, we saw those Appearances in the Sky . . . they are Streams of Light that suddenly shoot into one another and disappear for a minute or two."[2]

Ogle's convoy resumed movement into the channel but had barely gotten into the rougher swells before Russell's ship, the *Gambia Castle*, began taking on water and returned to Portsmouth. *Swallow*, *Weymouth*, and the smaller merchant ships sailed on without them. Back in port, shipwrights patched the vessel as best they could, and Russell stood out to sea, once again, but he made it only as far as Plymouth by February 20.[3]

Despite the earlier repair work supervised by Russell, Dudley, and Lowther, harbor inspectors at Plymouth condemned the craft. The Royal African Company, known to operate ships beyond their years of seaworthiness, had no choice but to replace Russell's leaky vessel. Captain Massey and his men debarked from *Gambia Castle* and waited until another ship arrived to carry on the voyage.[4]

Sometime in early March, the company paid £10,000 for a 250-ton galley-frigate known as the *Bumper*. Given that burthen, the ship would have measured 90 feet bow to stern and 23 feet at the beam. *Bumper* normally carried a crew of thirty and mounted twenty-two guns, probably a mix of 3-pounder minions and 6-pounder sakers. A ship-rigged vessel, *Bumper* had three masts with square sails, as opposed to fore-and-aft-rigged sails. The galley-frigate also stowed a full set of oars that could be extended from ports below its gunline to propel it during calms or inside narrow channels.[5]

Bumper, captained by William Menzies, had completed an active itinerary over the preceding three years with voyages to Guinea, Leghorn, Curaçao, and Barbados. Menzies left Deal on March 5, reportedly "for Guinea" though actually for Plymouth, where he delivered *Bumper* to Captain Russell. After assuming command of the ship, Russell renamed it *Gambia Castle* in keeping with its new role as a Royal African Company merchantman.[6]

Swapping ships on a single passage offered an ill omen for a voyage that may have already unsettled the crew. Under their charterparty, the men believed they had signed up for a single slaving mission to Africa, North America, and back. Experienced mariners had reason to dread such a triangular cruise under normal conditions. The slave business was revolting even to men hardened by service at sea, and could be as deadly for them as their human cargo shackled below deck. People in the eighteenth century thought that seamen died in "great numbers" each year on slaving voyages "from the intemperature of the climate, the inconveniences they labour under during the voyage, and the severity of most of the commanders." The steamy climates of Africa and the West Indies had nothing to do with crew mortality. Fearsome tropical diseases such as yellow fever and ague (malaria), were borne by mosquitoes that bred in the warmer environments. Other deadly diseases such as scurvy and the bloody flux resulted from poor diet, water, and sanitation. As for deaths from shipboard conditions, the assessment was sadly accurate. Captains of slave ships drove their crews hard, with little regard for the health and safety of their men. Many sailors on slave voyages suffered death by discipline. No wonder the *Gambia Castle*'s crew had reservations about their journey to the African coast. Nevertheless, the Royal African Company had hired their ship and was paying their wages. The men prepared for the voyage and prayed that fair winds would carry them home in a year or less. They were unaware of some of the company's instructions to Captain Russell that would impose an extended stay in the Gambia.[7]

Precious sailing time went to waste as the men offloaded five hundred muskets, 4 tons of iron bars, 40 gallons of brandy, and months of provisions from the condemned ship and stowed it on the newly christened *Gambia Castle*. John Massey contributed some of his soldiers to the labor pool, but the ship's mates, Dudley and Lowther, supervised the time-consuming work aboard the galley-frigate. The season had slipped past March before the crew had *Gambia Castle* loaded and the troops reboarded.[8]

HMS WEYMOUTH, GAMBIA RIVER, MARCH 31, 1721

Colonel Whitney hoped to make a strong impression upon his entrance into the Gambia, especially on the king of Barra, the African monarch who ruled the territory north of the river. James Island could not sustain the size of the factory's reinforced garrison and workers, so the company needed to establish a settlement on the north bank, across from the fort. Whitney and the company factors had to obtain the king's blessing to place the settlement within his domain, and it would take more than the customary *dashee* to appease him. The new governor transferred to HMS *Weymouth* after getting Ogle's and Herdman's agreement to divert the warship to Fort James. The 700-ton ship of the line, with guns lining two of its decks, presented the image of strength that Whitney wanted to convey. Unfortunately, *Weymouth*'s deep draft proved a disadvantage. The ship ran aground in the tricky sandbars off Barra Point, near the mouth of the Gambia. It took Captain Herdman's crew four days of fighting tidal flows to work it free.[9]

Despite the mishap, the greeting with the king went well. The African lord, pleased with his presents, consented to locate the British adjunct station at the town of Juffure (Jufureh), a Mandinka mud-hut village that would later gain fame as the birthplace of Alex Haley's ancestor Kunta Kinte. Whitney's inspection of the fort did not go as well, "not finding anything to inventory except seventeen old guns unfit for service." Fort James once boasted ninety guns and a £60,000 appraisal. Now the company carried it on the books at one-sixth that value. Two years earlier, a daring pirate, Howell Davis, gained entry to the fort by posing as a wealthy merchant. The governor, who had hopes of selling a cargo of slaves and ivory, discovered the ruse too late. He and the dozen men of the garrison put up a feeble resistance that the pirates easily overpowered. The governor relinquished the fort and allowed the pirates to "do all they desired." Davis and his cutthroats raided the storehouses and demolished much of the installation before sailing off. Adding insult to injury, half of the fort's garrison deserted and joined Davis's crew.[10]

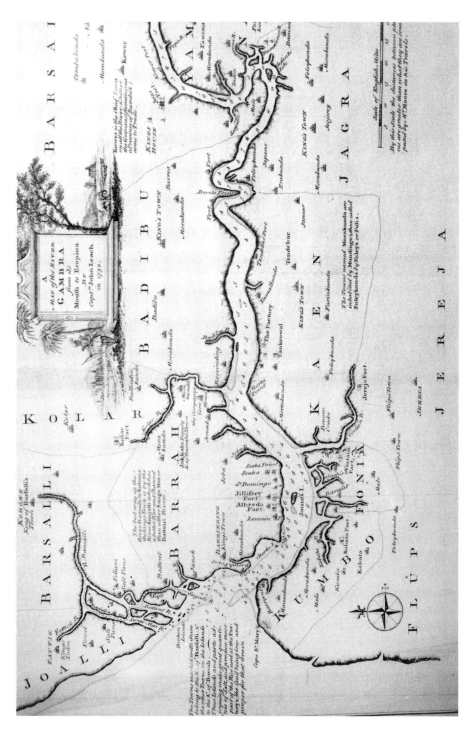

Gambia River. The Gambia River in the eighteenth century. Fort James is shown in the southern bend of the river. *John Leach, courtesy of Stephen C. Dickson*

The company's business operations mirrored the condition of the fort. With no duty on private traders, lower-cost interlopers were undercutting the company's margins—the surplus the company depended on to maintain its coastal fortifications. The expense of manning, supplying, and repairing the company posts weighted down the business with heavier operating costs. Private slave traders, settled at upriver locations, sold directly to independent merchants who sailed past Fort James to obtain better deals for slaves. John Atkins described these low-cost competitors as "loose privateering Blades" who were content if they earned enough to keep them supplied with "Strong-beer, Wine, Cyder, and such necessaries. . . . They all keep *Gromettas* (Negro Servants). . . . The Women keep House and are obedient to any Prostitutions their Masters command. The Men-servants work in the Boats and Periagoes which go a trading in turns with Coral, Brass, Pewter Pans, Pots, Arms, English Spirits, etc. and bring back . . . Slaves and Teeth."[11]

The company got squeezed on both ends—unable to acquire its human inventory at the lowest cost and undersold in the West Indies by discounting independent merchants. Out of 10,500 slaves embarked from West Africa the year before, the company shipped only 702, just 169 from the Gambia. The competition forced the Royal African Company to shift its focus to more-profitable trade in ivory and gold, leading to more neglect of its coastal garrisons. The Court of Assistants in London continued to issue inflexible guidance that often ran counter to local realities. Company agents at the stations and remote factories responded by applying stringent measures to minimize spending and reserve dwindling inventories of trade goods for the purchase of ivory and slaves, instead of buying foodstuffs for the garrisons. To reduce overhead, they replaced deceased personnel with slave laborers. The financial pressure on the company factors set the stage for the disturbing scene that would greet the *Gambia Castle*'s crew and passengers when they made it to the Gambia.[12]

GAMBIA CASTLE, PLYMOUTH HARBOR, APRIL 3, 1721

By the time Captain Russell's galley-frigate unfurled its sails and ventured out to sea from Plymouth, it had lost two months of sailing time behind Ogle's flotilla. Russell's crew and passengers had consumed over eight weeks of rations that should have been delivered to the storehouses at Fort James. The Royal African Company's Court of Assistants allowed their ships' captains a slim 14 percent margin on the expected proceeds of a voyage, and their instructions gave captains precious little latitude to adjust to changing circumstances. Russell realized that his earnings for the Gambia mission had shriveled before he had made it clear of the channel, a portent of more problems to come.[13]

Shipboard life brought immediate woes to John Massey and his troops. He would later declare that the departure from Britain "began the Date of his Misfortunes, here it was, that a wild Life was chang'd into a wretched one of Hardships." Captain Russell seems to have placed restrictions on rations, motivated by his desire to economize. Massey complained that the ship's captain and officers behaved "odly" toward their passengers and "denied them the Portion of Victuals and of Wine that had been promised them." The soldiers, unaccustomed to life at sea and deprived of a normal diet, started turning ill. "The Curses and Complaints of the dying Men was very lamentable to hear, nor could the Officers relieve them, being themselves in the same Condition." Halfway to its destination, *Gambia Castle* made a call at Madeira to replenish fresh water supplies. The brief visit dealt another emotional blow to Massey—the company's chaplain decided to abandon the mission and jumped ship. The army captain and his men felt the absence of the chaplain's comforting words as they suffered, because there was no longer "any one to pray by them." Left without spiritual counsel, the men prayed in their own way for the long passage to end. At the time, they could not appreciate that their situation was about to get worse.[14]

FORT JAMES, GAMBIA, MAY 9, 1721

Thirty-six days out from Plymouth, the *Gambia Castle* rode the incoming tide 22 miles from the mouth of the Gambia River to its mooring near the Royal African Company station. The galley-frigate anchored just off the islet, a mere speck in the river, 116 yards north to south and a little over 80 yards east to west. A twentieth-century Briton would later comment that James Island "is incredibly small and lonely. . . . On this bare and inhospitable spot stood the small fort which was to be the symbol of British suzerainty." Fort James, a modest fortress by any standard, had bastions on each corner and a tower for defense. It housed a cramped barracks and apartments for the factors and governor. The slaves who worked at the fort slept in separate quarters outside its walls. Storehouses, limekilns, and a forge were scattered around the eyot. To add protection, the British had built a half-moon gun emplacement at the northeast tip of the islet, and another at the western corner. The ordnance for these batteries had been removed by Howell Davis or rendered unusable. Captain Massey's longboat rowed to a landing spot next to the western battery on May 15 to remount the ordinance.[15]

The instant he stepped ashore, Massey discovered "a sterile place not affording any thing that was necessary for ye use of man." Instead of the mild temperatures of London, he encountered stifling 90-degree heat and dank conditions. The dry season still dominated the African coast, but the humidity hovered close to 70 percent. Even though the fort had few African slaves penned for transport, a macabre atmosphere hung over the whole place like a fog thickened with despair. The newly arrived army captain may have felt smothered by the oppressive climate and stench, but it was the news from the fort that left him aghast. Of his two subordinate officers who arrived with Ogle's convoy, Lieutenant Shute had died on May 5 and Ensign DeSoulies lay on his deathbed. Many of the enlisted men had also died "for want of due care." The surviving soldiers and artificers lay ill with no one to attend them—the surgeon, Peter Grahame, had passed away on May 8.[16]

Like any dutiful officer, Captain Massey brought his men ashore from the *Gambia Castle*, then went to work to improve the conditions for his suffering troops: fresh water and fresh provisions being the first priority. The islet had no well and was surrounded by miles of salt water. The nearest source of potable water was the hamlet of Jufureh, "a heathenish village not producing any thing to drink but water yt the Negro's daily wash themselves in." No sooner had his men moved into the barracks than waterborne illnesses struck them down. "In a few days after ye men was landed they were in Generall seas'd with a flux," Massey recalled. "Being forc'd to drink the Water of the Place, it threw them into strange Fevers and Fluxes; so that instead of building a Fort, [Captain Massey] used to see twenty Men at a Time rolling on their Backs in the Pains of Death." At one point, he remarked, "the men under my Command besides thirty black slaves have been without Water twenty four hours and when supply hath come it hath been half salt Water."[17]

The isolated and unhealthful environment hindered any means of obtaining a supply of clean water. However, the inability to procure ample rations stemmed from a more frustrating obstacle—the company factors.

Once Capt. Herdman had departed with HMS *Weymouth*, Governor Whitney had to deal with the company factors, though his faltering health left him in poor condition to negotiate. Massey and his soldiers soon discovered the stress the governor was under. Whitney, "being very old and hath not had one hours health since his landing," sought refuge aboard the *Gambia Castle* to recover from the fevers and infections running rampant at the fort and the new settlement at Jufureh. The first thing he asked for was bread from the ship's stores, none being available at the island outpost. Massey inquired why the governor did not order the company agents to release more provisions for the garrison or procure bread from the natives. The company contract with the army and merchant ships stipulated that the agents would feed and supply the garrison in a manner befitting British subjects. Could he not enforce it? Whitney explained that his authority extended only to "martial discipline and fortify[ing] a place for Trade." In all other matters, the company agents, whom Whitney called "mechanick Fellows," held sway. These merchants, "acting quite reverse to ye Company's proposals much augmented ye misery" by pinching costs and constricting sustenance.[18]

Days and then weeks went by with the governor confined to a cabin on the *Gambia Castle* and Captain Massey pleading with the factors to properly victual his men. He got nowhere. The agents were accustomed to feeding enslaved Africans only enough to keep them alive for transport and may have presumed that the soldiers could get by on the same allowance. Exasperated by the factors' indifference to his men's torment, Massey railed that "he did not come there to be a Guinea slave. . . . If they would not provide for them in a handsome Manner, he should take suitable Measures for the Preservation of so many of his Countrymen and Companions."[19]

The soldiers, driven by hunger and fear, proposed purchasing local provisions themselves on credit. "Some of the Weakly men that had Money due to them desired of ye Merchants to support them upon Acc't of their wages." The company agents refused—cash and goods had to be reserved for purchasing inventory. The hard-hearted factors countered with a suggestion that three or four of the complainers should be shot to set an example. The men thought about foraging the countryside, but by that time they were too feeble. "For tho' the Country afforded Fowls and Venison of several [s]orts, and other Provisions, which the Natives would have been ready to have sold them, yet they never tasted of them, being incapable of travelling through the parched Desarts to the Cottages belonging to the *Africans,* and especially in the bad State of Health they were in."[20]

Massey and his men resorted once again to the articles of their employment, drafted in London by the Court of Assistants. They pointed to the provision "That each Man after six Months Notice given should have his passage home at the Company's Charge." The local agents laughed off the argument and replied, "They should stay till they Rotted."[21]

Soon they did rot. Weakened by hunger, the troops began showing frightful symptoms of other maladies besides the bloody flux. Mosquito-borne tropical diseases such as ague (malaria) set upon the newcomers. The British Sick & Hurt Board would later describe the gruesome symptoms visited upon its victims:

> Obstructed perspiration, want of appetite and a headache. . . . The urine was then bilious and high-coloured . . . the belly costive. . . . After this the patient was either seized by a horror febris, or the fit began with a nausea and bilious vomitings, a cold damp sweat, a contracted pulse, and sometimes a dyspnea. To these succeeded the ardor febrilis. . . . The patient . . . was more or less weakened in proportion to his sweating. . . . Five or six hours after the first paroxysm went off, the patient was pretty hearty . . . till the third day, when the paroxysm seldom or ever failed to return. Soon, in spite of all the drugs, the fever became quotidian until diarrhoea or apoplexy carried off the patient.[22]

Governor Whitney had recovered enough by early June to leave the *Gambia Castle* and return to the fort. His presence lent more weight to the garrison's pleas for more provisions and fresh water. However, he had no more luck persuading the company factors to loosen their pocketbooks than before. His instructions from the Court of Assistants gave him latitude over the army garrison but not control over the agents or the company's purse strings. Stymied at every turn, Massey, who felt responsible for the misery of his men, became despondent. "He had then a very dismal Prospect before him, his Countrymen lying all Dead about him, his Victuals all wasted, no Water that he dare taste of, in a strange Part of the World, surrounded with Savages, whose Language he was a Stranger to, and no Possibility of his ever getting the Ship back to *England* again." An event aboard the *Gambia Castle* would rouse the captain from his feeling of hopelessness and present him with a more proactive solution to his company's predicament.[23]

GAMBIA CASTLE, JUNE 11, 1721

A beast was loose on the *Gambia Castle*. Discipline had cracked. The sailors had watched as the soldiers at the fort voided their guts or convulsed with fevers. They fared a little better than their compatriots in the fort, thanks to the provisions and water casks stored on the ship, but fear of the disease-ridden climate made them itchy to get away to more-healthful latitudes. A perceived betrayal stood in the way of their escape. "The Commander of ye Bumper aforementioned Contracted with his Men in England that they should not stay in Africa but make a Voyage to America and from thence to England but ye Merchants order'd that ye said ship should stay in ye Country as Guard ship wch would have Rend'red her for ever incapable of performing a voyage." The sailors had not signed on for a prolonged stay in the Gambian death trap. "We humbly presume," they noted, "that from time to time there hath been sevll Hundreds of Men Transported to their destruction in this part of Africa." History validated their concern. It took only four months in Africa for one out of five Britons to perish—three out of five within a year.[24]

The ship's captain, Charles Russell, had either deceived the crew about the terms of their charterparty with the Royal African Company or felt obligated to abide the factors' decision to retain the *Gambia Castle* at the slave station, his livelihood being at stake. The company would not load his ship with slaves or ivory, so he had no cargo to cover the crew's wages if he did sail. Furthermore, the company's terms might have exposed him to severe penalties should he deviate from its instructions. Russell turned a deaf ear to the sailors' complaints and fell back on "Barbarous and Unhumane Usage" to maintain order.[25]

Resentment and unruliness rankled below deck until a confrontation between the captain and the second mate, George Lowther, unleashed the bubbling discord like someone lancing a festered wound. Sympathetic to the men's plight and fed up with the captain's discipline, the second mate entered the captain's chamber to challenge the captain on their behalf. Lowther insisted that they had to get free from the clutches of the company agents. Russell, suffering the pressure from the demands of the factors and his own crew, shouted down his mate. Lowther "refused to stay in the Country." The captain's temper finally boiled over, and he decided to formally punish the mate. An ordinary seaman would have been subjected to a flogging, but confinement was a more suitable penalty for a gentleman-officer, preferably within the company fort and away from the ship's crew who sympathized with him.[26]

Perhaps the *Gambia Castle*'s crew got wind of what the captain intended, or they overheard the officers shouting. Regardless, the men took measures into their own hands. When Russell and Lowther emerged from the captain's chamber, most of the crew had already gathered on the deck, anxious to see what had developed. Russell ordered a few of the men to take the mate into custody. Lowther's supporters intervened. "The Men took up Handspikes, and threat'ned to knock that Man down that offered to lay hold of the Mate."[27]

Tense seconds ticked by. Captain Russell looked into the eyes of his crew. Aboard ship, a captain's will was law, and his directives required instant obedience. This time the men stood defiant. They had made their choice. Between captain and mate, they sided with the mate. Russell backed down. He dismissed Lowther and told the men to disperse. The immediate crisis passed, though a greater one gathered force.

The incident had ended without further violence, but it failed to resolve the crew's underlying grievance, and now they had an officer as a champion for their cause. The second mate and crew of the *Gambia Castle* had stepped over an invisible but fateful line, one that could not be easily recrossed. They had rejected the captain's orders and, having shattered the sanctity of command authority, turned loose a host of evils that would lead to terrible consequences.

CHAPTER 4

MUTINY

GAMBIA CASTLE, JUNE 11, 1721

Second Mate George Lowther had escaped his commander's wrath only through the intervention of an indocile crew. He knew enough to stay clear of the vexed captain and to let the first mate, James Dudley, handle the interactions with him, but Lowther still dreaded the incident's potential repercussions. Captain Russell had a vindictive streak and, at some point, would be in a position to inflict his vengeance. The junior officer could only draw solace from the ship's company. Roaming the deck, he saw the men's respectful glances and nods of the head, which told him that he and they shared a bond, an affinity born of a defiant spirit and a mutual desire to leave the Gambia.

Given the captain's hostility, Lowther could assume that his career with the Royal African Company would be terminated and his pay forfeited. Of greater concern, any confinement at the company fort would expose him to tropical diseases and easily equate to a death sentence. It was a hard fate for an officer who was only trying to uphold his duty and show loyalty to his crew. The mate might have resigned himself to enduring the captain's retribution, as befitting an officer, had he not been conspiring with someone who gave him hope of escaping his circumstances.

Over the preceding weeks, Lowther had found common cause with Capt. John Massey. The army officer had been making regular calls on Governor Whitney while the senior officer recovered from his fever aboard the *Gambia Castle*. During these visits, Lowther and Massey, who "was no whit the better reconciled to the Place," had opportunities to commiserate over the hardships and suffering of their men. The two officers thought themselves "bound in Duty to Relieve those poor wretches from a Visable and Tyranicall Calamity." The army officer talked of his men's desire to return to Britain, while the second mate relayed that the crew was "ripe for any Mischief."[1]

In time, these discussions had drifted from wistful thoughts to a serious conspiracy. "They aggravated one another's Grievances to such a Height, that they resolved upon Measures to curb the Power that controul'd them, and to provide for themselves after another Manner." Massey echoed Lowther's sentiment that they had to intervene to spare their men, but he could not sort out what to do on his own. Lowther had an idea—they could seize the ship. The scheme was not without precedent. Despair of being left to die in Africa had driven many others to desperate actions. Britain recorded twenty-one mutinies between 1718 and 1723, the west coast of Africa a setting for many of them. One starving company factor on the Gold Coast expressed his opinion that, given the choice, he would "rather to run a remote hazard of being hanged at home, than chuse a transfretation hither." Lowther's solution seemed straightforward and appealing. They could save their "Miserable Country Men" by sailing back to Britain, then justify their case before the Crown. The army captain convinced himself that the king would see their act as an honorable attempt to save lives. Massey later confessed that he did not think things through properly. "He acknowledged that he ought to have addressed himself to God for Directions how to act in Affairs so difficult, and to have sought the Assistance of Heaven, rather than that of Men."[2]

In the days preceding Lowther's altercation with Captain Russell, Captain Massey had shared a confidence with Colonel Whitney, who harbored the same anger and pique at the company factors. Massey intimated that they could embark on the *Gambia Castle* and, with the help of the crew, return to Britain. Whitney apparently expressed sympathy toward the idea. He was fed up with the Royal African Company and no longer felt any obligation to waste his time and his men's lives defending the desolate slave station. Massey came away from the discussion with the hopeful expectation that Whitney would support his and Lowther's conspiracy. The governor's presence and advocacy would give a huge boost to their case with the king.[3]

Governor Whitney may have offered his acquiescence to the plan, as he understood it, but that was given without full knowledge of all the plan entailed. Massey had not divulged that he and Lowther intended to wrest command of the galley-frigate away from Captain Russell. This misunderstanding would have tragic repercussions for John Massey and his men.

GAMBIA CASTLE, MORNING, JUNE 12, 1721

Aboard ship, Captain Russell and First Mate Dudley could sense trouble brewing ever since the failed attempt to punish the second mate. Hostile stares followed the officers wherever they walked. Where they should have been met with respect and deference, they encountered resistance and insolence. Dudley had to resort to shouts and threats to get simple orders executed. The bold and open contempt for discipline and command authority frightened the senior officers, and they knew whom to blame—George Lowther.

The captain concluded that to restore discipline, he first had to remove Lowther from the galley-frigate. Absent the second mate's leadership and disruptive presence, the crew could be cowed back into submission. Removing the second mate would not be easy. Russell had to formulate a plan that would get Lowther off the ship and then imprisoned at the fort, without giving the crew a chance to interfere. For that, he needed Governor Whitney's help and a contingent of soldiers. Russell was scheduled to attend a meeting among the factors, Whitney, and the king of Barra that morning. He ordered the launch to be readied to row him to Jufureh, where he planned to consult with the governor about confining Lowther.[4]

With so many crew members sympathetic to the second mate, word reached Lowther instantly that the captain was going ashore. There could be no mistaking the purpose behind the captain's visit with Governor Whitney. Lowther realized that the time had come for a decision. If he wanted to seize the ship, he had to do something before Russell returned with a guard. Otherwise, he would be in irons by evening. Even a decisive man of action had to pause over taking such a drastic step. Lowther understood that an act of mutiny would lead to an irrevocable break from the company, the navy, the king, and his family. Few mutineers ended their lives in peaceable comfort—nearly all died at sea or dangling from a noose. The junior officer knew the consequences could be dire, but he decided to follow through with his plan.[5]

To succeed, the mutiny required simultaneous actions by the ship's crew and the fort's soldiers. Massey needed the *Gambia Castle* to get off the island, and Lowther needed Massey's troops to bring off supplies, man the ship, and silence the fort's guns. If either side acted on their own, the endeavor would fail.

Lowther waited until Russell and the launch rowed across the river to Jufureh. By this time, he had sounded out his loyal followers and handpicked his men to take over the ship. He told them to find anything convenient to serve as a weapon and be prepared to act on his signal. The team of insurgents, clutching handspikes behind their backs and hiding knives under their shirts, gathered on deck without arousing suspicion. When the numbers were good and his followers ready, Lowther motioned for them to seize the first mate. The mutineers pounced on Dudley, disarmed him, and then shoved him into his cabin, where he remained confined. Lowther opened the weapons locker and handed out firearms to men he trusted to ensure that no one aboard would try to retake the ship. Most of the crew went along with the uprising. Nobody stood against it. Quick and neat, Lowther was now master of the *Gambia Castle*.[6]

The mutineers made no obvious motions to alert the fort or the other two ships, taking the precaution only of loading the guns. Lowther bided his time until the launch returned from Jufureh after dropping off Captain Russell. The unsuspecting rowers pulled alongside and asked why the ship's guns had been loaded. The mutineers answered, "To salute the King of Barra, who was expected to come on board to Dinner." Lowther scribbled a hasty message to Massey that they had to act, at once. He slipped the note to one of the boat's crew, someone the mate trusted. Lowther then ordered the launch to row over to Fort James and await further instructions. As soon as they pulled up to the island, the sailor with the note hopped out of the launch and hurried to find Captain Massey.[7]

FORT JAMES, FORENOON, JUNE 12, 1721

The sailor located the army captain inside the fort and handed over Lowther's note advising him "that he should repair on Board, for it was Time to put their Project in Execution." Massey jumped into action, and with firmness. He went straight to the barracks, where most of his men were either sick in bed or waiting their turn for guard duty. Though he had not shared his plans with them, the captain knew his men and their sentiments. Addressing those assembled, he put the case to them in simple terms: "You that have a Mind to go to England, now is your Time." The common soldiers would not have dared to consider such a thing, no matter how poor their circumstances, had not an officer taken the lead. Most of them, either sick or disgusted by their living conditions, answered favorably to their captain's suggestion. A few of the veterans, one of the sergeants among them, understood the implications of Captain Massey's proposal and declined to join the insurrection, though they did not interfere with the majority who sided with their commander. Massey counted his supporters. In total, one sergeant, two corporals, a drummer, thirty-five privates, and eight workmen joined the mutiny. Massey ordered the soldiers to throw on their uniforms, buckle on their gear, and grab their firelocks.[8]

The army captain moved quickly to secure Fort James. He and his rebel band hastened to the storehouses where the company factors locked up the provisions that had been denied them. Smashing in the door, the men gave the storehouse a quick inspection. They found plenty of wine but not much in the way of foodstuffs. It would have to do. The captain posted two armed guards at the door "and ordered that no Body should come near it."[9]

With the storehouse safeguarded, the rebels proceeded to Governor Whitney's apartment. Massey did not find the governor, who was meeting with Captain Russell and the factors at Jufureh and was oblivious to the mutiny. He did see Whitney's son and reassured the young man, who had been promoted to lieutenant in place of Shute and DeSoulies, by explaining he would be going home. Presuming the governor would join their cause, the mutineers gathered up Whitney's "Bed, Baggage, Plate, and Furniture." They even grabbed several of the governor's perukes, fashionable wigs with cascading shoulder-length curls. Massey supervised the collection of his commander's belongings to make certain Whitney would live in comfort during the return to Britain, an indication of how much he valued the governor's support.[10]

Next, the mutineers rushed to disable the fort's defenses before an alarm could be raised. They climbed stairs to the tops of the fort's bastions, where the guns were mounted. The fort's guns posed a deadly threat to the *Gambia Castle* and needed to be taken out of action for the mutiny to succeed. Massey did not want to destroy British armaments, even those belonging to the Royal African Company. It would not look good when time came to plead his case before the king. He found a simple solution to render the guns harmless with no permanent damage—dismount them. The task required a dozen men. A 6-pounder saker weighed about a ton, a 9-pounder demiculverin as much as a ton and a half. With strong backs and a heave, the mutineers tipped the guns off their carriages, leaving them temporarily useless.

In a matter of minutes, John Massey and his mutineers had taken control of Fort James without firing a shot and, apparently, without alerting the company factors or the ships moored nearby that an uprising was afoot. Massey had to get word to the second mate that he had his soldiers under arms and the fort in hand. He concocted a message that he sent back by the launch, likely one that he and Lowther had drafted ahead of time.

GAMBIA CASTLE, MIDDAY, JUNE 12, 1721

When the launch returned, Lowther immediately grasped the note's true meaning—Massey had taken the fort. The mutineers rejoiced. "We seas'd ye sd Bumper for ye use of ye Distressed." They soon turned their focus to getting away from the fort before the company agents and other ships organized a resistance. Lowther put a crew into the ship's longboat and told them "to go on Shoar to a Castle upon a small Island and to bring off from thence on board the said ship Captain John Massey and between 30 and 40 soldiers who were under his the sd [said] Massey's Command." The boat started rowing back to the fort, one of many trips they would make that afternoon.[11]

Lowther and Massey would later claim that "we sent to the Merchts in Order to have treated with them for ye sustenance of Life." None of the merchants on the island offered "to doe us Justice thereof." The assertion that they tried negotiating with the company factors had a bare morsel of plausibility, perhaps to give a veil of legitimacy in their future pleas to the king. The galley-frigate still had an abundance of iron and firearms in its hold that the mutineers would have willingly traded for necessities in the company storehouse. The factors would have likely countered that the ship's cargo was rightfully theirs too. In truth, the mutineers had possession of the storehouse and started looting it.[12]

Back and forth, the longboat rowed "to fetch off the Wine and Provisions from the sd Castle." The soldiers must have tasted a bit of satisfaction as they loaded eight pipes of wine on the longboat, equivalent to 1,000 gallons. The company agents had previously refused to issue the wine "for ye use of all ye white Men that was upon the Island . . . the country being so Unhealthy that it is impossible for White Men to Live in w'thout some Liquor to support nature." Instead, the factors tried "to sell the wine to ye artificers and soldiers upon Acct." No matter, the wine was theirs now.[13]

The two mutinous officers further claimed that "we delivered the Merchts what they required of ye ship's Cargo wch was ye Major part of the Cargo yt Remained." The company later disputed this dubious statement and contended that the mutineers stole all the supplies they had delivered plus more coming from the other ships. The helpless merchants could do nothing more than watch as the mutineers ferried boatload after boatload of supplies and drink to the galley-frigate. Massey's armed guards made sure of that.[14]

Once the storehouse had been emptied, the captain evacuated his men from the islet, a boatload at a time. First, they cleared the sick from the barracks, then more soldiers piled into the longboat. One of the army mutineers, Thomas Tucker, brought his wife and son on board, but the drummer, Robert Pattison, abandoned his wife at Jufureh. She slit her own throat three weeks later. After a few round trips, only the captain remained with a handful of guards.[15]

Throughout the afternoon, Captain Massey spoke with Governor Whitney, who by this time had returned to Fort James. Massey urged his superior officer to board one of the boats rowing over to the *Gambia Castle*. The governor's presence on the galley would be crucial in justifying their mutiny and their future appeal to the Crown for mercy. The old soldier refused to join. He had sympathy for Massey and his men fleeing the intolerable conditions at Fort James, but he could not abide a mutiny. Unlike the army captain, Governor Whitney could see no future for the soldiers and sailors aboard the *Gambia Castle* other than living outside the law as fugitives.

Whitney's decision dealt a ruinous blow to the mutineers and their cause, one that Massey felt personally. He had admired the colonel from their days in the 34th Foot and would later describe him as "a man of honour and integrity." Sadly, he could no longer call him a compatriot. Massey boarded the longboat for the last trip back to the galley-frigate.[16]

GAMBIA CASTLE, AFTERNOON, JUNE 12, 1721

George Lowther welcomed Massey aboard the ship, then heard that the governor would not be joining them. Massey might have considered giving the governor a little more time to think things over, but Lowther wanted to get away as quickly as possible. Before they could sail, they had to remove a few people from the ship, the governor's son among them. The young man and the governor's belongings were loaded back onto the longboat, less the perukes. Captain Massey could not resist holding back the stylish wigs or simply overlooked them. The mutineers also released James Dudley and a small number of crew members who refused to be a part of the mutiny.

When the longboat rejoined the mutineers, Lowther issued instructions to weigh anchor even though the tide was against them. The mutiny nearly came to an early and disastrous end due to some questionable seamanship. In their haste to get away, the crew raised one anchor but "slipp'd the other." The galley-frigate swung awkwardly in the channel, pushed upriver by the rising tide. Before the crew could react, the ship ran aground on a prominent sandbar off the western edge of the islet. Stuck fast, like a poacher tangled in vines, the *Gambia Castle* lay helpless against the sandbank.[17]

The grounding left the galley-frigate in a vulnerable position, unable to maneuver or turn broadside to a threat. One of the other ships could have fetched up against *Gambia Castle*'s exposed stern and raked it with a broadside. Luckily for Lowther and Massey, *Martha* and *Otter*, fearful of the more powerful ship, stood off at a respectable distance and opened fire rather than heave closer for a deadly salvo. Lowther's crew manhandled a gun to get shots off in the direction of the two merchantmen, but the ships fired "without doing Execution on either side."[18]

The heavier guns in the fort posed a far-greater threat to *Gambia Castle*. At this moment of crisis, Captain Massey stepped forward. He ordered sixteen men into the longboat and raced back to the islet. The armed mutineers retook Fort James. The loyal members of the garrison, the company agents, and the slave laborers stood back, intimidated by the small but aggressive party of soldiers. Massey's men scurried up to the tops of the bastions, where they had left the guns lying on the floor. Strong hands and straining backs lifted the guns back onto their carriage mounts and nestled the trunnions into the cradles. The soldiers loaded powder and shot into the guns, then shoved them forward to the embrasures on the parapet. They did not have to fire a shot. The moment that *Martha* and *Otter* saw the guns back in action and Massey's men occupying the fort, they drew off and ended the engagement. Massey's quick action saved the mutiny.[19]

Lowther and the *Gambia Castle*'s crew worked to rescue the beached craft while Massey's armed mutineers stood guard at the fort. Even with the help of the evening flood tide, the sailors could not free the galley from the bottom. The mutineers struggled into the night, but the ship could not be dislodged. Massey forcibly recruited workers from the fort and sent them out to the distressed ship in launches. The extra men and boats tugged, rowed, and dragged to work the ship loose.

Charles Russell used the hours of darkness to make one more attempt to retrieve his ship before the mutineers could haul it off the sandbar. He rowed out to *Gambia Castle* and hailed George Lowther. Russell asked to come aboard to talk things over, face to face, but Lowther refused. Massey even ordered him "to keep off" or his men would open fire. The displaced captain, sitting in his launch, shouted to the mutineers and appealed to them to return his ship. He offered any terms they would be willing to accept, if only they would end the mutiny and restore him to command of the vessel. His pleas failed to persuade. Lowther and the rest of the mutineers knew that matters had gone too far to be reversed with a mere change of heart.[20]

GAMBIA CASTLE, MORNING, JUNE 13, 1721

An early-morning rising tide and the added manpower finally heaved the galley-frigate off the sandbar. Once he could see the ship floating free, Captain Massey evacuated his men from Fort James for the second time. He took no chances with the ordnance. The soldiers pounded nails into the guns' touchholes, taking them out of service until an armorer could drill out the vents. Morning had dawned by the time Massey and his soldiers climbed aboard the *Gambia Castle*.

Chastened by the previous misfortune, Lowther waited for the tide to begin ebbing, then weighed anchor. This time the exhausted crew made certain to clear the sandbar. The loft gang scampered up the shrouds and unfurled the courses to give the ship more speed and maneuverability. The galley-frigate then steered for the mouth of the Gambia River under shortened sail. With the ship safely underway, George Lowther and John Massey could, at last, breathe easy and congratulate each other that they had pulled off their plan with no loss of life, despite the near brush with catastrophe. After most of the soldiers and sick had come aboard, the ship's crew had swelled to seventy-three, a lot of British lives rescued from the lethal environs of Fort James. Some of the mutineers might have felt some trepidation at abandoning their station. They faced an uncertain future, but it was better than their certain fate had they remained. All felt relieved to watch the miserable, disease-infested fort slowly dip below the eastern horizon and disappear beneath the Gambia's murky waters.[21]

CHAPTER 5

TURNING PIRATE

GAMBIA CASTLE, MOUTH OF THE GAMBIA RIVER, JUNE 13, 1721

Sailing close-hauled against the prevailing northerlies, the *Gambia Castle* plied its way between Barra Point and Baniyou Point, then out toward the distinct line delimiting the silten discharge of the Gambia from the blue waters of the Atlantic. The visible demarcation loomed like a boundary marker separating the misery of the African continent from the uncertainty of the open sea. It also reminded George Lowther of the troubling question that he and the rest of the men on the galley-frigate now had to answer: Whither to sail the ship?

In the run-up to the mutiny, Lowther and John Massey had conspired to seize the *Gambia Castle* and flee the oppressive hold of the Royal African Company. Massey, convinced of the rightness of their cause, planned on returning to London to plead their case before the Crown. Even as the two officers hatched their plot, Lowther could detect a bit of naïveté in his counterpart, a hint that the army captain lacked the intellect to sort through complex issues or fully appreciate their circumstances. The second mate had used Massey's simplemindedness to his advantage when he secured the army officer's help in gaining control of the ship, but since the mutiny, he realized that Massey's imprudence could be a liability. Massey still thought they should head for London. Apparently, he did not perceive how their situation had been changed by Colonel Whitney's refusal to come with them. Lowther understood—Massey's course pointed straight to the gallows.

If he wished to alter the plan, the second mate had to move with caution. The mutiny had obliterated any legal authority to command the ship, and he had nothing other than the respect of the galley-frigate's sailors to influence events. Half the men aboard were soldiers who had joined the mutiny under the presumption of going home and might still feel loyalty to the army captain. A confrontation with Massey and his armed company was out of the question. He had to rely on his powers of persuasion to orient the company of mutineers away from Britain.

Lowther called for the mutineers to gather on the weather deck, presumably after consulting with Captain Massey. Soldiers and salts climbed up ladders from the decks below and crowded around the stern castle to hear what Lowther and Massey had to say. Standing before the assemblage, the second mate reasoned that their futures were linked by a common crime, and no one's infraction was any lesser than another's. He then posed the question of how the company wished to proceed. Massey's desire to sail for Britain was well known, but Lowther took it upon himself to explain the reality of their situation. "It was the greatest Folly imaginable," he asserted, "to think of returning to England." The mutiny "could not be justified upon any Pretence whatsoever, but would be look'd upon, in the Eye of the Law, a capital Offence." Despite Massey's deluded optimism, he predicted that their arguments about maltreatment and broken promises would be quashed by the opposition of the Royal African Company, the Duke of Chandos, and the nation's maritime interests. The Crown would never tolerate mutiny. As for returning to Britain, Lowther announced his personal choice "not to run such a Hazard." Seeing the grim expressions in their faces and the dejection in their eyes, Lowther knew he had made a convincing argument and dashed any thoughts of heading back to London. The time had come to restore hope. He had a different plan. Circumstances had driven them to mutiny, but they now had the opportunity to become masters of their fate. If every British port was closed to them, they could sustain themselves by becoming predators on the open waters, for "they had a good Ship under them [and] a Parcel of brave Fellows in her. . . . It was not their Business to starve or be made Slaves. . . . If they were all of his Mind, they should seek their Fortunes upon the Seas, as other Adventurers had done before them." Lowther proved his conviction and commitment to the idea of turning pirate by stating that "if his Proposal was not agreed to, he desired to be set ashore."[1]

The second mate's reasoning and confidence struck a chord among the mutineers. If they were outlaws, why not live outside the law? Freedom to roam as they pleased, answering to no authority and dependent on no one other than themselves, sounded as enticing as a siren's melody to sailors accustomed to shipboard discipline and soldiers confined to a pestilential barracks. Without a captain's threat of flogging or a boatswain's raised cane to force them into toilsome duties, the mutineers could expect less regulation and more ease. They would forfeit any legitimate wage, but there were other ways to fill their purses. William Kidd, Henry Avery, Howell Davis, and Bartholomew Roberts had accumulated fortunes breaking into the plump chests of merchant sea captains. Liberty, laziness, and the promise of loot won them over to Lowther's side. "They one and all came into the Measures."[2]

The pirates had thrown off all vestiges of royal, commercial, and civil authority, but they were natural-born Englishmen and soon felt the need for some form of self-government expressed in writing. Lowther assumed the role of captain, though he understood that his position rested on the trust of the ship's company, not on any commission handed down from above. To establish command authority, he needed the entire crew to formally consent to their joint criminal enterprise and sign a voluntary yet binding pact. He and his men drafted a set of articles that would govern important shipboard issues. Once these were complete, each man signed or marked his name on the document and thereby acknowledged his new status as a pirate:

The Captain is to have two full Shares; the Master is to have one Share and a half; the Doctor, Mate, Gunner, and Boatswain one Share and a quarter.

He that shall be found guilty of taking up an unlawful Weapon on board the Privateer, or any Prize, by us taken, so as to strike or abuse one another, in any regard, shall suffer what Punishment the Captain and the majority of the Company shall think fit.

He that shall be found Guilty of Cowardice, in the Time of Engagement, shall suffer what Punishment the captain and Majority shall think fit.

If any Gold, Jewels, Silver, &c. be found on Board of any Prize or Prizes, to the Value of a Piece of Eight, and the Finder do not deliver it to the Quarter-Master, in the space of 24 Hours, shall suffer what Punishment the Captain and Majority shall think fit.

He that is found Guilty of Gaming, or Defrauding another to the Value of a Shilling, shall suffer what Punishment the Captain and Majority shall think fit.

He that shall have the Misfortune to lose a Limb, in Time of Engagement, shall have the Sum of one hundred and fifty Pounds sterling, and remain with the Company as long as he shall think fit.

Good Quarters to be given when call'd for.

He that sees a Sail first, shall have the best Pistol, or Small-Arm, on Board her.[3]

Given his experience in the Royal Navy, Lowther used the first and fourth articles to defuse a potential source of friction that often drove a wedge between naval officers and crews—the division of spoils. The Admiralty had prescribed methods for subdividing booty taken from a prize captured at sea, but captains and officers found ways to offload cargo and valuables before the Prize Commission could assess the amount of plunder to be split with the crew. Enlisted sailors usually walked away with only a slender share of the appraised value of the hulk and whatever loose goods they picked up from the main deck. The second, third, and fifth articles were intended to control riotous or cowardly behavior that could jeopardize the safety and harmony of the ship and crew, while the last three articles offered some assurances and incentives for courageous conduct. Interestingly, the articles said little about the routine operation of the pirate vessel. The ship still had a captain in charge and other subordinates in key positions who would perform traditional duties in managing the crew's activities. However, when it came to discipline, everyone aboard had a say in doling out punishment, a distinct departure from normal practice in the navy and merchant marine.[4]

With formalities handled, the crew flew into a whirlwind of activity to ready *Gambia Castle* for its new mission as a pirate ship. The galley-frigate needed a more open, less confined space on its main and weather decks to give gunners and matrosses freedom of movement for possible engagements. Partitions and bulkheads came down. Excess wood went overboard, and any casks, equipage, or supplies went down to the hold. On the weather deck, rails came off the gunwales, and private cabins in the stern castle were demolished and cleared. No one, not even the captain, enjoyed a personal sleeping space. As other historians have observed, there were no aristocrats among pirates. The remodeling left the weather and main decks flush and smooth from bow to stern, except for the guns lining the hull. The pirate company, anxious to put the memory of Fort James and the Gambia behind them, gave the reconfigured galley-frigate a new name, *Delivery*. In keeping with their status as sea rovers, Lowther's crew devised a new ensign. They "prepared black-Colours" to signify they were no longer subjects of the British king and to strike terror in the hearts of their intended victims. The pirates embellished the field with a skeleton to drive home the point to any merchant captain who might think of putting up a fight—resistance meant death.[5]

The pirate company had formed. The ship had been readied for action. Now, Lowther and his men had to decide where to search for prey. By turning south, *Delivery* could make an easy run along the Ivory, Gold, and Slave Coasts in a few weeks' sail, scooping up plenty of slave ships and heavily laden traders on the way. West Africa had already proven a lucrative hunting ground for the likes of Howell Davis and Bartholomew Roberts. Beyond that, the Indian Ocean beckoned with flush Arab dhows and large British East Indiamen loaded with goods for the European market. The southern route looked tempting, but Lowther knew that Chaloner Ogle and his two powerful warships patrolled those waters. The pirates had other options. Brazil and North America had active maritime traffic and a less active Royal Navy presence. However, the lure of the West Indies looked more promising. Spanish treasure ships and a rich commercial trade had drawn fabled corsairs and buccaneers to the Caribbean for more than a century, men such as Francis Drake, Piet Heyn, Francois l'Olonnais, and Henry Morgan. *Delivery* held adequate food supplies to last the six weeks it would take to cross the Atlantic. More important, the eight pipes of wine pilfered from Fort James would be enough to keep the men in their liquor for the entire passage. The decision was made: they would head for the West Indies.

Pirate captain George Lowther gestured to the ship's master and ordered him to turn athwart the northerlies and steer west. Deckhands braced the courses to change their orientation, while able seamen hurried up the shrouds to release the topsails. *Delivery* slowly nosed to port and plowed into the blue Atlantic.

Delivery, 13°10' North Latitude, 20 Leagues East of Barbados, Predawn, July 20, 1721

The neophyte pirates had enjoyed an easy, five-week midsummer passage of the Atlantic. After sailing abeam of the West African winds and currents to clear the Cape Verde Islands, *Delivery* caught the easterly trades and bore due west on a broad reach. Lowther had picked Barbados, the easternmost of the Windward Islands, to make landfall. Following age-old practice, he navigated by sailing along the latitude of his destination in the West Indies. Because mariners of his time had no means of accurately measuring longitude, he preferred to chart his course along a set latitude that he could maintain by taking noonday angular measurements of the sun and nighttime observations of the North Star. With steady winds and no obstructions in their path, the pirate crew set the courses and topsails, then stayed under sail all day. At night they ran with only the courses and a small watch on deck. The uniform and powerful trades gave them plenty of speed, though they could measure it only by throwing a log over the side and timing its passage down the length of the hull. *Delivery* averaged a comfortable 77 miles per day, while most of the inebriated pirates languished in their hammocks to pass the time.[6]

Lowther may have tried to follow the example of navy and merchant captains to break in the army lubbers to routine shipboard duties while *Delivery* cruised but he knew he could push the men only so far, since laxity prevailed over discipline. The crew, like most pirates of their time, used their freedom from authority as an opportunity to shirk shipboard responsibilities. Their captain adjusted his role from that of commander to one as director, issuing appeals to the men to see to their duties as necessary for the common good. A few weeks out, Lowther would have shortened sail in the evenings once he thought they approached Barbados. He did not want to chance upon a lee shore in the dark. The pirate captain took another precaution: keeping a lookout aloft.[7]

"A sail! A sail!" The sailor in the foremast top armor had spotted the shadow of yards and masts through the early-morning gloom.

"Where away?" Lowther responded to the lookout's cry.[8]

"Off the starboard bow." The alert lookout had just earned himself a fine pistol.

"All hands, hoay!" Lowther shouted, to turn out the entire company for its first potential action. Below deck, Massey and his infantrymen buckled on their gear, passed out cartridge pouches, and grabbed their firelocks. Hammocks came down, and personal chests were shoved out of the way. On the weather deck, experienced hands pulled on the buntlines to stretch the courses and give the ship a little more speed. Lowther wanted more canvas to get a closer look at the sighting before deciding whether or how to make his approach. Pulling out his spyglass, he could make out the shape of a southbound two-masted brigantine.

Across the open water, Capt. James Douglas, skipper of the *Charles* out of Boston, spied the silhouette of the galley-frigate as it lay on more sail. He had cruised well east of his intended call in Barbados until he could gain the right latitude, whereupon he intended to turn due west to make landfall, a common navigational practice. Unfortunately for the *Charles*, his course put him on the same path as *Delivery*. Observing an unexpected sail on the horizon was usually a benign event, though a lightly armed merchantman would view it with caution in pirate-infested waters. Most times, ships would hail one another once they got close and exchange news of weather or recent happenings in other ports. Assessing *Delivery*, Douglas worried that the larger ship approaching from his windward was not interested in pleasantries. Going over his options, the merchant captain considered running into Barbados, where he might find help. *Charles* was not far out, just 20 leagues (about 70 miles), but the three-masted galley-frigate carried more sail and could outrun his fully loaded brig. *Delivery* had already gotten too close in the dark before he discovered her. Douglas shortened sail and hoped for the best. His heart sank when the *Delivery* raised her black ensign at dawn. He was about to experience one of the most bizarre pirate encounters ever recorded.[9]

The particulars of the *Charles*'s seizure were not documented, though standard procedures for taking a prize suggest a tense though nonviolent surrender. The pirate vessel usually hove to windward of its prey in case the merchantman had a change of heart and tried to run. Instead of sending over a longboat, most pirate captains preferred to call over the merchant captain in his launch, then hold him hostage to ensure his crew's cooperation. Once Captain Douglas came aboard *Delivery*, Lowther inquired as to his destination and cargo. Lowther could not have been more thrilled by Douglas's answer. They had stumbled upon a ship with a cargo that pirates valued above all others—food. Lowther filled the longboat with some of his crew and sent it back to the *Charles* to begin emptying the contents of its hold, "which they plundered in a pyratical Manner."[10]

At this point, John Massey entered the picture. The army officer still clung to the hope, slender as it might have been, of receiving a royal pardon for the mutiny. Massey pointed out to Lowther that since sailing off with the ship, they had not committed an act of piracy or any other affront to their royal master until their seizure of the *Charles*. He did not want this incident to spoil one last appeal to the king. The *Delivery* still had iron bars and other trade goods from the Royal African Company in its hold. They could offload whatever they no longer needed onto the *Charles* and make it look like an exchange of goods rather than an outright robbery. Massey's suggestion gave the pilfering of *Charles* a thin veneer of veniality, perhaps enough to confound a charge of piracy in a court of law. To humor his co-conspirator, Lowther agreed to the ruse. For the better part of two days, the longboats went back and forth loading *Delivery* with "Casks of Mackerel and Sturgeon . . . and a Cask of Beer" while filling Douglas's ship with useless trade goods that would appeal only to an African chieftain.[11]

By the twenty-third, the pirates had finished looting the Boston brig. Notwithstanding their dubious "exchange of goods," the men of *Delivery* had completed their transition from mutineers to bona fide pirates; yet, before releasing Captain Douglas, Lowther and Massey asked a favor of the merchant captain. One can only imagine Douglas's shock and disbelief as they handed him a letter addressed to the king and asked him to deliver it to the governor when he arrived in port.

Massey had spent hours drafting a long-winded justification for his and his companions' mutinous action:

> To His Most Sacred Majesty George, by the Grace of God King of Great Britain, France and Ireland, Defender of the Faith andc.
>> May it Please Your Majesty,

The letter recounted a rambling list of grievances and complaints about the miserable conditions and deprivations suffered by the army captain and his troops while stationed in the Gambia. Massey included a few passages about the abusive treatment of Lowther and his crew by Captain Russell and the Royal African Company. He made repeated references to the high mortality of the men stationed at Fort James and the likelihood that disease and death were about to swallow the survivors. Fourteen paragraphs into the missive, Massey justified the mutiny as a lifesaving act:

> These Inevitable Proofes of Destruction forced me to Use my Utmost Endeavour to preserve the Lives of Yr Majesty's Dutifull subjects.

After several more paragraphs intended to explain away the theft of stores from the fort's warehouse, Massey finally got to the point:

> We therefore; humbly implore Your Majesty's Gracious Pardon for the Reliefe of Yr Majesty's miserable subjects who are now Tossing upon ye seas Depending on Yr Majesty's Unparelled Goodness and Clemency not daring to come near any Christian port.
>> But soe long as our small store will support us we shall live in Hopes that Yr Majesty's Royall Pardon will be Extend to ye Enlargement of Yr Majesty's miserable subjects who if not relieved before our small stores be Expended Necessity will oblige us to take some Irregular method we never designed.

The unexpressible miserys of Yr Majesties Dutifull subjects who now hopes to Receive Yr Majesty's mercifull Pardon is intolerable not haveing any Conversation nor hopes of any but what we have aversion to. But so soon as Yr Majtys Great Goodness shall grant yr Royall Permission for our return we will not only bring home ye aforesd ship and ye remaining part of her Cargo wth our Dutifull acknowldegmts of Your Majy's Gracious favour but will use our utmost Endeavours to perswead all Ships we meet wth yt use any Irregular practice to return wth us and as providence hath been pleased to Release us from Imminent death wee humbly hope yr Majty will take our Miserable Case into Consideration and Defend us from all other.

The Burthen of the ship we are in is about Two hundred and fifty Tunn Carry's Twenty two Gunns and hath on board one hundred men besides Officers [the actual total was seventy-three men], all wch humbly beg leave to subscribe ourselves yr Majesty's Dutifull subjects who always did and ever will vindicate Yr Majesty's succession and the Posterity of Yr Majesty's Royall Issue whilst we have Life, and shall in Duty Bound for Yr Majesty and Yr illustrious Progeny ever pray andc.

We humbly beg Yr Majesty will be pleased to order this Declaration to be Printed for the satisfaction of our friends and Relations.

On board the *Delivery* als [alias] *Bumper* in the Latitude of Barbados Distance seven Leagues, July 22nd 1721.
John Massey, George Lowther[12]

Douglas accepted the letter from the pirates, but before he could return to his ship, Lowther wrote out "a Sort of Certificate" addressed to the captain of a fictitious consort ship. The pirate captain handed it to Douglas and explained that it was a release paper that he could present to the consort ship's master, giving *Charles* free passage. To help Douglas identify the other pirate ship, Lowther described her as a forty-gun frigate and mentioned that their two ships would be cruising the waters east of Barbados for several more days. Lowther concocted the fiction to discourage a vigorous pursuit by the Royal Navy station ships in Barbados who might think twice before tangling with two heavily gunned pirate ships.[13]

A bewildered James Douglas finally climbed aboard his brigantine and ordered sails raised. *Charles* bore away for Barbados. As soon as he anchored in port on July 27, Douglas handed over the pirates' appeal for a royal pardon to Samuel Cox, the acting governor, who would forward the petition to the Board of Trade the next month. After speaking with the governor, he hurried out to the navy station ships moored in the bay and reported the pirate attack to the captains of HMS *Hector* and *Feversham*. The fifth-rate navy ships were not deterred by

Lowther's false claim of a forty-gun consort and put to sea the next morning. *Hector* and *Feversham* combed the eastern approaches to Barbados over the next four days but found nothing.[14]

The second part of Lowther's subterfuge worked better than the fiction of the consort ship. The moment that *Charles*'s sails had dipped below the western horizon, Lowther ordered all sails raised and directed the master to steer north-northwest for Dominica, leaving the station ships with nothing but empty ocean to search. This would not be the last time that Lowther would use deception to make his escape from the scene of his piracies.

CHAPTER 6

DIVISIONS AND DEPARTURES

DELIVERY, SOUTHEAST OF DOMINICA, LATE JULY 1721

The call of the lookout brought George Lowther forward to examine the latest sighting of land off the port bow. Peering through his spyglass, the pirate captain could make out a dark irregular shape emerging from the dazzling blue of the tropical sea. The land mass grew in stature as the pirate ship drew closer, and its color began burnishing through the haze until the brilliant green of its forested slopes saturated the landscape. The high peaks and lush vegetation matched the plot for the pirates' destination—Dominica.[1]

Working off Captain Russell's charts for the promised voyage from Africa to the West Indies and, possibly, some maps left by Captain Menzies from his trips to Barbados and Curacao, Lowther plotted *Delivery*'s entrance into the Caribbean through one of the passages next to Dominica. He likely stayed windward of the island, since the west side of Dominica could be tricky with wind gusts channeled through the gaps in its highlands. Also, a cautious pirate would want to keep any threats coming from Saint-Pierre, on the northern end of Martinique, in his lee. Dominica was populated only by Caribs and occasional French woodcutters from the neighboring islands, making for relatively safe sailing along its rocky eastern coast. Rounding the northern cape, Lowther turned *Delivery* south toward a 500-foot extinct volcano on the end of a short peninsula. Just past the headland, the pirate ship entered Rupert's Bay, a 3-mile-wide haven on the northwest end of

Dominica frequently used by European convoys making their first landfall after their Atlantic crossings. The pirates dropped anchor one or two cable lengths (about 200–400 yards) from shore in 7 to 20 fathoms.[2]

The eager crew swarmed ashore, splashing through the surf or ferrying to the beach in the longboat. After six weeks of fouling the decks, the men could relieve themselves on dry land wherever they pleased without hearing backlash from their deck mates. Massey's ex-soldiers thrilled at the chance to walk on stable ground, a relief for lubbers who had yet to adapt to life on a constantly teetering ship. The free-roaming men plucked wild limes and oranges that dangled from tree boughs just off the beach. The fresh fruit provided a delightful addition to their unsparing diet of biscuits and salted meat, lately supplemented with salted fish. They also adopted the habit of squeezing the juice into a mixture of rum and sugar to make a more palatable rum punch. What they did not appreciate at the time was the vitamin C packed in the citrus fruit, which forestalled the onset of scurvy, a horrible disease that carried off seafarers by the thousands.[3]

The pirate leaders, Lowther and his cohort John Massey, let the men frolic for a while before attending to some important business. The long sail from the Gambia had drained much of the ship's supply of water, and the casks needed refilling. Pulling the men away from their diversions, the captains oversaw the lifting of the water barrels from the hold and their transport to the island. Three rivers drained into Rupert's Bay. The largest one held brackish water, but the two smaller streams

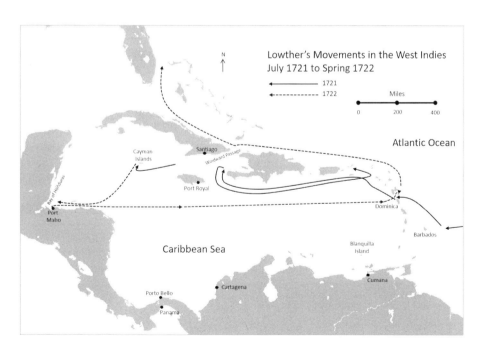

West Indies, 1721–22. Lowther's movements in the West Indies, July 1721 to spring 1722.

rippled with freshwater runoffs from the nearby hillsides. Crew members dumped out the last putrid dregs left over from Africa, then replenished the barrels with pristine drinking water. In short order, all of *Delivery*'s fully stocked water barrels were lowered back into the hold for the next stage of the pirates' adventure.[4]

While they relaxed in the pleasant bay, fortune dropped another treat in their laps. A sloop flying French colors turned into the bay, probably making its first landfall, too, since leaving Europe. Lowther examined the inbound sloop, then decided to use deception to seize it rather than make an outright assault. Why risk a fight when a little duplicity can achieve the purpose? The pirates threw out English colors and hid most of the crew below deck to put the merchantman at ease. When the vessel approached, the captains exchanged a friendly hail, telling the other their port of origin, destination, and principal cargo. Lowther might have honestly stated that they had come from Africa, but the rest of his greeting was a lie. The French captain volunteered that they carried a plentiful load of brandy and wine, to which Lowther replied that he would consider purchasing some of the cargo. The chance to make a quick sale for some hard English currency proved too enticing a proposition for the Frenchman to pass up.[5]

Lowther suggested that the French come over in their longboat while *Delivery* sent an officer back to inspect their cargo. This time, John Massey stepped up to participate in the piracy by posing as the buyer and performing the faux negotiations. A half dozen of the French crew came aboard *Delivery* and "were imediately bound and confined." With hostages secured out of sight on *Delivery*, Massey rowed over to the sloop and met with the French captain. He listened as the merchant captain recited his inventory and "ask'd the Price of one Thing, and then another, bidding Money for the greatest Part of the Cargo." Having toyed with the Frenchman long enough, Massey leaned into his ear to whisper, "They must have it all without Money."[6]

The Frenchman got the message. He had been hoodwinked and, with part of his crew already held prisoner on the pirates' ship, had no choice but to acquiesce to the robbery. Lowther sent the longboat over with ten "double armed" men under the supervision of Sgt. John McDonald to bring the sloop to anchor next to *Delivery*. The French crew then endured the pillaging of their ship, an experience akin to being eaten by rats: slow, painful, and revolting. The sea bandits, at anchor in a remote bay beside a largely uninhabited island, could take their time searching the sloop for anything of value. First came the cash, about £50 of English currency from the captain's quarters. "Massey and Lowther locked up the sd Money in an iron bound Chest which was called the Companys Chest to the lock of which Chest there were two keys and the sd Massey kept one and the sd Lowther kept the other." Massey also discovered a pair of gold buttons among other valuables. Next, the pirates emptied the merchantman's hold. They hauled out "three and thirty Anchors of Brandy" (10 gallons each) and "about six hogsheads of Clarrett" (63 gallons each). Though inexperienced as buccaneers, the *Delivery*'s crew may have reveled in the excess, as William Snelgrave reported another pirate crew had done with a similar find of wine casks. "They hoisted upon the deck a great many half hogsheads of claret, and French Brandy, knocked their heads out, and dipped cans and bowls into them to drink out of. And in their wantonness threw full buckets of each sort upon one another." In their occasional sober moments, Lowther's old tars combed the sloop for naval stores that might prove useful: spare yards, cordage, sailcloth, gunpowder, tar, paint, etc. The other men, working at their leisure, rifled the French crew's personal chests, then helped themselves to any fancy shirts or finery they uncovered. The captives sat in the roundhouse with their hands bound the whole night and into the next day while the pirates ransacked their vessel and quaffed the stolen brandy. The victims were eventually set loose, but, without a cargo, they would return home with few personal possessions and no pay, except a £5 tip Lowther left for their courteous submission.[7]

Flush with water, food, and spirits, the pirates weighed anchor and raised their courses to depart Rupert's Bay. They cleared the headland, then unreefed the topsails to catch the stiff easterlies as Lowther had the master bear northwest into the Caribbean Sea. Easy scores in Barbados and Dominica in little more than a week buoyed the inebriated crew's confidence. Prospects looked good. As they drank themselves into a stupor and a few men sat watch, the crew of *Delivery* settled down, feeling reassured about their future course as swashbucklers—all but one.

DELIVERY, SOUTHEAST OF SANTA CRUZ, EARLY AUGUST 1721

The few nights since Dominica did not pass undisturbed for John Massey. Despite a propensity for self-justification, he could not disguise his role in the piratical looting of the French sloop or rationalize his acts as anything other than wanton theft. It tore at his conscience. A British chaplain who would later get close to Massey heard him confess his misgivings about this time in the West Indies. "In this disconsolate state his night was often so troublesome to him as days, for, as he himself said, he seldom shut his eyes, but he dreamt that he was sailing in a ship to the gallows, with several others round him." Lowther noticed the moodiness of his partner and tried to keep Massey engaged in their pirate enterprise. Though Lowther was the senior mariner and captain of the ship, he still thought of Massey as a coequal leader of the company. Lowther discussed plans and ideas with him, but the army captain seemed to become more distant with each passing day. Lowther's concern for his partner was soon disrupted by another ship sighting.[8]

The sharp-eyed lookout had picked out the bare mast of a boat against the backdrop of the unpeopled island of Santa Cruz (modern-day Saint Croix). Upon closer examination, Lowther determined that the boat was anchored and, therefore, defenseless. The pirate crew pulled down the English colors, and up went the black ensign. The galley-frigate turned to starboard to make a run at the helpless vessel moored offshore.[9]

The boat's crew made no attempt to defend their craft. It would have been pointless. The men jumped overboard, swam to shore, then fled into the woods. The boat fell to the pirates with no effort. Lowther thought the easy capture might be a good opportunity to include Massey in decision-making. He turned to him and asked his opinion about "What they should take?" The army captain replied with disinterest, "He might do as he pleased." As for himself, he "understood no more how to be a Pirate than to be a Mountebank." Lowther disregarded the snide remark and sent some of his experienced mariners over in the longboat. The men climbed aboard the abandoned boat but found little to scavenge. They called back to say that the boat was newly built and may not have been to sea yet. Even without a cargo the hull had value, so the pirates manned it and brought her off as a prize. Lowther might have been tempted to sail the boat to the nearby Danish port of Charlotte Amalie and sell it. However, the evidence suggests that he continued his westward course and dropped off his prize along the way, since there is no further mention of it.[10]

Delivery made good speed during daylight, cruising due west inside the Caribbean while taking advantage of the strong following winds that filled its sails and a steady current that pushed it along. Nights were different. The numerous islands and shoals circled on Lowther's charts loomed as potential hazards that forced the crew to lower the topsails and partially reef the courses during the night watches. Work was slack. No sails to set at night and few adjustments during the day. With an overpopulated crew to share the minimal duties, most men sat idle and drunk. Seafarers normally had innumerable tasks to keep the ship and its rigging and cargo in good shape. All ships leaked, and pumps had to be manned on occasion to clear water from the bilge. Sails and shrouds had to be mended and replaced. Wooden surfaces had to be cleaned, scraped, painted, tarred, patched, or replaced. Pirate crews attended few of these functions. Why mend canvas when you can steal sails off the next prize? For that matter, why worry about the ship when you can take a new one?[11]

Lowther worried. As captain, he knew that their lives and livelihood depended on keeping the ship in sailing and fighting trim. Too much neglect would leave them trailing their prey or worse, unable to escape a pursuing man-of-war. He managed to get men to take care of most tasks, but without the threat of a flogging or a boatswain's cane to encourage mindfulness, he had to look the other way if one of the gallants wasn't properly furled, a brace became twisted, or a bowline had frayed. He had other worries. *Delivery* had to seize merchant ships to keep the men and ship stocked with necessaries, and the responsibility of finding the next target rested on him.

Working their way south of Puerto Rico and across the Mona Passage, the pirates kept searching for sails on the horizon. Lowther, in his unrelenting quest for prizes, plotted a course farther westward toward the more heavily trafficked routes between Jamaica, Hispaniola, and Cuba. He kept asking Massey for suggestions but got apathy in return. Lowther could see a steady decline in Massey's spirit as he lost faith in their venture. Even with the pressures of being captain on his shoulders, his partner's worsening attitude was becoming Lowther's biggest headache.

Massey spent his days lounging in his hammock, frustrated and wracked by guilt. He had stature among the pirate company but no useful input. His combat experience counted for nothing aboard a ship, and he had no way to exercise command when he had not the least idea of how to run a sailing vessel. The fruits of his piracy only added to his disgruntlement, "tho' here he liv'd very well, yet his Heart was uneasy." His despondency grew as the ship plowed along the south coast of Hispaniola until an odd idea popped into his head. It occurred to him that thirty-nine of the seventy-three-man crew were soldiers trained for land warfare. Could they not be used to attack a town rather than a ship? Drake and Morgan had plundered cities and walked away with fortunes in ransom money from townspeople desperate to be rid of them. He approached Lowther with the suggestion, arguing that with thirty men he could seize a French or Spanish habitation "and bring aboard the Devil and all of Plunder."[12]

The pirate captain thought it lunacy. Corsairs had every advantage when snatching an overloaded merchant ship at sea—more speed, more guns, more men, etc. Setting a force on land, on the other hand, ran countless risks. They would not know the lay of the land or whether the town had guns at its gate. An armed militia could contest their movements, or a hostile ship might appear while half the crew was ashore. Lowther rejected the idea, though he took time to reason with Massey instead of rebuffing the idea outright, humoring him as a master carpenter might an enthusiastic apprentice. The army captain relented—for the time being.

DELIVERY, SOUTH OF SAINT DOMINGUE (MODERN HAITI), MID-AUGUST 1721

Massey may have deferred to Lowther's judgment, but he had not forgotten his dubious scheme of seizing a town. Far from it, the idea had further metastasized in his troubled mind. Where was the honor in plucking random merchant ships at sea, he wondered? Assaulting and capturing a land objective felt like a more worthy and lucrative endeavor to the army officer. It would allow him to use his military talents and add to his stature as a leader among the pirate company. Coasting along the shore of a French colony, Massey became enamored by the thought of striking a blow against part of a Bourbon realm. Behind Lowther's back, the army captain talked up the prospect of a shore raid among his followers, mostly the soldiers of his old company, who may have felt as out of place on the galley-frigate as he did. Massey understood the risks of sowing division within the company of pirates, but it appears his actions were propelled by a deep personal motivation. Capturing a French colonial town would do more than haul in loot; it would be an honorable act supporting their royal master against his enemy, the French king. Surely, he reasoned, King George would see the service to the Crown of such an enterprise and extend his gratitude to the adventurers who could accomplish so daring a raid. In his own convoluted way of thinking, Massey fixed on the land raid as his path to escape the nightmare of piracy and retrieve his self-esteem—a desperate lunge for redemption.

Massey confronted Lowther with his supporters in tow and demanded that his proposition receive a hearing before the entire company. Lowther had to consent to a general conclave. He did not command the ship or the pirate company. Major decisions had to be determined by general consensus, and Massey's supporters were within their rights to bring the issue before the assembly of pirates. Arguments for and against a landing bounced back and forth across the deck. The debate rent the company between soldiers and seafarers, Massey and Lowther. After giving the land operation a hearing, the issue came to a vote. The majority sided with Lowther, and "the Affair was over-ruled in Opposition to Captain Massey." With the decision having gone against him, Massey became fractious. He could not abide losing his chance at redemption, and his supporters stuck with him. The whole ship's company separated into opposing camps. Reasoning and logic gave way to passion and temper. The two factions "were all ready to fall together by the Ears, when the Man at the Mast-Head cry'd out 'A Sail! A Sail!'"[13]

The fortunate sighting doused the flaring tension among the pirates. They now had a common target to focus their ardor. *Delivery* had worked its way into the Windward Passage and chanced upon a small ship out of Jamaica bound for Britain. Lowther ordered his experienced sailors aloft to throw out more canvas while Massey's men strapped on gear and loaded their firearms for a potential boarding. Catching more of the steady easterlies in its sails, *Delivery* ran down the smaller vessel after a few hours' chase. The merchantman hove to once the pirates closed in gun range and raised their dreaded black ensign. The pirates then indulged themselves in the ritual of plunder, "feasting upon what they found and looking in the Trunks and Coffers belonging to the Officers, Passengers, and others, and taking such Things as appeared best for their Purpose."[14]

This time, Lowther and his crew took more than mere possessions. Two men from the merchant vessel were forced to remain aboard *Delivery*. Pirates often held merchant sailors against their will, especially if they had particular skills. Carpenters, physicians, and even surgeon's assistants were invariably turned into "forced men" because of the critical need for their services on pirate ships. Sometimes, pirate captains wanted to plus up their crews to fill vacancies left by death, injury, or desertion. The process of coercing reluctant sailors to join a pirate crew became an unpleasant, often-cruel experience for the new men. The record left no mention of specific measures applied against the two forced men, only that they had to leave their ship for *Delivery*. However, the next interaction suggests that the threat of death may have been persuasive. Once the forced men were secured, Lowther proposed sinking the merchant ship along with its crew and passengers. This is the only known occasion that Lowther showed an inclination to murder any of his captives, at least English ones. Luckily for the victims, Massey—the likely source regarding the incident—interposed on their behalf. The crew stood with Massey this time, unwilling to stomach the thought of turning into deliberate murderers. Lowther released the vessel, and it continued its voyage on to Britain, empty handed.

The capture may have calmed the internal crisis on *Delivery*, but the hard feelings among Massey and his supporters persisted, though another piece of good luck kept them distracted. The next day, lookouts spotted sails belonging to a schooner, a two-masted vessel rigged with fore and aft sails. The pirates displayed their black flag, but the schooner turned and fled. For the second time in two days, *Delivery* had to chase its prey. With more masts, square sails filled with wind, and less cargo, the pirates could outpace their intended victim. The schooner's advantage rested on its ability to sail a point closer to a headwind than a ship-rigged vessel. In this situation the schooner's captain would have turned east and tacked against the wind or, as mariners liked to say, "clapped on a wind." Lowther and *Delivery*'s master had to rely on good seamanship to snare the elusive craft. They lost ground tacking back and forth to windward, but their superior speed allowed them to keep the schooner contained to windward. The contest between pirate and prey came down to a matter of space and light. If the schooner had enough sea room to stay beyond gun range until nautical twilight, it could slip away from the galley-frigate in the dark. Unfortunately for the schooner, Lowther was able to pin it against a shore, probably near Cape Tiburon, the southwestern tip of Hispaniola that projects into the Windward Passage. The schooner's crew, who turned out to be smugglers, beached their craft and abandoned it, leaving the contraband cargo to fall into the pirates' hands.[15]

Lowther and his crew helped themselves to their latest prize and the goods in its hold that the smugglers had intended to sell illegally in a Spanish port. The pirates refloated the schooner, with the idea of using it as a consort for *Delivery*, but John Massey had other ideas. The army captain stood before Lowther and the rest of the pirates and "declare'd his Resolution to leave them." He wanted the schooner, he wanted his share of the company's plunder, and he wanted to strike out on his own with as many of his supporters who were willing to join him. Lowther, by this time wearied of his partner's attitude and disgusted by his divisiveness, agreed to split the company and sacrifice their latest prize just to be rid of him. Massey addressed the assemblage and asked any who wished to go with him to stand by his side. Only twelve soldiers and one mariner, Alexander Thompson, chose to leave the pirate company, proof that most of the soldiers and nearly all the old *Gambia Castle*'s crew had higher regard for Lowther. Before departing *Delivery*, Massey used his key to open the company chest and withdraw his stake of cash, about £20, the Frenchman's gold buttons, some fancy silks, and the perukes he had pilfered from Colonel Whitney. The long, flowing wigs may have been a minor indulgence on his part, a luxury that he could not quite part with. They would cost Massey dearly at his future trial, since they were the only pieces of stolen property that the court could link to him personally.[16]

The breakup of the pirate company illustrated a common problem among pirate crews. They were not formal communities held together by institutions or customs, but, rather, loose confederations of criminals who had thrown together. They had no laws beyond a short set of rules forbidding certain conduct, and majority-rule votes over major issues. Pirate captains and ships' officers like Lowther managed only the running of the ship, though their positions were no more secure than the general mood of the crew allowed. The crew of *Delivery* had no method for reconciling internal schisms other than to let the company split apart.

The detached pirates climbed aboard the schooner and cast off from *Delivery*. Captain Massey boldly proclaimed that they would seize the first ship they encountered, but reality dictated a different course. With a crew of thirteen lubbers and one sailor, they could barely manage to steer in one direction without springing a mast or capsizing. Notwithstanding his bravado, Massey intended to terminate his pirate days and turn himself in at the nearest British port. He directed Alexander Thompson to head for Jamaica.

Standing on *Delivery*'s deck in the Windward Passage, Lowther watched his former partner sail southwest, in the direction of Jamaica, he guessed. He waited until the schooner's masts disappeared under the horizon, then ordered the ship's master to turn into the wind and sail east—opposite the direction they had followed over the previous weeks.

BRIGANTINE MARY, DARTMOUTH, ENGLAND, AUGUST 21, 1721

Capt. Charles Paris, master of the Royal African Company packet boat *Mary*, rode the incoming tide into the Dart River estuary and past the fifteenth-century castle guarding its entrance. The brigantine had spent the preceding seven weeks sailing from the Gambia on an urgent mission. The moment that *Mary* safely docked inside Dartmouth's harbor, its primary passenger, Charles Russell, hurried into town to board an express coach for London. He carried letters from Colonel Whitney and the company factors at Fort James, Henry Glynn and William Ramsey. Russell was also burdened with some awful news. A week later, he arrived at Africa House on Leadenhall Street.[17]

Notes from Russell's interview with the company Court of Assistants and secretaries were not kept, but the meeting must have been dreadful and humiliating for the merchant captain. He faced both professional and financial ruin: lost ship, lost crew, and lost cargo. The news was no less heartbreaking for the assistants and the Duke of Chandos. They had invested heavily in the recovery mission to the Gambia with both currency and hope. All that vanished once the mutineers absconded with the *Gambia Castle*. Instead of restoring the company's fortunes, the declining situation at Fort James and the Gambia River mission led the company to close three upriver factories the next year. By January, only twenty-two soldiers would be left alive at Fort James. Colonel Whitney would not be among them. He died on October 6, 1721, a heavy charge for the £500 salary that lured him to the Gambia.[18]

The Court of Assistants dismissed Russell after digesting his report. He remained in town, but the company gave no thought to offering him a new ship. A surprising piece of intelligence would change their minds a month later.

CHAPTER 7

PROWLING THE GREATER ANTILLES

GOVERNOR'S RESIDENCE, SPANISH TOWN, JAMAICA, AUGUST 21, 1721

For Sir Nicholas Lawes, longtime resident and current governor of Jamaica, few issues vexed him more than the unending depredations "committed by pirates of all nations who infest those seas." He had repeatedly warned the Council of Trade and Plantations in London that "pyracys and robberys" committed by Spanish *guardacostas* such as Augustin Blanco, and British buccaneers such as Benjamin Hornigold, had been choking the island's commerce for years, "insomuch that there is hardly one ship or vessell, coming in or going out of this Island that is not plunder'd." The degree and persistence of these attacks at sea exceeded what could be tolerated or excused, and he knew where to place the blame. "This in great measure," he wrote, "I impute to the neglect of the Commanders of H.M. [His Majesty's] ships of warr, who are said to be appointed for the suppressing of pyrates and for a security to this Island, and protection of the trade thereof, but in reality, by their conduct, have not the least regard to the service they are designed for."[1]

After the War of the Spanish Succession came to an end in 1714, piracy burst forth and flourished in the Atlantic basin, fueled by the excessive number of unemployed mariners, many with experience as sanctioned privateers, and compounded by the neglect of the British Admiralty. Charles Johnson, the main chronicler of early-eighteenth-century pirates, wondered about the ineffectiveness of Royal Navy station ships in catching sea robbers infesting nearby waters. "Tis strange that a few Pyrates should ravage the Seas for Years, without ever being light upon, by any of our Ships of War. . . . Pyrates at sea . . . know what Latitude to lie in, in order to intercept Ships . . . and by the same Reason, if the Men of War cruise in those same Latitudes, they might be as sure of finding the Pyrates, as the Pyrates are to find the Merchant Ships." Sir Nicholas had his own theory—the captains of the station ships were too busy carrying private cargoes for profit to see to their duties. He also complained that the navy's private commerce undercut the legitimate business of Jamaica's merchants. "The men of warr's transporting goods and merchandize," he noted, "otherwise would be done by vessells belonging to the Island." The governor's stated powers gave him authority to direct the missions of the station ships, however, he had little success in getting them to go after any sea bandits. Lawes protested to London that "tho' the Commanders thereof, by their Instructions are directed to advise and consult with myself and the Council: yet they have no other regard for wt. is resolved upon, than is consistant with their own private gains." A year earlier, Lawes had a notable confrontation over contraband trade with the Royal Navy Jamaica Station chief, Cdre. Edward Vernon. George Lowther's former commander had prevented Jamaican port authorities from confiscating an illicit cargo of French indigo because the navy intended to escort the shipment, presumably for a substantial stipend. Feeling no pressure from the Admiralty and preoccupied with commercial prospects, the navy captains had little incentive to chase the elusive corsairs. "The taking of pirates," one observer commented, "is but a dry business, unless they catch 'em by extraordinary good fortune with a prize fresh in their mouths."[2]

Lawes and the Jamaican Assembly took matters into their own hands by commissioning two sloops to patrol their coasts to make up for the Royal Navy's inaction. Their efforts began producing results. Private traders first captured Charles Vane, then Calico Jack Rackham and his crew, including Anne Bonny and Mary Read. Commodore Vernon got more involved and snared the Spanish guardacosta, Simon Mascarino, recently commissioned by the governor of Santiago de Cuba to interdict foreign traders in the Caribbean, and with a fresh prize in his mouth.[3]

More good news came from the harbor when Governor Lawes heard that a schooner with fourteen pirates had come into port claiming they had chosen to mend their ways. Sir Nicholas normally dealt harshly with pirates. He had already strung up Vane, Rackham, and ten of his crew, though not the two women. A few months hence, he would authorize the mass hangings of forty-one Spanish guardacostas. However, he agreed to interview the reformed pirate leader. Lawes listened as John Massey justified his part in the African mutiny as an attempt to save the lives of his men. Massey confessed to his brief career as a sea robber but mitigated his crimes by mentioning that he had taken the first opportunity to depart from Lowther and his gang. The governor came away impressed by Massey's sincerity. His offer to help hunt down his former partner, George Lowther, may have convinced the governor to deal graciously with him and give Massey a chance to redeem himself.[4]

Massey's intelligence that Lowther was roving the Windward Passage prompted Lawes to order out HMS *Happy* in search of the newly reported pirate. The governor's orders carried more weight, given that Edward Vernon had previously departed the Jamaica Station. Massey joined Lt. Joseph Laws, commander of the ten-gun sloop, as it sortied from Port Royal on the morning of August 22 to patrol the southern and western coasts of Hispaniola. Standing on *Happy*'s weather deck, the former army captain might have entertained second thoughts about tangling with *Delivery* in a vessel half its size and with half the number of guns, but the navy lieutenant did not hesitate, feeling confident in his ship's fighting skills against an ill-trained, undisciplined band of buccaneers. *Happy* slipped out to the Caribbean, tacking its way toward Jamaica's eastern tip against easterly winds. They rounded Morant Point on August 25 and from there bore northeast toward Hispaniola. *Happy* enjoyed fair weather and reached Cape Tiburon three days later to begin hunting *Delivery*.[5]

AFRICA HOUSE, LEADENHALL STREET, LONDON, SEPTEMBER 22, 1721

At last, good news! A report just arrived from Barbados set the Royal African Company's Court of Assistants abuzz. HMS *Feversham* "hath lately taken on that Coast a Pyrate Ship carrying 16 guns," identified as the *Gambia Castle*. The joyous company officials hastened to take advantage of this coup and recover their lost galley-frigate. They rushed a letter to Charles Russell with specific instructions to proceed "without a moments loss of time" to Portsmouth. Upon reaching the harbor, he was to hand instructions to Captain Wilkinson, master of the company ship *Crown*, to sail for Barbados with himself as a passenger. The company gave Russell three important missions once he arrived in Barbados. First, he should coordinate with the company's local agents "in the recovery & taking possession of Our Ship the *Gambia Castle*" to ensure that the High Court of the Admiralty did not condemn the ship and award it to the Royal Navy as a prize. Next, the company wanted him to inventory the ship and its cargo to prepare *Gambia Castle* for a return voyage to London. Finally, the assistants wanted him available to the Barbadian court to give "evidence & information . . . particularly as to the behaviour of George Lowther the mate & Capt. Lt. John Massey . . . in order to their being brought to justice for their Piracy & Robbery as the Law directs." The Court of Assistants made their wishes clear: they wanted Lowther, Massey, and their fellow mutineers hanged. Within a few days, Russell dashed to Portsmouth to begin his journey to the West Indies, grateful for the astonishing opportunity to retrieve his lost command and, perhaps, restore a bit of his reputation and finances.[6]

DELIVERY, SOUTH COAST OF PUERTO RICO, LATE SEPTEMBER 1721

Massey, Laws, Russell, and Wilkinson would come back disappointed. *Delivery* was not in the Windward Passage or secured in Barbados—it was cruising 550 miles east of Cape Tiburon in the Caribbean Sea, south of Puerto Rico. Lowther, showing his skill as an elusive commander, left the British ships combing waters he had vacated for safer coasts. The sail to windward dodged his pursuers, but it had taken weeks longer than the westward run of August. Zigzagging against headwinds and a stiff current, the galley-frigate plodded eastward. The crew had more work spilling wind from the courses, lowering and raising the topsails, and pulling over the mizzen yard and sail; each time the master turned the helm to the opposite tack. At night, *Delivery* tried to catch offshore breezes, but usually the crew had to drop anchor to keep the current from pushing them back half a day's distance. That required the crew to winch the anchor off the bottom each morning to get underway. Lowther may have used this time to break in more of the soldiers to the duties of a seaman. The old *Gambia Castle* hands likely encouraged their inexperienced shipmates to help aloft simply to spread the workload among more of the crew. More men pitching in meant more time for each crew member to relax and drink his share of brandy and rum.

Pirate captains had to do more than avoid navy station ships. The ship and crew needed food, water, spirits, clothes, naval stores, etc. to maintain themselves on the sea. They could get those necessaries only by seizing merchant ships. The pressure to keep the company of adventurers well stocked with loot weighed on Lowther until the sighting of a pair of ships near Puerto Rico. Throwing out British colors, *Delivery* steered toward the two ships. The quarry briefly turned away but soon gave up the chase against the speedy galley-frigate. When Lowther drew close, he hailed the two vessels. The reply came back in Spanish. The exchange soon revealed that *Delivery* had stumbled upon a Spanish guardacosta and a small Bristol ship they had just taken.

Spanish authorities licensed the guardacostas to enforce the kingdom's onerous trade monopoly on its New World possessions. For centuries, Spain had kept its American colonies beholden to the mother country for all manufactured goods by awarding exclusive trading rights to the Seville house of trade and imposing an embargo on all foreign goods. The regular sailings of the galleons brought overpriced armaments, clothing, and wine to the West Indies and returned with over ten million silver pesos from New World mines and the expenditures of the colonists. Great Britain wedged its way into some of this trade under provisions of the Treaty of Utrecht at the end of the War of the Spanish Succession. Spain had to grant the British an *asiento* to sell 4,800 enslaved Africans a year in the West Indies, along with one 500-ton shipload of British goods, a *navío permiso*. Britain's legitimate traffic in the Spanish West Indies paled in comparison to the thriving smuggling operations that involved British, North American, Dutch, and French traders. Foreign merchants slipped into Spanish ports, bribed local officials, and sold manufactured goods at prices well below the exorbitant charges for items coming off the galleons. Jamaica's economy boomed as the fruits of contraband trade flowed through the hands of the island's merchants, eventually reaching six million pesos a year.[7]

Colonial *alcaldes*, under provisions of Spain's 1720 Proyecto trade policy, granted commissions to the guardacostas to dampen the illicit trade and to reap the spoils when they returned with prizes. These privateers cruised the Caribbean Sea and the Straits of Florida apprehending interlopers from other nations, then hauling them to a Spanish port. Friendly courts condemned the vessels and their cargoes, earning the guardacosta commanders handsome payouts and the alcaldes freshly confiscated guns to mount in their fortifications. British contraband traders naturally resented the interference in commerce, but captains who had rights of passage to sail between British-held islands and carried lawful cargoes got caught in the guardacostas' seines too. The Spanish corsairs impounded their ships if they had on board so much as a purse of *pesos de ocho*, the most widely circulated currency in the New World. The licentious behavior of these Spanish privateers infuriated the British and would precipitate the War of Jenkins' Ear eighteen years later.[8]

Lowther's crew had no concern for rights of passage, the asiento, or the Proyecto. They were natural-born Englishmen who took a dim view of Spaniards capturing one of their own country's ships, even though they themselves engaged in the same conduct. British colors came down and the black ensign went up. Gunports opened. The crew ran out a broadside's worth of minions and sakers. A platoon of heavily armed soldiers lined *Delivery*'s weather deck. Backed by an overwhelming display of firepower, Lowther challenged the guardacosta commander by what authority he could justify taking a British vessel, then "threat'ned to put every Man of them to Death" if they could not show cause. The terrified Spaniard could produce only his vaguely worded commission, probably issued by the alcalde in San Juan. He claimed rights of seizure because the Bristol ship was caught in Spanish waters (i.e., the Caribbean Sea). The Spanish captain could see that his argument made no impression on Lowther. He and his crew assumed the worst until someone noticed the black ensign. Relieved that he had not been intercepted by a man-of-war, the Spaniard appealed to the British pirates "as great Rogues as themselves," for some professional courtesy. The appeal went only so far. Lowther spared their lives but not their ship. The Spaniards endured the routine of being transferred to *Delivery*, bound, and locked below deck. Meanwhile, the British pirates ransacked the guardacosta ship. In this instance they helped themselves to a plentiful stash of cutlasses, pistols, and grenades from their fellow sea robbers, as well as the standard fare of ship's stores and any loose coins and valuables. Lowther had the guardacosta crew brought up from the hold and then dumped into a launch. Packed into the small boat, the Spaniards were released off the coast of Puerto Rico, perhaps feeling fortunate that they at least came away with their lives.[9]

Captain Smith, master of the Bristol ship, soon came to realize that *Delivery*'s crew, far from coming to his rescue, only further perpetrated the piratical acts of the Spaniards. His cash wound up in the company's iron chest while his crew's personal possessions and the ship's cargo got stolen. He and his men had watched with trepidation as the pirates set the Spaniards adrift. Their anxiety rose further when Lowther turned to Captain Smith's men and announced that they were now part of his crew—no discussion, no pleadings, and no choice. *Delivery* cut loose the two prizes. A small detail in *Delivery*'s launch stayed with the ships until they had drifted off a safe distance, then fired both vessels. Lowther had no use for the ships and did not want to leave evidence of the robbery for someone to notice. The Bristol sailors cringed in anguish as the flames torched their ship, subsiding only when the fiery hulk slid below the surface. Normally, pirate crews gave their detained captives a choice between joining the pirate company or taking a beating. Honest mariners endured long periods of stress as the company men alternated between tempting them with promises of easy living, if they signed on, and frequent whippings, if they refused. The record does not state if Lowther went through the formality of having the Bristol men sign the articles, or whether he had the recalcitrant thrashed. The result was the same. *Delivery* had new crew members.[10]

The reinforced pirate company continued its eastward journey, sailing beyond Puerto Rico into the Leeward Islands' sea-lanes. Within a few days, they fell in with a 30-ton sloop out of St. Kitts. Charles Johnson, in his book on "pyrates," provided no details on the location or the manner of the seizure. Given that the sloop was sailing from St. Kitts, the encounter would have occurred somewhere near the Virgin Islands, if the sloop had been bound for Britain or North America. Lowther, again, confined the crew while his men rifled the sloop of any valuables. As before, the pirate captain informed the merchant seamen that they would be held aboard his ship to share the same fate as the Bristol men. However, when Lowther took a look at the sloop's sleek lines, he considered a different solution than sending it to the bottom. *Delivery* was gaining stores and weight with each plundering. The two recent seizures had more than replaced the thirteen men who had abandoned the pirate company with Massey. Lowther calculated that he now had enough men to crew both vessels. By converting the sloop into a consort, he could unladen *Delivery* to keep it in better sailing trim. There were tactical advantages too. He would gain more flexibility in sighting and running down his prey with two vessels rather than one.[11]

The pirates tore into the sloop, knocking out bulkheads and stripping its deck to turn it into more of a fighting vessel. The sloop needed more armament than a typical merchantman would carry, while *Delivery* had more than it needed. The galley-frigate came with over twenty guns and had picked up more ordnance from its prizes. To strengthen the sloop, *Delivery*'s crew hoisted over swivels and a few guns, most likely lighter minions. Once the conversion was complete and the sloop was crewed, the two vessels set course for their next destination.

The pirate captain, with the support of the company's majority, voted to suspend their sea roving in favor of a little time ashore. The ship's hold contained ample supplies of food and wine. The company chest had been filled with cash, and the men were amply girded with pistols, daggers, and swords. More than anything, they needed fresh water and rest. Lowther figured that *Delivery* could use some maintenance as well. The pirates searched for a quiet bay where they could careen their crafts and take their leisure on land. Mindful that his ship carried stolen merchandise collected over several months, Lowther might have had his eye out for a convenient outlet to unload their inventory. He could not simply sail to the nearest harbor. Finding a safe anchorage meant staying away from port authorities who might set local militia against them, fire on the galley-frigate from a fortification, or call in a navy station ship. Having robbed British, French, and Spanish vessels, the only nearby unoffended islands left to the pirate company were Danish St. Thomas and Dutch St. Eustatius. Yet, even within some of His Majesty's possessions, pirates could still find welcoming officials, merchants, and locals. Blackbeard found a ready customer for his plunder in the governor of North Carolina. Nassau, Bahamas, thrived on a pirate economy until Woodes Rogers drove the buccaneers out three years earlier. A future governor of Bermuda remarked upon his arrival at the island colony, "Pyrates in former days, were here made very welcome, and Governors have gain'd estates by them."[12]

Bribes could get local officials to look the other way, but a pirate ship could not enter a port without attracting unwanted attention. The rovers had other options. If they could not sail to a market, the market might come to them. The Bermuda governor noted a "correspondence betwixt the pyrates and those people that go from hence (as well as from the other Plantations) to those [Virgin] Islands where they pretend to rake salt" but return with stolen merchandise. The future governor of St. Kitts would spend three weeks inspecting the Virgin Islands in 1724 and come away suspicious of the islanders' familiarity with sea bandits. "Altho' I cou'd gett no possitive proof that the inhabitants of these Virgin Islands (especially at Tartola and Spanish Town) aid and assist the pirates, who frequently come amongst them; Yet there is a strong presumption, that they hold correspondence with them, and furnish them with provisions."[13]

No record mentions where *Delivery* alighted that fall, though Lowther only had to turn leeward between Round Rock and Ginger Island to enter Drake's Channel and find dozens of secluded bays in the Virgin Islands. North of the channel, the west coast of Virgin Gorda offered well-protected coves with easy access to the fleshpots of Spanish Town. Farther west by south, the lee shore of Peter's Island had two excellent harbors lined with sandy beaches. Continuing southwest, Bight Bay, a deep harbor nearly enclosed by Norman's Island, could be "as calm as a bath" even while stiff breezes churned the channel. Lowther might have gone farther, bypassing the rocky coast of Puerto Rico and sailing as far as

Samana Bay on the north shore of Hispaniola, where Bartholomew Roberts had rested his crew earlier in the year. However, the Virgin Islands lured the pirate captain and his crew with everything they required: seclusion, soft beaches for careening, comfort, and outlets for commerce and carousing. Experienced mariners from the ship's company or some of the forced men who knew the islands could have directed Lowther to some of the choicer spots.[14]

Delivery pulled into an out-of-the-way cove sheltered by high ground on two or more sides for protection from the winds and the unwelcome glances of passing ships. An anchorage close to a sandy beach completed the setting for the pirate company. The men pitched in to prepare the galley-frigate for a long overdue cleaning, knowing that the quicker they finished careening, the more time they would have to frolic. It could take the entire crew of a twenty-man merchant ship to clean and repair its hull. *Delivery*'s crew numbered near a hundred. The experienced seamen and ex-soldiers shared the work in shifts, but that still left dozens with idle time and an eagerness to indulge cravings for long-denied pleasures. The men had a ready opportunity to make overnight trips in the launches to Spanish Town, Charlotte Amalie, or one of the fledgling settlements on St. John or Tortola where the coins spilled from their purses as quickly as the brandy from their tankards. One contemporary observed the propensity of a typical British sailor to speedily exhaust his wages on flowing liquor and compliant women. "His Furlow is commonly but a night or so; and 'tis well for him it's no longer, for he needs but a week to spend a twelve months pay in reversion."[15]

Local traders knew that pirates were notoriously easy marks and soon visited the careening bay in loaded periguas and dinghies to take advantage of the buccaneers' profligacy. *Delivery*'s crew bartered for local goods with looted merchandise they were pleased to be rid of. Bolts of linsey-woolsey or a kilderkin of nails could be exchanged for a basket of fresh vegetables. The bandits were no better with cash. For a few shillings, traders bought pounds worth of finery, tools, or excess gunpowder from the crew. The same shillings, in turn, dropped back into the traders' hands for pennies worth of rum punch sold to the buccaneers. The sea robbers might have known they were getting skinned, but couldn't care less. Seamen and especially pirates saw little value in the accumulation of wealth. A sixpence spent to fill a cup was better than a guinea sitting in a chest.[16]

Unbeknown to the pirates and their trading partners, Parliament, at that moment, was working to outlaw their commerce. In October the king approved a new act intended to further suppress piracy by declaring that persons who "trade with any pirate, by truck, barter, exchange, or in any other manner," were guilty of piracy themselves and subject to the same extreme penalties. News of the law would not reach the West Indies for several weeks and would not take effect until spring, but the sea robbers were already living on borrowed time. Parliament had finally begun tightening the noose around the libertine bandits who had wreaked so much havoc upon Britain's maritime trade.[17]

Oblivious to the legislative actions in London, Lowther's crew finished cleaning *Delivery*. As the workload slackened, the revelry surged. The men lounged in the sand under the shade of sailcloth canopies, soaking in the warm breezes and answering to no one but themselves and their insatiable appetites. They had thrown off their masters and superior officers. They had removed themselves from all civil regulation. They had abandoned king and country. Free of anyone to tell them otherwise, the pirate company decided it was "Time to take their Diversions, which consisted in unheard of Debaucheries, with drinking, swearing and rioting." Immersed in an excess of libations, they may have emulated other pirate crews by snapping off the necks of bottles with their cutlasses rather than wait for a corkscrew to circulate. The besotted sea bandits tested the limits of their liberty by flouting custom, convention, and the ultimate authority—religious faith. The men seemed to relish blasphemous conduct, "striving who should outdo one another in new invented Oaths and Execrations." Cotton Mather, a famed Puritan divine, described the progress of such behavior: "He rushes upon the Grossest Abominations. Riot, Revels, Debauches grow familiar with him . . . his Impiety improves into Malignity." The pirates wallowed in their freedom but made little use of their time. Weeks passed, blurred by dissipation.[18]

The buccaneers were free from governmental control but not from necessity. Eventually, Lowther and his men realized they had to rove the seas again to sustain themselves with loot to be stolen from other mariners. The canvas canopies came down, and the wine barrels went back into the hold. Climbing up the rigging, the men bent on the courses, topsails, and gallants. Sometime in late fall, the galley-frigate and converted sloop weighed anchor and slipped out of the protective cover of their secluded bay. Captain Lowther directed the master to catch the trade winds and bear leeward. The pirate company was headed to the western Caribbean, where Lowther would encounter a new partner, a pirate with a murderous heart who would earn a vile reputation as one of the most brutal of a savage lot.

CHAPTER 8

A PIRATE ADMIRAL

Downcast and glum, John Massey, former captain in the British Army and reformed pirate, stood before Gov. Nicholas Lawes. His expression spoke to his unhappiness as he asked the governor's leave to return to London. Three months earlier, he had sortied aboard HMS *Happy* to assist in the capture of George Lowther and his pirate band, but the navy sloop returned to Port Royal on September 1 empty handed. With that failure, his last chance for redemption had slipped from his fingers. Massey had lived in Jamaica under the indulgence of Governor Lawes, who had overlooked his past acts of mutiny and piracy in recognition of his genuine contrition and willingness to apprehend his former partner. The former army captain might have been grateful for the governor's forbearance, but he remained mired in depression like someone with his feet stuck in sand as a tide of gloom submerged him. Massey eventually concluded that he could escape his melancholy only by erasing the stain of piracy from his reputation. Convinced of his righteous motivations, he decided to plead his case before the court and stake his fate on the monarch's clemency.[1]

The governor tried to dissuade him from rashness. Massey would face powerful enemies at home. The Royal African Company, the British Army, and the nation's merchant class were not predisposed to forgiving acts of mutiny or piracy. Massey persisted. Word had reached Jamaica that the Duke of Portland had been named to replace Governor Lawes, and Massey could not count on official protection if he stayed in the West Indies. Lawes relented, then went to the trouble of endowing

Massey with some funds and writing a letter of recommendation on his behalf. He commented on Massey's efforts to apprehend his former pirate company and recommended him to the mercy of the authorities in London. Letter in hand, John Massey boarded a ship bound for London sometime in early December. He may not have been the only former pirate to leave Jamaica. Alexander Thompson, the lone mariner to depart the pirate company with the army captain, also found passage to London.[2]

DELIVERY, GRAND CAYMAN ISLAND, END OF DECEMBER 1721

Cruising south of Grand Cayman, *Delivery* and its sloop consort stood well out from shore to give the dangerous reefs off their starboard a wide berth. Capt. George Lowther scanned the frothy coastline as he searched for a place to shelter his ships. He had already passed Cayman Brack and Little Cayman for lack of safe anchorages. The breakers along Grand Cayman looked as forbidding as a snarling mastiff, but the tall coconut trees covering the island offered good prospects for water and other provisions. The pirate company had been at sea for a few weeks in their passage from the careening island and needed a stopover to refresh their water casks.

Nothing is known for certain of *Delivery*'s route to the Caymans. Lowther could have stayed north of Puerto Rico and reentered the Caribbean Sea either through the Mona Passage, west of Puerto Rico, or the more westerly Windward Passage, between Hispaniola and Cuba. However, having twice sailed south of the Greater Antilles, he may have preferred to travel through familiar waters. No matter which route he took, Lowther and the crew maintained a lookout for the Royal Navy station ships operating out of Port Royal as they passed north of Jamaica. No record exists of any ship seizures, but the pirate company may have taken some Spanish vessels as they passed the larger islands without leaving mention in any British publications from which pirate historian Charles Johnson drew most of his accounts.[3]

Delivery and the sloop cleared the southwestern point of Grand Cayman, then turned athwart the wind to get in the lee of the island, where they found a safe roadstead. The man tossing the lead to sound the depths reported a rocky bottom. Ships' captains preferred to moor away from rock-strewn seafloors, where anchor cables could sever and snap when dragged. Fortunately, Lowther could peer through the warm water as easily as if it was an aqua-tinted window, and found several patches of sandy bottom. The galley-frigate dropped anchor above one of the smooth spots a convenient distance from shore in 8 fathoms.[4]

The pirates swarmed ashore to find a congenial place where the "climate and soil are singularly salubrious." They located a water source not far from the beach and began replenishing the casks. After that, the men spent their time in diversions, and on Grand Cayman, the chief pastime was catching turtles. The Caymans in the early 1720s had few, if any, permanent settlers but drew frequent visitors from other locales who culled large supplies of the amphibians from the plentiful lagoons and estuaries. The chance to feast on turtle instead of salt pork delighted the rovers, who filled their bellies with fresh meat and copious amounts of rum punch.[5]

Lowther planned only a brief stay-over at Grand Cayman, not a prolonged period of rest. Once the men had satisfied their gluttony, *Delivery*'s crew prepared to sail. However, before they raised anchor, a small boat holding thirteen men entered the road. To the amazement and amusement of Lowther and his company, the boat proudly displayed a black flag—another band of pirates, albeit a pitiful one. Far from intimidating a merchantman, these sea bandits looked more in need of a rescue than a prize. Edward Low, the leader of the squad, introduced himself to Lowther and proclaimed his intention of earning a fortune by robbing at sea. "Lowther received them as Friends and treated them with all imaginable Respect." Impressed by Low's pluck, the pirate captain invited them to sign the *Delivery*'s articles and join their company.[6]

Some pirates, such as George Lowther, went on the account to get out of difficult circumstances, some out-of-work mariners took up the life to escape poverty, while others found themselves forced into pirate crews. Edward "Ned" Low was different. "Nature seem'd to have designed him for a Pyrate." Born in Westminster, Low and his eldest brother committed petty thievery from their child years onward, progressing into break-ins and strong-arm crimes. The brother would end up hanged at Tyburn, but another brother brought Low to Boston and got him a job as a ship rigger. In 1714, Low married a local woman, Eliza Marble, in a ceremony officiated by Benjamin Wadsworth, a future president of Harvard College. Sadly, Ned Low was not destined for a domestic life. Eliza died in childbirth, and Low lost his job at the shipyard. Bitter and angry at his turn of fortune, he decided to leave Boston and his newborn daughter, also named Eliza. He signed on with a merchant ship that sailed to the Bay of Honduras to collect a shipload of logwood, possibly attracted by the high pay. Commercial voyages to the bay fetched premium wages because of the dangers posed by Spanish guardacostas, who viewed the logging operations as larceny from territory rightfully belonging to the Spanish Crown. Low's career as a merchant seaman did not last long after they reached the bay. He had charge of a boatload of thirteen men making runs between ship and shore when he asked the captain's permission to come aboard for dinner. The captain ordered him to make another run to shore because the cook did not yet have the meal ready. Low took offense to the captain's order. He grabbed a musket and fired a ball at him, though with errant aim. He missed the captain but blew the head off another shipmate. Now a murderer, Low shoved off with his small band in their open boat. To survive on their own, Low and his team captured a slightly larger vessel the next day and adopted the profession of piracy. They made a black flag and declared, "War against all the World." The jaunty gang bent their course for the Cayman Islands, where they had a chance, yet fortunate, encounter with Lowther and *Delivery*.[7]

Besides welcoming Low into the company, Lowther made the extraordinary decision to name him as his lieutenant. The newcomer's promotion had less to do with Low's swagger than some critical intelligence he brought the pirates. Low described the numerous merchant vessels coming in and out of the Bay of Honduras with their holds loaded with tons of logwood and their captains' chests filled with bags of coins to pay the itinerant loggers who worked the rivers feeding into the bay. The core wood from the logwood tree, *Haematoxylum campechianum*, was highly desired by European textile mills to dye their fabrics. The active trade produced £60,000 of revenue a year from an otherwise empty forest wilderness. The tree could be found only in the Yucatán Peninsula, with major logging centered on the bay indented into its Caribbean coast. The seashore extended over 400 miles from Cabo Catoche, near Cancún, to the Gulf of Amatique in Guatemala. Such a long littoral would normally require extensive patrolling to snare multiple prizes, but Low shared another promising bit of intelligence. A long reef system and several coral atolls restricted sailing ships to three passages from the bay to the sea. Furthermore, the ships had to navigate those outlets in the face of steady easterlies. A pirate ship stationed windward of the channel exit would have any merchant ship at its mercy.[8]

As with any major decision, Lowther brought up the proposal to venture to the Bay of Honduras before the entire company. Ripe prizes, narrow passages, and favorable winds promised easy hunting for *Delivery* and its crew—the pirates voiced their hearty approval. Lowther charted a course toward what is now the coast of Belize. Eager crewmen jumped into action, anxious to ransack new victims and split more plunder. Men jammed handspikes into the capstan and wound the anchor off the bottom. The loft gang climbed the shrouds to unreef the courses, topsails, and gallants. Deckhands hauled on the braces to catch the wind in the sails while the captain told the quartermaster to set the helm on a southwesterly course. *Delivery* and its sloop consort bore away from Grand Cayman for more-lucrative seas.

DELIVERY, WESTERN CARIBBEAN SEA OFF THE YUCATÁN PENINSULA, JANUARY 10, 1722

The pirates made a quick 530-mile run from the Caymans toward the bay, pushed by the unrelenting easterlies in that part of the Caribbean. As a careful and skilled mariner, Lowther would have maintained his course southwest to the latitude of one of the passages through the barrier reefs, then doglegged due west on that parallel. The northernmost exit of the Bay of Honduras, Grand Bogue Channel, left the bay next to Key Chapel, then steered past Mauger Key at the northern end of Turneffe Atoll at latitude 17°40' N (north). Lowther would have to be cautious about approaching this passage. Any ship coming from the east had to stay alert to avoid getting pushed onto lee shoals by a following wind. Famed navigator Capt. Nathaniel Uring had wrecked on these reefs two years earlier from lack of caution.

Another narrow passage from the Belize River meandered between several keys in the center of the bay before swinging round the southern ends of Turneffe Atoll and Four Keys Reef at 17°06' N, but this route would have been too challenging for any ship's captain without having a knowledgeable pilot aboard. Lowther's most reliable option was to drop farther south. Following a southwesterly bearing, he might have stopped at Ruatan Island to refresh his water, an uninhabited spot frequently visited by corsairs. From Ruatan, *Delivery* could raise the northern coast of Honduras in a day and follow it west, keeping the hills of the mainland off his larboard until he reached the Zapadilla Keys at latitude 16°02' N. This chain of islets marked the southernmost extension of the barrier reefs and the safest entry into the bay. Both the northern and southern channels carried enough traffic to offer the sea robbers plenty of looting opportunities, but the southern one was Lowther's best choice and the likely scene of his next piracies.[9]

Lowther adopted new tactics for the logwood boats coming out of the bay. Instead of searching for the merchant ships in open waters, *Delivery*'s crew could lie in wait and let the prey come to them. A successful ambush depended on early detection of the target vessel and an advantageous position from which to spring the trap. The St. Kitts sloop gave the corsairs an important edge by providing early

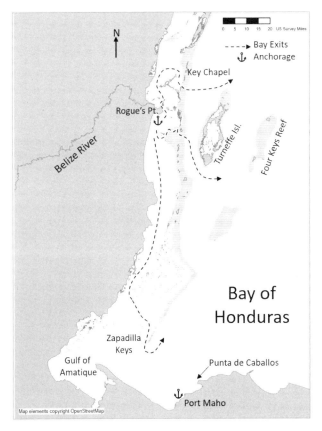

Bay of Honduras. The Bay of Honduras, showing channel exits and Port Maho.

notice of any merchant ship in the channel. English pirates had a history of using multiple ships in tandem. Sir Henry Mainwaring noted, "A little before day they take in all their sails, and lie a-hull, till they can make what ships are about them. . . . They keep their tops continually manned, and have signs to each other when to chase, when to give over, where to meet, and how to know each other, if they see each other afar off." The single-masted sloop could lie several miles southeast of the Zapadilla Keys, with its hull and mast blending into the background of the Honduran mountains. The early-morning hours and an eastward position would further help the pirate scouts by illuminating a target ship's sails while putting glare into the eyes of the prey's lookouts. From its vantage point, the 30-ton sloop could detect ships exiting the bay without being seen, then signal *Delivery*, standing over the horizon from the keys, that a prey had fallen into its trap.[10]

On January 10, *Delivery* received a signal from its consort that a 110-ton merchantman had turned the keys. The deck crew immediately raised anchor and threw out all its canvas, while others cleared the spaces below deck for action. Given the distances and winds, Lowther would have stationed *Delivery* off Punta de Caballos, near present-day Puerto Cortes. Lowther's tactical plan is not known for certain, but a clever pirate would set a course northwest, instead of bearing due west to the Zapadilla Keys. The buccaneers would have wanted the merchant ship out from the protected waters of the bay and plying northward with the reefs in their lee as *Delivery* popped over the horizon and alerted their quarry to the danger. By the time the chase started, the galley-frigate would have a favorable intercept angle and the wind in its starboard-rear quarter. Ship-rigged vessels achieved their fastest speeds while catching the wind on a broad reach, faster even than having the wind to their stern, because all the sails could catch the wind directly without being slackened by the mizzen sails.

Capt. Benjamin Edwards, master of the Boston merchant ship *Greyhound*, grew alarmed as he watched the large frigate draw closer on an angle that would soon bring it within gun range. His heavily laden ship sailed abeam of the easterlies and could not outrun the frigate, nor did he have any maneuver options to avoid the menacing ship. Edwards had the reefs to his lee, and if he came about to starboard or clapped on a wind (i.e., sailed close-hauled against the wind), he would only close the distance to the frigate. Edwards could only hope that the unknown ship had no evil intent.

Once *Delivery* came within range of *Greyhound*, Lowther decided it was time to show his colors. He had no need for deception. The merchantman was cornered—time for intimidation. The black ensign went up, men armed with firelocks crowded the weather deck, and a gun crew fired a shot across the prey's bow. The ship did not heave to. Lowther upped the threat. This time, *Delivery* "edg'd down and gave her a broadside" to demonstrate its firepower and willingness to use it.[11]

Edwards refused to yield. Rather than relinquish his ship and crew to the clutches of pirates, he chose to fight them off. *Greyhound* had only six guns and a crew of fourteen, but the New Englanders girded for battle. With such a small crew, the merchant ship could man only one, possibly two, of its guns. Edwards needed the rest of the crew to manage the sails and man the helm. While the pirate ship waited for them to haul down their topsails and courses, *Greyhound*'s crew charged their guns. The crew did their best to sight the guns and, at Edwards's order, fired at the galley-frigate.[12]

Lowther and his men stood on the deck, dumbfounded by the plume of smoke belching from the merchantman. An instant later they heard the booming report and saw the splash of the shot that clearly had been aimed at them. It took a moment for the shock to wear off. The pirate company had suited up for battle several times, but only to threaten, never to actually fight. Lowther shouted orders to man all the port guns and mount more swivels on the gunwales. Confusion broke over the deck as the untrained and undisciplined buccaneers scurried around to find unfamiliar battle stations. Men collided with each other and crammed the stairways to the gun deck to help man the 6-pounder sakers. Gunners shouted for someone to bring up more powder and shot from the magazine. Only Lowther and a few other pirates had ever handled a naval gun. The master gunner of the *Gambia Castle*, Alexander Ker, had refused to join the mutiny and stayed in Gambia, where he died in September. That left the pirates without anyone truly skilled in naval gunnery. The pirate captain had to go from gun to gun to ensure that each one had at least three men to load, manhandle, and aim the piece. Lowther and a few other navy veterans coached the gun crews. Without training and drills, the men fumbled through the process of swabbing the bores, charging the gun with the right amount of powder, and ramming the bullets. Once the guns were loaded, the gun crews yanked on the lines and tackles to haul the guns against the ship's hull. The most-experienced men then sat behind the barrels and instructed the men with handspikes to wedge the barrel left or right to align the gun with the distant merchant ship. Lowther cautioned the gunners to aim at the target ship's sails and rigging. He wanted the merchant disabled and helpless, not heavily damaged or its crew killed. It took some time, but *Delivery* finally had the ten guns ready. On the captain's orders, *Delivery* unleashed its broadside.[13]

Neither side scored effective hits in the early exchanges. In these circumstances, the pirates would have called up for specialized munitions in lieu of round shot. Bar shot, double-head, or chain shot were linear-shaped projectiles that tumbled through the air once fired from a gun. Flung into the target ship's rigging, these bullets could more easily sever lines or tear out sections of a sail. *Delivery* kept firing broadsides at *Greyhound*, but the Boston ship could fire only a round or two back at the pirates. The battle had an inevitable result. With damaged sails and rigging, Captain Edwards could not maneuver as easily as *Delivery*, and soon the sea bandits drew close. Edwards could see dozens of armed men on the deck getting ready to forcibly board him. After an hour-long battle, Edwards "order'd his Ensign to be struck."[14]

Lowther sent a strong boarding party over to the *Greyhound* before Captain Edwards had a change of heart. The next events strongly suggest that his new lieutenant, Edward Low, had charge of the men taking possession of the merchantman.

The pirates climbed aboard *Greyhound* and immediately unleashed their pent-up emotions on their captives. Using knotted ropes, handspikes, pistols, cutlasses—anything that could inflict pain, they "whipp'd, beat and cut" the defenseless sailors. Sea bandits often whipped merchant crews that had put up resistance, if only to discourage such defiance. This drubbing went beyond the normal punishment and certainly exceeded any of *Delivery*'s previous encounters. Once Low discovered that the ship sailed from Boston, he pummeled the captives with redoubled force. Captain Edwards received a particularly savage thrashing. "Two of the unoffending sailors were triced up at the foot of the mainmast and lashed until the blood ran from their backs." The brutality persisted until the captors exhausted themselves. Eventually, the longboat brought the merchant seamen over to *Delivery*, where the rovers imprisoned them in the hold. The bandits then "rifled the ship." After Greyhound had been looted of all portable items of value, Lowther ordered the ship burned—no sense leaving evidence of a crime.[15]

The next stage of the pirate ritual prolonged the captives' ordeal. The merchant seamen were brought on deck and then asked to join the pirate company and sign their articles. The buccaneers began with appeals. They tried to mimic country gentlemen in their embroidered waistcoats, plumed hats, and silk sashes stolen out of the chests of previous prizes, while bragging of their easy lifestyle. One of Low's future captives described their attempts at persuasion. They "set before me the strong Allurement of the Vast [fortunes] they should gain, and what Mighty Men they designed to be and would fain have me to joyn with them and share in their Spoils." However, when temptation failed to produce volunteers, the buccaneers resorted to their true natures and inflicted more beatings and threats. Willing or not, five men were forced to join the crew: Christopher Atwell (first mate), Charles Harris (second mate), Henry Smith (carpenter), Joseph Willis (apprentice), and David Lindsey (able seaman). Lowther selected them because they had special skills that the company could utilize. Sea robbers habitually retained skilled mariners and artisans to serve their needs. Atwell and Harris were literate and knew the basics of navigation. Lowther could use someone besides himself to plot positions and set bearings now that they had more than one ship to manage. Smith, the carpenter, could help with repairs to the ships. Captain Edwards and the remaining crew of *Greyhound* went back into the hold.[16]

Delivery and the consort sloop reset their ambush outside the bay exit. The victims kept coming. Over the next few days, the pirates snared two brigantines out of Boston. Low's animus toward New Englanders continued to show. They burned one and sank the other. Captain Ayres, out of Connecticut, fared no better a day or so later. Lowther and Low burned his sloop too.

The pirate company enjoyed easy pickings outside the bay, but Lowther may have become a little wary of their success. He had a habit of not lingering in one place. Fortunately for him, the two passages out of the bay offered a convenient solution. *Delivery* could shift 130 miles between the northern and southern channels and continue raiding the logwood ships without making its presence obvious. All the while, the buccaneers kept the forced men busy topside and alternated between entreaties and threats to induce them to join the company. The second mate from the *Greyhound*, Charles Harris, began to show signs of second thoughts. A man of small stature but knowledgeable of seamanship, Harris had duties that put him in contact with Lowther and Low. It was not unusual for pirate captains to station forced men at the helm, where they could perform an important job under a watchful eye. Harris did not take a hand in plundering the brigantines and Ayres's sloop, but he saw how easily the lawless adventurers could support themselves on the sea.[17]

The Bay of Honduras continued to offer up logwood ships for *Delivery*'s consumption. A sloop out of Jamaica, Captain Hamilton master, fell into their hands. The bandits pilfered it, taking the usual supplies and contents of personal chests. When the looting ended, Lowther took an admiring look at the sloop's seaworthy design and decided to hold on to it as a prize rather than torch it. By now, the company may have needed more space to store its stolen goods and imprison the growing number of captives. A Virginia sloop came next. The captain and crew of this vessel were spared Low's vendetta against all New Englanders. After the sloop had been plundered, Lowther and Low released the Virginia crew without the customary thrashings and allowed them to sail off, a courtesy Low would never have extended to a Bostonian. The company seized a seventh victim within another couple of days, an 80-ton sloop out of Rhode Island. Once again, Lowther decided to keep the sloop as a prize.[18]

Lowther used the occasion to reorganize the company and his burgeoning fleet. He wanted to convert the Rhode Island sloop into a consort and use the St. Kitts and Jamaica sloops as tenders. These sloops, built from Jamaican red cedar, were lighter than the typical oaken ships and brigs coming out of Europe and the North American colonies. Merchants who plied the Caribbean valued the sloops for their shallow drafts and maneuverability, essential qualities for negotiating the reef-bound Bay of Honduras. Pirate captains such as Lowther appreciated the same features. To turn the larger sloop into a proper consort, the crew had to add armament. They mounted eight carriage guns on the weather deck, then supplemented its firepower with ten swivel guns that could be cradled on stanchions placed at various positions along the gunwales. Lowther turned the up-gunned sloop over to his protégé Edward Low, the first of several pirate leaders who would trace their criminal lineage to his mentorship.[19]

The Jamaican sloop also needed a master, and Lowther gave the command to Charles Harris. The twenty-five-year-old mate of *Greyhound* had succumbed to the buccaneers' psychological pressure over the previous fortnight and signed the company's articles. The lure of a free-and-easy lifestyle had turned his head from the evil practices that sustained it. Harris had grown envious of the corsairs' ostentatious apparel and the absence of hardship in their daily routines, while forgetting the suffering they inflicted on his former shipmates below deck. The pirate code had a seductive appeal to someone coming from the privations of a mariner's life. Another forced man who famously went on the account, Bartholomew Roberts, expressed the logic of adopting the pirate code. "In an honest Service there is thin Commons, low Wages, and hard Labour; in this, Plenty and Satiety, Pleasure and Ease, Liberty and Power; and who would not Ballance Creditor on this Side, when all the Hazard that is run for it, at worst, is only a sour Look or two at choaking. No, a merry Life and a short one, shall be my motto."[20]

Once command relationships had been established within his pirate fleet, Lowther felt the time had come to slip away from the lucrative sea-lanes they had been prowling so successfully. The Virginia sloop he had released would soon be spreading the alarm and might have tipped off a navy station ship that *Delivery* lurked about the bay. The company of adventurers had filled the holds of their ships with stolen goods, supplies, and prisoners. Lowther decided that his small fleet needed a change of scenery and mission, if only for a spell. He ordered *Delivery's* helmsman to set a southerly course, and the galley-frigate along with its consorts left the bay's passages astern. Lowther intended to go only a short distance and only for a short time, but he would not return to the Bay of Honduras for more than a year—the galley-frigate would never return.

CHAPTER 9

PORT MAHO

DELIVERY, PORT MAHO, COAST OF HONDURAS, END OF JANUARY 1722

The company of corsairs had enjoyed a run of good fortune. Merchant ships had fallen into their grasp so fast the men hardly had a chance to finger their loot before the next prize came into view. As much as they relished their newfound bounty, Lowther decided to suspend their marauding. A couple of months had passed since the pirate company had given their ship a thorough cleaning. In general, sea rovers were not mindful of routine maintenance—their creed connoted laxity more than diligence. Still, Lowther determined the galley-frigate had to be scraped, repaired, and retarred to keep the ship trimmed for speedy pursuits. They now had a carpenter on board, Henry Smith from *Greyhound*, who had the expertise to properly supervise the careening and repairs. The pirate captain also figured the crew could use a little shore time to relax without having to key up for another ship seizure or worry about running into a navy station ship. To careen *Delivery*, the buccaneers would need a secluded anchorage deep enough to moor the 250-ton ship. The harbor's bottom had to be sandy to allow the crew to heel the ship on its side. For a prolonged stay the men required a source of fresh water. Rather than search for an offshore island, Lowther turned south into what is now the Bahía de Omoa to locate a suitable protected bay along the coast. As he scanned to his west, he could see the low Guatemalan coastline bearing to the northwest, but it offered no harbor. To his east the Honduran mountains crowded against a shore that bore to the northeast. *Delivery* followed this shoreline east by north until they came upon a coastal plain beneath the highlands. Lowther found a small anchorage protected from the easterly winds and current by the shore and from the north by a mangrove point that jutted into the Caribbean. The charts identified the harbor as Port Maho, modern-day Omoa, though the previous Mayan-Spanish settlement had disappeared years earlier.[1]

The three consort sloops dropped anchor below the mangrove point while the crew of *Delivery* warped the galley-frigate into a secluded cove between the brackish woodland and the coastal strip. The loft gang went up the shrouds to unbend the sails and strip the masts and spars. The canvas sails were carried ashore, then spread out to form canopies for overhead cover. Before the men could get about cleaning the hull, the ship had to be offloaded, a tedious and time-consuming project that involved pirates, forced men, and prisoners. One by one, barrels of salt pork, water, tar, flour, rum, etc. had to be tied off to the masts with lines and tackle, then winched out of the hold by deckhands turning a windlass. The men rigged lines from the yardarms to swing the barrels off the deck onto the longboats that ferried them to shore, where the casks could be rolled to a storage tent. After the supplies and provisions had been lifted out of the hold, the crew removed the ballast. *Delivery* still had tons of iron bars left over from its mission to the Gambia that had been kept to stabilize the ship. All of it had to be raised from the ship's bottom and ferried ashore by prisoners and inebriated crew members. The heavy weight forced the crew to man the capstan to wind up the iron. Poor supervision soon caused a problem. The men dumped the iron near the water's edge on soil composed of silt. "So soon as they landed it, the Earth trembled at their wickedness, that it Caved all in, and as fast as they endeavoured to carry their good higher up, it still Cav'd the more in & sunk." Carelessness cost the sea bandits tons of iron ballast that would have to be replaced with rocks. Small matter; the pirates could force the prisoners to do the hauling. However, the company had to show more care with the guns. The sakers weighed a ton apiece and had to be set on solid ground.[2]

It took several days, but the company finally had the ship ready for the next phase of the operation. A few water casks and other heavy objects left on the ship were shoved to the side nearest the shore to help tilt *Delivery* in that direction. Next, the crew ran long lines and tackle from the masts to shore, then secured them to well-rooted trees. Pirates and prisoners grasped the lines attached to pulleys and heaved until *Delivery* heeled to one side, exposing half of its bottom. The ends of the lines were either tied off to stakes or other trees to hold the ship on its side. A dozen men or more, standing on the keel, began breaming the wooden bottom to remove the gaggle of barnacles and seaweed that had affixed itself to the ship. The process involved holding lighted torches to the accretions to loosen them from the planks, then scraping off the sludge. Henry Smith, the carpenter forced to join the company, examined the boards for any evidence of damage from naval shipworms (*Teredo navalis*), pesky vermin that could chew through the bottoms of wooden vessels. Smith and a few helpers dug out the worms and either patched or replaced the cankered boards. Once the hull had been cleaned, repaired, and caulked, the men lubricated the surface to ease friction with the water and give the ship more speed. They slathered on a stinking mixture of brimstone, tallow, and pitch that had the added benefit of killing the worms, at least for a while. The crew gathered again after the bottom had been coated, easing the tension on the lines and tackle so *Delivery* could right itself in the cove. After warping the ship out of and then back into the cove, the pirate company repeated the careening and breaming of the other side.[3]

With more than enough prisoners and forced men to perform the drudgery, the buccaneers spent their time relaxing onshore, smoking tobacco and draining the supply of wine and rum punch. Those with idle time and motivated by mischief may have explored the coastal strip for any settlements or Mayan villages. Lowther's crew could be expected to search for any chance to frolic with local females or plunder native food stores. Whether or not they made any contacts with the Mayan Ch'orti people who inhabited that corner of Honduras, the natives were certainly aware of their presence. Raids by English, French, and Dutch privateers over the preceding century had driven the Ch'orti and Spanish settlers away from the coast and forced the abandonment of Port Maho and Punto de Caballos. Alert natives, fearful and resentful of the sea intruders, sent word to the interior that several pirate ships were moored at Port Maho.

The crew of *Delivery* had no sense of danger. They had enough heavy guns, firelocks, and swords to fight off a battalion of militia, or so they believed. Showing their customary overconfidence and neglect, they had posted no sentries for early warning of an approaching enemy. The sea rovers stayed busy watching the prisoners toil on the heeled ship, swilling their cups and relaxing in the shade until the sound of snapping twigs and rustling branches roused them from their reverie. Turning their heads toward the forest growth behind them, the pirates observed a mob of natives emerge from the woods armed with a mix of machetes, bows, arrows, and a few muskets. Shock and fear coursed through their veins. They realized, too late, that the natives had caught them defenseless. The great guns that could have leveled dozens with a single blast had been separated from their carriage mounts and lay unattended in the sand. Few of the pirates had bothered to load a pistol with fresh powder or carry a sword. The muskets had been piled under a tent. No one tried to organize a resistance. The pirates jumped to their feet and fled to the water with the roaring throng chasing at their heels. Splashing for the boats and swimming for the sloops, the corsairs cried out for help.[4]

Lowther could see at once that everything and everyone left on land was lost. The natives swarmed over the shoreline and pursued the panicked buccaneers into the water. *Delivery*, lying on its side, could not be saved. Lowther called to the men breaming its bottom to use their torches to set fire to the ship. The crews of the sloops swept in to save as many men as they could. Their guns and firelocks kept the native mob at bay while they pulled survivors out of the water. The pirates and prisoners who were able to reach the sloops assembled on the decks and surveyed the horrific scene. The barrels of pitch that had been used to bream *Delivery* had ignited. Flames licked up the flanks of the galley-frigate and soon ignited the entire ship. Onshore, the natives romped through the tents, looting whatever they could carry off. Anything they could not lift, they smashed. The prisoners and forced men may have enjoyed a moment of bittersweet satisfaction as they witnessed the irony of the pirates' plunder getting plundered. The buccaneers could do nothing more than cringe as the natives destroyed or made off with all the goods, supplies, cash, armaments, wine, food, and possessions they had stolen over the previous six months. In the time it took to load and fire a gun, Lowther's crew had gone from a prosperous company of adventurers to an impoverished gang.

The pirate leader assessed the new reality. Flames engulfed the powerful twenty-gun galley-frigate, and with its loss the bulk of their firepower and cargo capacity also went up in smoke. The existing records do not identify any casualties among the pirates, though some deaths can be inferred by Lowther's next action. He consolidated the entire company onto the 80-ton Rhode Island sloop. Space became cramped aboard the sloop, which measured little more than 50 feet in length and 20 feet at the beam. Furthermore, the smaller company could not guard the large number of prisoners without risking a takeover. Lowther turned the other two sloops over to Captains Edwards, Ayres, and Hamilton and the masters of the brigs. All the prisoners, except the forced men retained by the pirates, joined the merchant captains on the two small sloops after the sea robbers had removed their guns and most of the provisions. The buccaneers reconfigured the Rhode Island sloop with ten guns and eight swivels, then uploaded the extra stores into its hold. Once the personnel and armaments had been parsed between the sloops, the three vessels left Port Maho. The freed merchantmen sailed for Boston, where they would share the news of Lowther's depredations in the Bay of Honduras and his misfortunes at Port Maho.[5]

Lowther's sloop stood out to Bahía de Omoa as the pirate captain gathered all the buccaneers on deck for a major decision that required a vote of the entire company. Lowther proposed leaving the western Caribbean for safer waters. Word of their activity would soon be reaching the ears of the Royal Navy, he reasoned. Because of their diminished fighting capacity, they could not risk an engagement and needed to seek their fortunes somewhere else. Several crew members, especially the mercurial Ned Low, likely harbored questions about the captain's leadership after the disaster at Port Maho, though a vote to replace him was not forthcoming. Lowther had proven his seamanship and had provided well for them since the mutiny in Africa. The majority of the crew stuck with its captain, for now.

Relieved by the crew's support, Lowther renamed the sloop, his new flagship, *Ranger* and ordered the helmsman to steer an easterly course. The pirates headed back across the Caribbean to the Windward Islands. The next few weeks would stress the crew and Lowther's leadership near to the point of fracture.

HMS SWALLOW, CAPE LOPEZ, GULF OF GUINEA, WEST AFRICA, FEBRUARY 5, 1722

The pirate-hunting mission dragged on, accompanied by misery and frustration. Exactly one year had passed since Capt. Chaloner Ogle had left Spithead with HMS *Swallow* and *Weymouth* to sweep the pirate menace from the west coast of Africa. In that time, Ogle had roamed from Sierra Leone to the Gulf of Guinea, lost most of his crews to disease, and had accomplished nothing. A critical shortage of sailors had forced Ogle to leave Captain Herdman and *Weymouth* at Cape Coast Castle while he took *Swallow* back to the Windward and Gold Coasts to impress seamen from the slave ships working the African shores.

The Royal Navy ships were on the trail of the infamous Bartholomew Roberts, later known as Black Bart. Roberts had inherited command of the pirate ship once led by Howell Davis, the buccaneer who had ravaged Fort James in the Gambia. After Davis had been killed in July 1719, his crew elected Roberts to take his place, even though he had once been a forced member of the crew. Roberts then rampaged across the West Indies, North Atlantic, and Africa, seizing an astounding 140 ships and over two hundred smaller craft. Cruising the West African coasts from windward (west) to leeward (east) and back, Roberts had learned of the Royal Navy's presence but deftly avoided Ogle while taking and plundering ships for nine months.

By January, Captain Ogle feared that the notorious pirate had eluded him and flown to Brazil. However, when he arrived at Whydah with a replenished crew, he picked up a crucial piece of intelligence. Roberts had just plundered several ships off the port the day before and headed eastward into the Gulf of Guinea. Ogle followed the scent and at the dawn of February 5 spotted the masts and rigging of Roberts's three ships while they refitted at Cape Lopez, the southern point of the gulf. *Swallow* approached the pirates from the north but had to steer westward to avoid a sandbar, which took them away from the coast.[6]

The pirates mistook *Swallow*'s maneuver as an attempt to flee, all the evidence they needed to identify a target vessel. Roberts ordered his lieutenant, James Skyrm, to pursue what they assumed was a well-stocked Portuguese merchantman. Skyrm set out in a powerful thirty-two-gun consort ship with a reinforced crew of sixty mostly inebriated buccaneers, twenty-three slaves, and sixteen French prisoners.

The navy captain correctly surmised that the pirates had taken after *Swallow* with the idea of plucking an easy prize. He played to their misjudgment. Ogle ordered his helmsman to continue bearing farther out to sea, and instructed the deck officers to shorten the sails enough to let the pirate ship slowly close the distance between them. The chase continued into midmorning. The agitated pirates pranced around the deck, cursed at the wind, and lashed the forced men in their desire to catch the large ship, not noticing that the pursuit had taken them out of sight and earshot of the cape. Unsuspecting of their opponent's cleverness, Skyrm and his men threw out their black ensign and fired their chase guns at the fleeing vessel.

Judging the moment propitious, Ogle signaled the crew to open the engagement. The helmsman threw *Swallow* into a hard turn as the deck crew yanked the braces to reorient the courses and topsails. The sudden maneuver turned *Swallow* athwart the rovers' path. The ports on the gun deck flew open. Crews ran out eleven 18-pounder culverins along with the eleven 9-pounder demiculverins and three 6-pounder sakers on the weather deck and quarterdeck. Before Skyrm and his crew had a chance to drop their jaws and take cover, *Swallow*'s broadside erupted in flame and smoke. A split second later, iron shot smashed through the bow of the pirate ship and rattled down the lengths of its decks, knocking guns off their carriage mounts and dismembering several of the crew.

Skyrm realized too late that he was caught in a battle with a well-armed warship. He tried to turn away while some of his crew fired a few shots in the direction of *Swallow*. A running battle ensued, but the navy crew handled their ship more skillfully and their guns more effectively. The pirate ship took more hits and lost more of its rigging. Skyrm and those swaggering in their rum-fueled courage were all for coming alongside and boarding the navy ship. The more sensible crew saw the lunacy of the idea. The thought became moot when *Swallow* drew close enough to deliver more devastating fire. The main topmast crashed to the deck, costing the pirates their maneuverability. Amid the wreckage, some of the old hands urged fighting on, preferring death in battle to choking at the end of a rope, but the rest of the crew gave up and begged for quarter.

After tending to the wounded and washing the blood and gore off the decks, the sailors shackled the remaining pirates inside the hold. The navy seamen spent several days securing the captured pirate ship. Ogle manned the ship with a skeleton crew and directed them to a nearby island. The British captain then turned back to Cape Lopez to deal with Roberts.

On the morning of February 10, *Swallow* rounded the cape. Roberts and most of his men assumed their consort ship was returning. By the time they recognized the Royal Navy ship, Roberts had lost his chance to flee. He roused his besotted mates and stood out to the gulf to engage *Swallow*, leaving one of his ships and a merchant vessel at anchor. Roberts could see that most of his men were still drunk from the previous evening's debaucheries and in no condition to fight a well-armed warship. Rather than trade broadsides with the navy ship, he planned to go straight for *Swallow* under full sail, give it a broadside, then fly past it to the open sea. He hoped his flagship, the *Royal Fortune*, could sail better against the prevailing westerly winds and allow him to escape into the Atlantic. The pirates threw out all their canvas and steered directly for the man-of-war. The two ships slid past each other, great guns blazing. *Swallow* immediately came about and began to chase *Royal Fortune*, which had gotten the worse of the exchange. Roberts had cleared the navy ship, but he and his drunken crew failed to sail close-hauled as well as *Swallow*. The warship soon drew close and delivered another broadside. A chunk of grapeshot ripped through Roberts's throat, killing him on the spot. Without his leadership, the pirates lost heart and struck their colors, though not before throwing their captain's body overboard.[7]

The capture of *Royal Fortune* capped a triumphant six days of action. Capt. Chaloner Ogle had won a lopsided victory against an enemy that had more ships, guns, and men than he did. He and his sailors had seized three pirate vessels, killed thirteen buccaneers outright, wounded dozens more, and captured 268, all without suffering a single casualty. Roberts, the most feared and successful pirate in the Atlantic basin and master of a fleet of pirate vessels, had been vanquished in humiliating fashion by a single navy ship. For all their bravado the pirates fought with the skill and fervor of ordinary bandits. They proved no match for the Royal Navy. John Atkins, *Swallow's* surgeon, who observed the action, reasoned that their pathetic resistance stemmed from their lack of discipline. "The Pyrates, tho' singly Fellows of Courage, yet wanting such a Tye of Order, some Director to unite that Force, were a contemptible Enemy."[8]

Roberts's crew endured the melancholy ordeal of having their fates determined by the High Court of the Admiralty. After sifting out the slaves, prisoners, minor offenders, and objects of pity, the court condemned seventy-two pirates to death. Of these, fifty-two were hanged in several mass executions, most at Cape Coast Castle, the Royal African Company station on West Africa's Gold Coast. The other twenty had their sentences commuted to work in the mines, though all expired in short order.[9]

Ogle reaped the fruits of victory upon his return to Britain. The king appointed him Knight Companion of the Order of Bath, and the treasury rewarded him with a £5,364 disbursement of prize money, a sum that included a bounty that he was supposed to distribute to each man on the expedition. The figure seemed suspiciously small. The calculated prize value barely exceeded the price of one of the condemned ships. The treasure, armaments, stores, goods, and personal effects accumulated by Roberts over months appear to have been pilfered before the Admiralty could inspect the prize and assess its value, most likely at Ogle's personal direction. Not content with what he had already filched from Roberts's treasure chest, Sir Chaloner refused to pay out the bounty owed to his crew members. It took the court and treasury, intervening on behalf of the men, to pry £1,940 out of his hands to pay what was due his sailors. Ogle's conduct stood in contrast to Lowther, who stipulated articles in his pirate compact about how booty was to be shared among his crew. Apparently, Lowther had a better sense of fairness than Captain Ogle.[10]

AFRICA HOUSE, LEADENHALL STREET, LONDON, FEBRUARY 1722

The stupefied Court of Assistants of the Royal African Company passed the letter from one hand to the next. Each director reacted first with disbelief, then with rage. The cheek! The gall! Who does this mutinous pirate think he is? The offensive letter, delivered by local post, had been written by John Massey. Besides eliciting shouts of anger and disbelief, the note provided the company with its first notice that one of the chief perpetrators of the infamous mutiny of the *Gambia Castle* was in London living as a free man.

Upon his arrival in England, John Massey had set about the restoration of his name in his own peculiar, guilt-ridden, self-righteous way. He wrote a confession to the Royal African Company "wherein he imprudently relate[ed] the whole Transactions of his Voyage, the going off with the Ship, and the Acts of Pyracy he had committed with Lowther." Massey attributed his rash and ill-considered actions to the poor treatment and desperate conditions he and his men suffered under the supervision of the company's factors. Though he "own'd that he deserved to dye for what he had done," he still offered his services to the company if they could find it in their hearts to forgive him. "But if they resolved to prosecute him, he begg'd only this Favour, that he might not be hang'd like a Dog." He asked, instead, to be shot like a soldier.[11]

The fuming Court of Assistants replied immediately to Massey's letter—just not with the degree of sympathy he had hoped for. The company vowed "that he should be fairly hang'd."[12]

The army captain's behavior continued to diverge from what would be expected of a fugitive or someone with any sense of personal well-being. Massey went to the chambers of the chief justice the next day to inquire if a warrant had been sworn out for his arrest. When the clerks replied that they had no such warrant, he explained that he thought one would be coming shortly, then kindly gave them the address of his residence on Aldersgate Street, not wanting to cause the authorities any trouble in locating him. As he predicted, the tipstaff knocked at his door a few days later to bring him into custody.

Massey's appearance before the magistrate did not flow as smoothly as the Royal African Company might have wished. No witnesses could testify to any crimes committed by him. The only evidence before the court was the letter he had penned, but the court had no way to link Massey to the letter. Finally, the frustrated magistrate asked the accused directly, "Did you write this letter?" Massey answered affirmatively and elaborated on the facts described in the letter. That was enough for the court. The magistrate formally charged him "with Robberies or Piracies on the High Seas in the West Indies" and committed him to Newgate Prison on February 24. Massey found himself confined within the walls of London's most notorious hellhole, crowded among the city's debtors, thieves, felons, and those awaiting execution. One man described the place as "a bottomless pit of violence, a Tower of Babel where all are speakers and no hearers."[13]

While Massey mingled with the outcasts, the Royal African Company scrambled to come up with evidence of his criminal activity beyond his voluntary statement. They feared that the flimsy case against the former army captain could not justify holding him indefinitely in pretrial confinement. Colonel Whitney was dead, and they had dispatched Captain Russell to Barbados. They needed to find someone who could testify to the charges until they could bring Russell back to London; otherwise Massey might be released on bail. Luckily for the Court of Assistants, someone learned that Alexander Thompson, the ex-pirate who left Lowther's company with Massey, was in the city. They approached the former mariner with an enticing offer: they would pursue a pardon for his acts in the Gambia and West Indies in exchange for his testimony against Massey. Seeing a pathway to evade the gallows, Thompson accepted. On March 2 he dictated a lengthy statement about the mutiny on the *Gambia Castle* and the early acts of piracy in the West Indies, recorded in the presence of Lieutenant Lloyd, one of the king's attendants. Thompson added one crucial detail at the end of his statement; that Massey had pilfered Colonel Whitney's perukes at Fort James. This information gave prosecutors testimony of an overt crime committed by Massey himself that could counteract a possible defense that he had only gone along with the pirates and not participated in any robberies. Satisfied with Thompson's deposition, the Royal African Company petitioned the king to issue a pardon to Alexander Thompson, so soon as he could testify in court. Lieutenant Lloyd forwarded the petition to the king, along with his recommendation that it be granted. Thompson's statement proved enough to justify holding Massey in Newgate for the next six months.[14]

A dejected John Massey sat among the riffraff in Newgate and ruminated on his misfortune while his former partner in mutiny, George Lowther, worried that he might find himself caught up in another mutiny—on the opposite side.

CHAPTER 10

TROLLING NORTHERN WATERS

RANGER AT SEA, MARCH–APRIL 1722

The weeks since the disaster at Port Maho crept by under a cloud of tension and doubt for George Lowther. He had convinced the pirate company to shift their prowling to the Windward Islands, 1,750 miles due east of Port Maho, a manageable distance except for the persistent easterly winds and currents of the Caribbean. At first, *Ranger* hugged the northern coast of Honduras, clapping on the wind during the day and catching offshore breezes at night to make headway. Once they reached Cabo Camarón, the coast bent south to Cabo Gracias a Dios. The sloop had to leave the mainland behind and strike out toward Dominica and Guadeloupe. Lowther left no journal or log of *Ranger*'s movements, so the pirates' route can only be guessed. They could have jogged northeast back to the Cayman Islands, then sailed along the southern coasts of the Greater Antilles, a path both familiar and well trafficked by merchant ships. It was also frequented by four Royal Navy station ships. Lowther most likely took a direct bearing along the sixteenth parallel to the Windward Islands, which would carry the company a safe distance south of Jamaica. If he had selected this track, he underestimated the time it would take *Ranger* to cover the distance against the prevailing winds and currents, all of it beyond the sight of any appreciable land formation where the sea rovers could take on water and hunt turtles. Day after day, *Ranger* tacked against the wind to starboard, then came about to port then back again, sailing 2 miles for every mile it closed the distance to the Windward Islands.[1]

The one bright spot in the arduous voyage was the sailing performance of *Ranger*. The sloop, modeled in the form popular among Caribbean traders with its single raked mast and streamlined hull, handled the winds with ease. Because it was fore-and-aft-rigged, *Ranger* could sail a point closer to the wind than square-rigged ships such as *Delivery*. The gaff-rigged mainsail attached to a long boom and could swing to port or starboard to catch the wind at a better angle. The backward-tilted mast, positioned slightly forward of midship, had a yard supporting a square-rigged course and topsail. The sloop featured an extended bowsprit that allowed for a large triangular staysail, jib, and jib topsail forward of the mast. *Ranger*, likely built with sturdy yet light red cedar, could keep pace with square-rigged ships running before the wind, outsail them against the wind, and negotiate channels too shallow for the brigs and frigates. These characteristics explain why over half of all pirate attacks between 1710 and 1730 were conducted from the decks of sloops.[2]

Ranger plunged steadily east, but the crew began showing signs of strain from the long passage. The rovers found the middle of the Caribbean Sea as barren of merchant vessels as it was of islands. Supplies of fresh water, food, and rum grew thin, along with the crew's patience. The sea bandits, who valued their leisure, had to put in long hours on watch as *Ranger* sailed close-hauled day and night to avoid getting pushed backward by the current. Even in times of ease and plenty, the pirates could be an unmanageable bunch. Charles Johnson once observed, "It was with great Difficulty that they could be kept together, under any kind of Regulation; for being almost always mad or drunk, their Behaviour produced infinite Disorders." In times of distress, the crew could be even more heedless and hostile. Edward Low, Lowther's lieutenant, itched to get command of his own roving vessel. He spread discontent among the men and troubled Lowther with his murderous, insolent attitude. Pressure mounted on Lowther. The men looked to their captain to find prizes and provide for their needs. Discontented pirate crews were known to replace their captains by vote or mutiny. Many of the old crew from the Gambia had come to regret their show of support for him after the loss of *Delivery*, while Low stirred up his former colleagues and made known his willingness to take over. The pirates had already demonstrated their proclivity for throwing off authority. Duty and loyalty carried little weight among them. Famed mariner Nathaniel Uring once remarked, "Such unthinking, ungovernable Monsters are Sailors, when once from under Command." Who knew what they might do at the prompting of someone as demented and cruel as Low?[3]

Lowther's reputation and navigational skills may have kept him in command. Stuck in the middle of the Caribbean Sea, the crew may not have trusted anyone else to bring them to a safe landfall. The pirate captain spent his days and nights keeping one eye on the horizon and the other on his crew as *Ranger* tacked to the east.

HMS *GREYHOUND*, CUBA, APRIL 20, 1722

The Royal Navy frigate HMS *Greyhound* eased into Cuban coastal waters west of Havana on a sensitive mission. Its crew had come not to defend British merchant ships from Spanish guardacostas or pursue Caribbean buccaneers, but to trade contraband goods stored in its hold with the local population. The Admiralty had stationed *Greyhound* at New York to protect shipping in the North American colonies; yet, Capt. John Waldron had sailed the twenty-gun frigate 1,400 miles from its duty station to Port Maria (Mariel) to carry on a bit of private commerce. He had already manned a second vessel with part of his crew and sent them to trade along the coast, wanting to make the voyage as lucrative as possible. Welcomed into port, the crew exchanged a consignment of flour from a Jewish merchant in New York for a sizable sum. At 3:00 p.m., Captain Waldron invited a number of what he assumed were local merchants aboard the ship for a lavish dinner to celebrate the transaction. A half-dozen Spaniards dined in the cabin with Waldron, his lieutenant; Edward Smith, the surgeon; the New York merchant; and a few other petty officers. Another dozen Spaniards lounged on the weather deck with a small number of seamen after the rest of the crew went below for their meal. The visitors, pirates masquerading as traders, jumped the handful of sailors remaining on deck and subdued them. At the same moment, the Spaniards in the cabin drew pistols and daggers to take the ship's leaders prisoner. Waldron tried to resist, but a Spaniard plunged a dagger into his chest. Chaos broke out in the cabin, and the pirates opened fire, killing the surgeon and another sailor. Lieutenant Smith, though wounded, jumped out a window and climbed down a side ladder to make his escape. The Jewish merchant suffered a more gruesome fate: the pirates carved him into quarters. Taking weapons from the cabin and quarterdeck locker, the Spaniards fired on the British crew, who responded to the commotion and "drove them down into the Hould."[4]

As quickly as the land pirates seized control of the Royal Navy frigate, they had to abandon their juicy prize. Waldron's consort sloop arrived on the scene by pure coincidence. The Spaniards had time only to confiscate the captain's chest before fleeing to shore, a £10,000 consolation for what had been a daring and successful seizure of a powerful warship.

Waldron's death and the momentary loss of *Greyhound*, besides embarrassing the Admiralty, laid bare the Royal Navy's inattention to its true mission, an oversight that Sir Nicholas Lawes, the Jamaican governor, had previously complained about. Parliament had passed the "Act for the More Effectual Suppressing of Piracy" to address the navy's lackluster performance in protecting commerce and specifically prohibited the kind of private trading that Waldron and *Greyhound* had tried to conduct. "Any captain, commander, or other officer of any of his Majesty's ships . . . [who] receive on board, or permit to be received on board . . . any goods or merchandizes whatsoever, in order to trade . . . shall upon his being convicted thereof by a court martial, lose and forfeit the command." The act had gone into effect on March 22 for people trading with pirates, but the stipulations against navy personnel using His Majesty's ships for personal trade were delayed until September 29. Waldron had answered a last call to swell his purse by carrying illicit goods to Cuba when he ran afoul of the Spanish pirates. After this incident, other navy captains got the message. Henceforth, the Admiralty would expect its officers to concentrate on clearing the seas of buccaneers, and those who wished to augment their navy incomes would have to earn it by taking their share of prize money from the capture of pirate vessels. The next commander of HMS *Greyhound*, Capt. Peter Solgard, was one who would take the message to heart.[5]

RANGER, WINDWARD ISLANDS, EARLY MAY 1722

"Land! Land!" the lookout shouted.[6]

"Where away?"

"East, by the bow."

Lowther must have sighed with relief when he heard the lookout's call. The interminable passage had ended with him still in command. He had brought *Ranger* to the Windward Islands but needed to produce results quickly before the crew's temporary relief vanished. After a brief stop to water and forage, Lowther turned his attention to patrolling the islands for prey. He targeted ships traveling between Barbados and North America. This sea-lane ran north from Barbados windward of the islands before catching the Antilles Current, which carried the ships north of Puerto Rico, Hispaniola, and Cuba all the way to the Gulf Stream off Florida. Lowther positioned *Ranger* near Deseada Island (modern-day La Désirade), a 7-mile-long table-rock land mass lying east of Guadeloupe. Deseada stood at the outward bow of this commercial route, ensuring that the merchantmen would skirt past the island within easy grasp. *Ranger* did not wait long before it pounced on a brigantine captained by a man named Payne. The brigantine turned out to be a rich capture, yielding plenty of food and booty. Ransacking the ship, the sea robbers offloaded any needed stores and began rebuilding their personal stashes of loot. The rum flowed once more, "which put them in better Temper." The buccaneers finished despoiling the brigantine of everything they could use, then "sent her to the Bottom."[7]

For pirate captain George Lowther, the immediate leadership crisis had passed. The men were in their cups. The disgruntlement dissipated. He had demonstrated, once again, his seamanship and ability to find prey. Lowther felt a huge weight come off his shoulders, just not enough to allow him to relax. He knew that his position as leader of the pirate company would not be secure so long as Ned Low remained on board.

The pirate company had hardly consumed Payne's brigantine when it convened an all-hands meeting, a session that may not have been at Lowther's request. The buccaneers debated about where they should hunt for more prizes. The crew voiced their preference for shifting up to North American waters. Summers in the temperate zone sounded better than the heat of the West Indies. As pirate chronicler Charles

Johnson noted, "The Pyrates generally shift their Rovings, according to the Season of the Year." Ranging northward promised richer cargoes and the chance to scoop up plenty of forced men from the fishing fleets on the Grand Banks. Ned Low's influence may have played a part in the argument too. A cruise up to New England would give him more opportunity to indulge his vendetta against the good citizens of Boston, Providence, and Gloucester. The majority voted to depart the West Indies. Before they embarked on another long journey, Lowther sent the men ashore on Deseada to top off all the water casks and forage for more local produce.[8]

Bearing west-northwest, *Ranger* rode the strong current north of the Greater Antilles for several days, pushed along by the prevailing easterlies. Passing below the Turks and Caicos Islands, then the Bahamas, the sea rovers had more opportunities to restock their food supplies. "The Pyrates often take their rise here, or if not, seldom fail in the Course of their Adventures to visit these Seas. There are Multitudes of little Islands and Kays . . . that afford Refreshments of wild Hog, Cow, Goat, Sheep, Parrots, Guanas, Turtle, and Fish." As they approached the coast of Florida, the buccaneers caught the Gulf Stream, which carried them north at a speedy 2 knots. Surging northward, Lowther and crew entered the "Horse Latitudes," so named because ships sailing from Europe to the West Indies were often forced to throw their livestock overboard at this point in their passages. Lowther also noted a change in the wind patterns. North of the Tropic of Cancer, the steady easterlies gave way to variable winds that could shift to all points of the compass. The variable winds persisted until they passed north of St. Augustine, Florida, at which point westerly winds prevailed. The three-week sail from Deseada had been uneventful but also unproductive. That changed once *Ranger* cruised north of the Virginia capes.[9]

RANGER AT SEA, THIRTY-EIGHTH PARALLEL, MAY 28, 1722

Sailing up the Gulf Stream well east of Delaware's Cape Henlopen, Lowther combed the sea-lane between New England and Cape Hatteras. *Ranger* soon ran down a merchantman that had taken the same route from the Caribbean. James Flucker, master of the brigantine *Rebecca*, was on his way from St. Kitts to Boston when the speedier *Ranger* caught up with him. The seizure yielded a surprise for the pirates. *Rebecca* carried a crew of seventeen and six passengers, including five women, who were certainly terrified at the prospect of being at the mercy of eighty-some cutthroats. The company of adventurers consisted of thieves, robbers, and drunks but not rapists. They treated the females with courtesy while they looted their personal belongings and the ship's stores for the better part of two days. Captain Lowther may have entertained the women and Flucker that evening to help ease their pain from the robbery. Many pirate captains enjoyed socializing with more refined company than they could find among their crews. Captured merchantmen and passengers likely grimaced and suffered silently as their captors carried on like gracious hosts and served them drinks from stock pilfered from other unfortunates.[10]

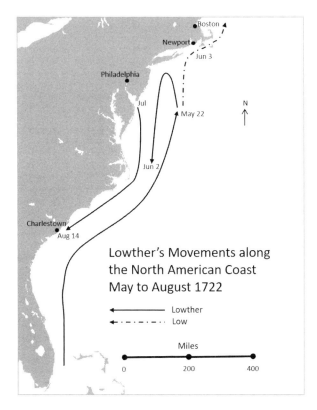

Lowther's Movements along
the North American Coast
May to August 1722

Atlantic Coast, 1722.
Lowther's movements along
the North American coast,
May to August 1722.

The capture of a seaworthy brigantine brought out a reckoning within the pirate company. Edward Low, who champed at the bit to take charge of his own vessel, and George Lowther, who had taken his fill of grief and aggravation from his lieutenant, decided to end their five-month partnership. The two agreed on an amicable split—half the men would go with Low, and the rest would stick with Lowther. The experienced captain made certain that he retained *Ranger*, whereas Low seemed content to take the brigantine *Rebecca*. The following day, the pirates transferred two guns and some swivels from *Ranger* to give Low's new command a little more firepower. Next came the division of the crew. About forty-five men, roughly half of the company, joined Low, including Charles Harris, the former merchant mate turned pirate. More surprising, Francis Spriggs went aboard the brigantine to serve as Low's quartermaster. It was thought that Spriggs had been with Lowther since their time together on the *Gambia Castle*. If so, his departure indicated that Spriggs thought his prospects looked better serving under Low than his former shipmate. His later conduct would reveal that Spriggs tended more toward Low's level of violence than Lowther's more restrained approach to captured men.

Three men from *Rebecca*'s crew were forced into service with the sea rovers. Lowther kept Robert Willis with him on *Ranger* while Richard Rich and Joseph Sweetser went with Low. The melancholy forced men found themselves sharing berths with what another forced man described as "a vile Crew of Miscreants, to whom it was a sport to do Mischief; where prodigious Drinking, monstrous Cursing and Swearing, hideous Blasphemies, and open defiance of Heaven, and contempt of Hell it self, was the constant Employment." Flucker, his mate John Smith, the remaining crew, and the five women stayed aboard the brigantine that parted from Lowther's sloop at the end of the day. The two pirate leaders separated on good terms and may have agreed to rendezvous in the West Indies in the winter season, but for now they went in different directions. Low took a beeline for Massachusetts. Showing his usual caution, Lowther charted a diverse course for the waters off Long Island, where he swept up a few fishing vessels, "which was no great Booty to the Captors." He then turned farther south to patrol the Gulf Stream while giving himself more separation from Low.[11]

RANGER, AT SEA OFF CAPE HATTERAS, JUNE 2, 1722

Peering through his spyglass, Captain Lowther inspected the distant sails called out by the lookout. He detected a small northbound galley, an obvious merchant vessel. The pirate captain had situated the sloop in a good spot, a pinch point in the sea-lane where any ships bearing toward New York, Boston, or London from the West Indies had to bend their paths around Cape Hatteras. He stood a certain distance from land to stay within the Gulf Stream, which was 5 degrees warmer than the coastal waters. Ships usually rode the Gulf Stream north and often tested the water's temperature to ensure they stayed in the current—a technique that Lowther's crew likely performed for the same purpose. Lowering the spyglass, Lowther could see that his patrol plan had produced quick results. He ordered the helmsman to intercept the small merchantman. The sea rovers closed quickly on their prey, using the sloop's superior speed and maneuverability. Once *Ranger* gained an advantageous position, likely windward of the prey, they hoisted the black flag to signal the galley to submit.[12]

Capt. Peter King, master of the *Mary* galley, was returning from Barbados to Boston and had just rounded Hatteras when he crossed paths with the well-armed sloop. Sailing a slower craft, he had little hope of escape, but he still refused to yield. The little galley fired at the pirate sloop—his way of returning intimidation with defiance.[13]

For a second time, Lowther had a fight on his hands, though Captain King's reply failed to daunt him. He called the bluff and ordered the sakers run out. *Ranger* responded with a more powerful broadside. That was all it took. The *Mary* "yielded herself a Prey to the Booters."[14]

Despite their resistance, King and his crew suffered no beatings. The buccaneers went through a perfunctory robbery as though they were taking toll on a ferry. Perhaps, Captain King's inventory placated their anger. The next morning the sea bandits lifted from the galley's hold "13 Hogsheads and 1 Barrel of Rum, 5 Barrels of Sugar, 4 Trunks and a Box of English Goods, several Cases of Loaf Sugar and Pepper." Rum punch all around! The pirates also relieved Captain King and his men of £4–£500 of currency and plate.[15]

The galley's inventory included more than merchandise and supplies. Lowther's crew removed six Black people from *Mary* and forced them aboard *Ranger*. Their fate remains a mystery, though it can be guessed. Pirates often seized slaves from the merchant ships they captured, many of them involved in the disagreeable trade. The buccaneers seldom, if ever, took pity on the Blacks shackled below deck. In almost all cases, slaves freed from merchant ships were not set free: they were sold by the pirates at convenient ports or to passing slavers, kept as slaves on board ship, or, the most favorable outcome, forced to join the crew. Even when attached to a pirate company, they were reduced to second-class status and denied an equal share of booty. Their luck would be no better should a navy ship retake them from their pirate captors. Viewing the slaves as mere booty, most navy captains resold them for profit, as Ogle had done to the twenty-seven African slaves he took from Bartholomew Roberts.[16]

The pirates finished looting the galley by late morning of June 3, and Lowther released Captain King and his crew with no further disruption or damage. The galley made it into Boston harbor eleven days later. The master lost his investment and the crew their wages, but their treatment under Lowther's control would stand in stark contrast to the suffering wrought upon the victims of his protégé.[17]

REBECCA, AT SEA OFF BLOCK ISLAND, JUNE 3, 1722

Ned Low and his crew enjoyed a productive day cruising the waters east of Long Island. They picked up and ransacked two vessels, one captained by a man named Hall and another belonging to John Hance out of Perth Amboy. The pirates released Hall because he was westward bound and would not be able to raise an alarm until he reached New York. The sea bandits' demeanor changed when they took a sloop trying to enter the sound. The cutlasses came out the moment Low discovered that Capt. James Cahoon was sailing to his home port of Providence. New Englanders were not to be spared. Beyond the customary beatings with the flat sides of their blades, Low and his men slashed at Cahoon and wounded his hand. When the bloodlust cooled, Low decided to use Cahoon's sloop to rid himself of the five women and the other prisoners left over from *Rebecca*, except for Captain Flucker, whom he kept on board. So near to shore, Low took the precaution of disabling the sloop "from carrying Intelligence." The buccaneers cut down the sloop's rigging, removed the mainsail and foresail, then forced the wounded Cahoon to saw off his bowsprit and boom, leaving the sloop virtually helpless. In similar fashion, Low's men hamstrung Hance's vessel "and turned her adrift."[18]

Time had come to leave the scene of their piracies. Low cast Cahoon and Hance loose and raised sail to bear east. However, he did not account for the slight winds, which failed to carry him out of sight from Block Island.

James Cahoon used his seafaring skills to steer his crippled sloop to the island that night. The island's residents, not waiting for daylight, dispatched a whaleboat at midnight to alert the Rhode Island authorities to the presence of the pirate ship.

The whaleboat got into port by seven o'clock in the morning, and the cry went out across the colony. "Our Governor immediately ordered the Drum to beat up for Volunteers, and two of the best Sloops then in the Harbour to be fitted out." By sunset, two well-armed sloops sortied from Newport to run down the pirate brigantine, still becalmed off Block Island.[19]

The sloops out of Rhode Island were a little too late. *Rebecca* slipped away to the east during the hours of darkness. Low and his men put into shore in the vicinity of Buzzard's Bay to replenish their water casks and steal local livestock, then sailed past Martha's Vineyard and Nantucket. On their way, they snatched up several men out of fishing vessels "whom he plunder'd, and robb'd of all their Cloaths and Provisions, and used them very Barbarously." One of the small sloops had five Native Americans in its crew, who suffered even worse. Pirates shared an unwritten rule not to murder any captives or forced men—it was bad for business. Low, however, did not construe the rule as extending to Indians. The buccaneers trussed up the Native Americans and tossed a line over Rebecca's yardarm. After haltering two of them with a noose, the crew hauled the pair up into the rigging. Thomas Mumford, one of the Native Americans from Nantucket, had to watch his kinsmen twist and jerk above the deck until they choked to death. He was spared summary execution by the sea rovers but forced to join their crew, though he refused to do anything more than menial tasks despite their routine abuse. For thirteen months, Mumford, who could barely converse in English, submitted to beatings and curses from the sea bandits. He then endured the added humiliation of sitting in the dock beside some of his abusers when the High Court of the Admiralty put several members of Low's company on trial for piracy. Fortunately, other forced men were able to persuade the court that Mumford was no more than a hapless victim of the buccaneers, caught up in the madness taking place on the seas.[20]

Low and his company left Nantucket behind and continued northeast toward Nova Scotia. In mid-June, *Rebecca* pulled into Port Roseway (modern-day Shelburne, Nova Scotia) to round up more forced crew members from among the cod fishermen who frequented the harbor during fishing season. They abducted several "Young Nimble Men," including twenty-year-old Philip Ashton from Marblehead, who would leave a chilling account of his time as a forced man with Low's company. Reinforced with captive fishermen, the pirates discharged Captain Flucker and returned *Rebecca* to him in favor of a Marblehead schooner. Low had already declared the brigantine to be "a dull sailer." He took over his new flagship, a two-masted fore-and-aft-rigged vessel he named *Fancy*, and departed for Newfoundland.[21]

By the time Low left Nova Scotia, the whole coast of New England buzzed in panic over the pirates' depredations, as if someone had seen the devil's apparition in church. "The Pirate Lowe upon our coast," the *Boston News-Letter* heralded. Only two months earlier, Capt. Benjamin Edwards had brought news of Lowther's and Low's robberies in the Bay of Honduras and their horrible mistreatment of merchant seamen. The latest reports from King, Hance, and Cahoon that Lowther and Low had made their way north set mariners and Massachusetts port authorities on edge. Boston sent out another sloop to join the Rhode Island captains scouring the northern waters for the two notorious sea bandits, but they returned to port later without making contact with either *Ranger* or *Fancy*.[22]

Low had left the vicinity, but where was Lowther? Since his seizure of Captain King's brigantine at the beginning of June, he had disappeared. Lowther had been cruising a busy sea-lane, but no reports of *Ranger* trickled into colonial ports for the rest of the month. Three facts suggest a possible answer: Lowther's sloop had not been cleaned for over six months, the pirates had six enslaved Black people aboard, and *Ranger* was lying near the coast of North Carolina. Lowther may have decided to sneak into a secluded cove on the Albemarle, Pamlico, or Core Sounds and careen his sloop while negotiating an exchange of his newly acquired slaves for some fresh provisions. The pirate Blackbeard had found North Carolina residents and government officials receptive to such bartering only a few years earlier. Lowther would resume his prowling about four weeks later, an interval consistent with the time it would take to rest his crew and refit his sloop. He would return to the Carolina sounds not long after his reappearance, but his next stay would not be by choice.[23]

CHAPTER 11

DISASTER IN THE CAROLINAS

FANCY, ST. JOHNS, NEWFOUNDLAND, JULY 2, 1722

The pirate schooner threaded its way into the deep harbor through a heavy fog, a common meteorological occurrence along the Newfoundland coast. The occasional splash of the sounding lead was the only noise to be heard from the deck as the pirates crept into St. Johns. The expectant buccaneers entered the port, hoping to swoop down like a sea hawk on a helpless merchantmen lying in repose, and pluck more seamen to force into *Fancy*'s hold. St. Johns was a popular station for fishermen working the Grand Banks and a convenient port of call for vessels sailing between Britain and North America, which also made it an attractive target for corsairs. As Capt. Edward Low and his men peered through the dissipating mist, "they spy'd a large Ship riding at Anchor in the Harbour." They judged the square-rigged ship to be 4–500 tons burthen and thought it would make a "Boon Prize." With the prey stationary, Low opted for a subtle approach and a sudden boarding of the unsuspecting ship. *Fancy* coasted toward its target when it passed a small fishing vessel heading out of port.[1]

The fisherman gave them a friendly hail, "Hoy!"[2]

"Ahoy!"

"From whence came ye?"

Low responded with a lie to avoid raising an alarm. "Barbadoes, with a bonny load of rum and sugar. What be the large ship in ye harbour?"

"Tis the navy frigate Solebay."

The answer sent shivers down the pirates' spines. Instead of pouncing on a tasty mackerel, they were about to tangle with a fierce shark. "The very Name of a Man of War struck them all up in a Heap," a forced man aboard *Fancy* related, "and lest they should catch a Tartar, they thought it their wisest and safest way, instead of going into the Harbour, to be gone as fast as they could."[3]

Fancy came about as quickly as the deck crew could yank on the booms and the helmsman could throw over the rudder. Once they turned the bow toward the harbor exit, the men threw out all the canvas the schooner carried to make full speed out of St. Johns. Word of their hurried departure reached the captain of HMS *Solebay*, a twenty-gun sixth-rate ship, and he put the frigate to sea in pursuit of the suspected pirate. *Fancy* made its escape, but Ned Low's recklessness nearly cost him and his crew their lives by risking an attack on an unknown vessel that turned out to have a 240-man crew.[4]

Philadelphia, July 22, 1722

Andrew Bradford, publisher of the *American Weekly Mercury*, had come to the city wharf to gather news of the port's comings and goings for Thursday's edition. There had been little to report of late. He observed Jonathan Swain, a captain from nearby Cape May, dock his small sloop, and went over to speak with him. Swain brought some disturbing news that confirmed earlier reports. Pirates were lurking in Delaware Bay. Ten days earlier, the paper had recounted, "A brigantine has been observed to stand in and off our Capes about 2 leagues southward" of Lewes, Delaware. People working farm fields near the shore could see the brigantine standing under its topsails and "supposed [it] to be a Pyrate." Swain's information drew a more ominous picture. A sloop and the suspicious brigantine had been cruising the Delaware Bay for three weeks. On July 8, the two unnamed sea bandits had advanced "Ten or Twelve Leagues" up the bay and seized a large sloop. The two pirates brought their prize back down the bay and anchored offshore, where they unnerved the residents as they caroused and "beat Drums all Night."[5]

Upon further investigation, Bradford determined that just one other vessel had entered Philadelphia's port in the past week, the sloop *Little Joseph*, belonging to Charles Hargrave. Bradford spoke with Hargrave and learned that *Little Joseph* had departed Philadelphia two months earlier, bound for St. Kitts, but had to return with nothing left in its hold. Hargrave explained that he had been stopped three times by pirates who had rifled his sloop, forcing him to shorten his voyage.

The *American Weekly Mercury* broadcast the alarm four days later. "Our trade is entirely stopped." The pirate sloop and brigantine had set a virtual blockade of the Delaware Bay, Bradford warned. He attributed their brazenness to their "not fearing Disturbance from the Men of War." The Royal Navy had no ships at Philadelphia, preferring to station them out of New York. That meant Philadelphia's security depended on HMS *Greyhound*, the frigate that had been taken by Cuban pirates three months earlier—an uncomforting thought. Bradford descried the Royal Navy's lax patrolling and repeated the charge that the navy captains "love Trading better than Fighting."[6]

Throughout the summer of 1722, port cities from Philadelphia to St. Johns felt the grip of terror from Lowther's and Low's roving and robbing. Some governors sent out armed sloops to drive off the pirates, while others bemoaned the navy's inability to protect commercial shipping. In the end, their relief came only when the buccaneers sailed off for more-lucrative seas.

The pirate leaders in the Delaware Bay went unidentified, though their depredations look like Lowther's handiwork. The sloop could certainly have been *Ranger*, but a question remains about the brigantine. Lowther may have thrown in with another buccaneer for a time, or the brigantine may have been a prize that he used as a consort before turning it loose. Whether or not Lowther was the one harassing shipping in the Delaware Bay, the troublesome pirates left the area shortly before Lowther made his presence known a few hundred miles away.

RANGER, OFF CHARLESTOWN, AUGUST 13, 1722

Southerly gales had dominated July weather as a summer high-pressure system stalled over Bermuda, but Lowther took advantage of a break in the wind pattern to shift his pirate crew south. They cleared Cape Hatteras, then cruised down the North Carolina coast past a seemingly endless chain of barrier islands. In 1722, Beaufort, North Carolina, was no more than a fishing village, and the Cape Fear River was only sparsely settled. Just one significant British port existed below Hatteras—Charlestown. Any search for well-larded merchant ships needed to focus on British America's most active slave-trading port. Besides importing slaves to work lowland fields, the growing colonial town carried on active commerce with West Indies islands and exported furs and rice to British markets. Three years earlier the citizens had thrown off the governance of the colony's Lords Proprietors in favor of a royal governor and in June had voted to incorporate their town, though the Crown disallowed the measure the next year.

Charlestown had attracted previous pirate encounters. The infamous Blackbeard had blockaded the harbor for several days in 1718 and lifted it only after the town paid him a ransom in sorely needed medical supplies. Since then, the navy had stationed a sixth-rate ship in Charlestown, HMS *Blandford*. The frigate had just completed a patrol up to Quiqueton (Hampton), Virginia, and back to its home station on July 20. Lowther could see that the presence of the station ship would prevent any prolonged obstruction of Charlestown's commercial traffic, but he figured that *Ranger* could still pick off a ship or two and sprint away before *Blandford* could stir from its moorings.[7]

A convenient chart stolen from one of his recent prizes or a forced man with knowledge of Charlestown's tricky channel may have helped Lowther plan an ambush. The town's harbor ran west to east from Smith's and Rhett's docks on the Cooper River past Fort Johnson, then out to the Atlantic between Sullivan's Island and the tidal marshes of Boone's Island (now James Island). At its outlet, the channel took a 90-degree turn to the south and ran 6 miles close by Caffen Island (later Cummins and then Morris Island) before exiting to the east between a pair of breakers. A long bar had formed east of the main channel, interspersed by several shallow swashes and channels. One of these, the North Channel, ran next to Sullivan's Island. Though narrow, this channel had enough depth to allow a light sloop, such as *Ranger*, to approach unseen from the east to the pivot point in the main channel. A clever pirate captain could lie in wait behind the cover of Sullivan's Island for an unsuspecting merchantman to leave the harbor and turn south. Once the prey swung to starboard to follow the main channel, the pirate sloop could pounce on its stern.[8]

On the evening of August 13, Lowther drifted toward the bar with Sullivan's Island hard on his starboard, aided by the light of a three-quarter waxing moon. The lightning and thunder earlier in the day had passed and the weather had calmed. In such narrow waters, he would have sent the launch ahead with a crew to tow *Ranger*

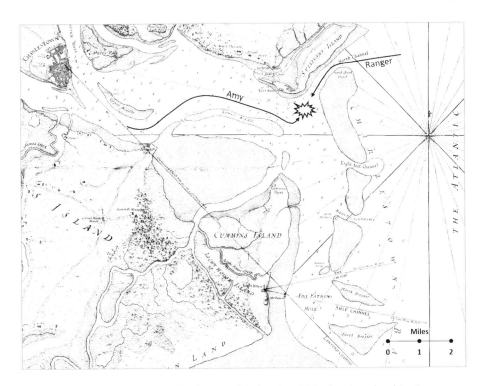

Charlestown Harbor, 1780. Charlestown Harbor in 1780, showing the shipping channel south of Cummins Island and the North Channel next to Sullivan's Island. *William Faden, courtesy Library of Congress*

into the North Channel. He listened carefully as the man tossing the lead from the launch called out the number of fathoms to the bottom. He had to be sure the sloop had enough clearance not to ground itself. "Five . . . Four." This close to shore, everyone felt tense. "Three . . . Three . . . Two." Pulled along gently by the oars, *Ranger* threaded its way through the constricted waterway. "Two . . . Three . . . Three." Once Lowther could see the end of Sullivan's Island and knew he had a clear route into the main channel, he would have called to the launch to stop rowing. The crew dropped anchor in only 3 fathoms, with the shoals just 100 or so yards off their port and the island an equal distance to starboard. Seeing that he had to charge at his prey straight out of the channel, Lowther repositioned one of his guns to serve as a bow chaser. *Ranger* moored in an ideal ambush position, with its mast obscured by the island's palmetto trees and just a short distance from where a slow brig might pass across its bow. After reefing the sails to make *Ranger* harder to see, most of the crew went through their routine for an upcoming assault on a merchant vessel—getting drunk and passing out in their hammocks. Not everyone reveled. Lowther maintained a certain level of vigilance and care. The quartermaster kept a watch on deck at night, and a lookout scanned the channel and the open ocean for any ships that might necessitate a rapid departure. The pirate captain, after passing instructions for the watch, retired to his own hammock to await the dawn.

BRIGANTINE *AMY*, REBELLION ROAD INSIDE CHARLESTOWN HARBOR, DAWN, AUGUST 14, 1722

Rays of sunlight peeked through the trees and marsh grasses on Boone's Island as Capt. John Gwatkin, master of the brigantine *Amy*, stepped on deck. He had checked his tidal charts the night before and noted that the morning ebb tide would begin shortly after dawn. Gwatkin had passed instructions to his crew to be ready for an early departure should the winds and weather allow. *Amy* had left the Charlestown dock twelve days earlier and shifted downriver to Rebellion Road, where they had been moored ever since, held up by easterly winds and contrary weather. From the deck, Gwatkin checked the sky. The storms of the previous day had passed, and light breezes were coming in from the southwest. Satisfied that the winds were favorable for exiting Charlestown's harbor and negotiating the main channel, he ordered his crew to unmoor and set the courses to depart. *Amy* was bound for the Thames, laden with barrels of rice harvested from the numerous farms and plantations lining the interior rivers. The ship safely cleared Fort Johnson on the south side of the harbor and steered east toward the Atlantic. The captain sent part of his crew up the shrouds to set the topsails to help *Amy* gain speed and enable the brigantine to maneuver more easily.[9]

Gwatkin was not a Charlestown native. He resided in the hamlet of Ratcliffe, in Stepney, on the east side of London. Sometimes known as "sailor town," Ratcliffe sat along the Thames next to the Limehouse dockyard, where HMS *Assistance* had been refurbished in 1715. Captain Gwatkin followed the naval tradition of his hometown and spent years as a mariner and a little time as a sea rover too. In 1718, the Admiralty had awarded him a letter of marque as captain of a 150-ton, ten-gun galley named *Resolution*. After his brief stint as a privateer, he returned to his customary employment as a merchant sea captain, a duty that brought him to the South Carolina colony. Heading toward the gap between the dunes on Sullivan's Island and the tidal marshes of Boone's Island, Gwatkin felt upbeat to begin this homeward journey, which he expected to take him back to his "well-beloved" wife, Elianor, though events would unfold differently than he imagined.[10]

North Channel off Sullivan's Island, Morning, April 14, 1722

The lookout in *Ranger*'s foretop spotted glimpses of white sails glowing in the early-morning light through the branches and fronds on Sullivan's Island, giving the first hint of a ship in the channel.

"A sail, coming out."

The call stirred the pirate crew into action. The decks were cleared and powder was brought up for the guns. Men jammed handspikes into the capstan and started lifting the anchor off the bottom. Forced men either helped set the rigging or went below into the hold. The loft gang raised the gaff-rigged mainsail and lowered the course from its yard. Wind filled the sails, and *Ranger* advanced down the North Channel. Lowther came forward and pulled out his spyglass to get a good look at the vessel once it came into view. Slowly, a square-rigged brigantine edged past the intervening palmettos, giving the pirate captain a chance to appraise his intended target. Lowther shouted directions to the quartermaster to adjust *Ranger*'s speed and course to intercept the merchantman's path just aft of the brigantine. That would give them an advantageous position to accost the prey.

Amy's lookout shouted a warning to Captain Gwatkin that a sloop had appeared coming from the far side of Sullivan's Island. The merchant captain raised his own spyglass to inspect the vessel coming from a direction no commercial craft would use. He did not like its appearance: stripped, well armed, and with lots of men running around on its deck. Out of precaution, he called his crew on deck and ordered powder and shot to be brought up from the hold. He held course for the harbor exit but kept his spyglass focused on the sloop.

Now in clear sight of the brigantine, Lowther decided to apply some intimidation to force the merchant ship to come to. The crew raised the dreaded black ensign on the staff, where it fluttered and snapped in the breeze. Lowther ordered the bow chaser charged with powder and loaded with shot. At his command, *Ranger* sent a shot across *Amy*'s bow.

The merchant crew scrambled to ram powder and round shot into their port guns. Captain Gwatkin, an experienced privateer, assessed the situation. No doubt he was facing a pirate, but he saw something his opponent failed to recognize. The pirate captain had taken a position well designed to surprise an unsuspecting victim, but one that put him in a disadvantageous posture for executing a naval engagement. Time to seize the initiative! Gwatkin yelled for the helmsman to reduce speed and steer closer to the narrow channel where the sloop was emerging. The captain ordered the crew to run out the guns.

Lowther grew alarmed. *Ranger* was charging bow on toward the prey, but the brigantine was shifting closer, not away. Still caught in the North Channel, Lowther realized that he had no room to maneuver. The merchant ship drew close, showing the pirates its guns like a big mako shark baring its teeth. Too late, the pirate captain and his crew watched the opposing ship cross their bow. They had "caught a tartar."

Boom! Boom! Boom! Boom! Iron shot smashed through *Ranger*'s bow. The bullets ripped down the decks and through the rigging, ricocheting off the guns and shattering everything else in their paths. The force of the blasts carried away planks, weapons, and body parts from the bow all the way to the stern. It took the dazed corsairs some time to shake off the shock and their wooziness. When they looked around, they saw chaos. Dismembered men cried for help. Blood smeared the deck and sails. Debris was scattered everywhere. Lowther had one thought—get away. He scanned toward the shoals and then the island and saw that *Ranger* had no direction to go but forward. He called to the quartermaster to steer as close to the island as he could, hoping to slip astern of the ship and away from another broadside.

Gwatkin observed the telling effect that *Amy*'s broadside had on the pirate sloop. He was not finished with it. Using his tactical skills, the merchant captain "stood after him to clap him aboard." Gwatkin performed one of two possible maneuvers depending on how he wanted to play the southwesterly wind. He may have halted *Amy*'s forward motion by reorienting his mainsails to catch the wind from one angle while orienting the foresails to catch the wind at an opposite angle, thereby forcing the sails to counteract each other, a maneuver known as lying to. Alternatively, Gwatkin may have ordered the helmsman to come about and attack the sloop using its starboard guns. Either way, Gwatkin had Lowther trapped against Sullivan's Island while he delivered another punishing broadside.[11]

More shots punctured *Ranger*'s hull. Splinters flew in all directions. More men screeched in agony. Lowther could see no escape and no way to keep the merchant ship off with only a bow chaser. He made a snap decision. The pirate captain shouted to the quartermaster to run *Ranger* onto the beach. The quartermaster threw the helm to starboard, and the sloop slithered to a stop on the sandy bottom. "Get out!" "Abandon ship!" Lowther yelled for the men to grab their firelocks and climb into the launch. Many simply jumped overboard and splashed for the shore. In their hurry, they left the wounded and the bodies of the dead aboard the helpless *Ranger*. Once they reached the beach, Lowther shepherded his remaining men to the protective cover of the dunes.

The crew of *Amy* cheered and shouted their derision at the fleeing pirates. They had beaten the sea bandits who dared to rob them. Their captain wanted more. It was not enough to drive the buccaneers off—he wanted to end them. Gwatkin ordered men into his launch with torches and buckets of pitch, with the idea of firing the sloop. He had the anchor dropped to hold *Amy* in the channel, then climbed into the launch to take charge of the pirate sloop's destruction. Barking commands to the rowers and the man at the rudder, he directed the longboat toward the island where *Ranger* lay pitched in the shallows.

Onshore, the pirates caught their breath behind the dunes and stayed out of sight. Still within reach of its guns, they had to keep themselves hidden from the brigantine. Lowther poked his head above the sand after a few minutes to survey the situation and caught sight of Captain Gwatkin and his men rowing toward *Ranger*. A new threat! Lowther feared that the men in the longboat intended to destroy or take over the sloop. If they succeeded, he and his men would be stranded on an island next to a busy port that would soon send parties to hunt them down. Stede Bonnet had been recaptured less than four years ago on the island, then hanged in Charlestown. No one wanted that fate. The buccaneers reacted quickly. The men with firelocks leveled their pieces and fired at the longboat. At that range, they would have been lucky to hit a target the size of the sloop, much less a launch, but their volume of fire could make up for their inaccuracy. The men fired as quickly as they could reload.

The bullets splashed into the waves or skipped over the surface past the launch. Captain Gwatkin told his men to ignore the fire and keep to their rowing. Seconds ticked by as the mariners drew close to their objective, but a random shot struck Gwatkin before they could get to *Ranger*. The men in the launch heard the gruesome *Thwap*, then watched in horror as their brave captain slumped lifeless into the bottom of the launch. Looking at their fallen captain and then at the continuing bursts of musket fire from the beach, the leaderless sailors lost heart. "The *Amy's* men did not think it proper to proceed any farther." They rowed back to their ship as quickly as they could heave on the oars. The mate, a man named Rowe, had the anchor raised and drew off, leaving the beached sloop to the pirates.[12]

The relieved buccaneers gathered on the shore to watch the merchant ship that had nearly destroyed their vessel sail out to the ocean. Lowther and his quartermaster immediately took charge of the recovery, a task that would take them the rest of the day. Bodies of the dead were removed and laid out in the sand—no time for ceremony. The crew did what they could for the wounded, but without a surgeon among them, most bled out. Some torn limbs could be amputated and tied off, once the wounded man had consumed enough rum to put him into a stupor. Men with minor wounds got bandaged and then put to work on the sloop. *Ranger* needed hull repairs: holes plugged and loose planks replaced. New sails and rigging could be put up later. The more urgent matter was getting *Ranger* refloated by the next high tide and before someone notified HMS *Blandford* about their presence. Men carried stores and excess weight to the beach and emptied water from the bilge, using the chain pumps. That evening they ran a line from *Ranger* to the fully manned launch. Once the tide neared its crest, the men pulled on the oars, and the rest of the healthy crew put their shoulders to the sloop's hull. Straining with all their might, the crew worked *Ranger* off the beach and towed it back into North Channel. The corsairs brought all the barrels and stores back onto the sloop, egged on by Lowther, who was anxious to clear the area. The men soon had *Ranger* restocked. The pirate captain ordered the sails raised. The damaged sloop and its frazzled crew steered northeast for the more isolated coves on the North Carolina shore, where the company of pirates could attend more to the needs of their vessel.

Survival was now the preoccupation of George Lowther and his band. The pirates limped along the coast in search of a hideaway to lick their wounds. *Ranger's* egress from Charlestown put the pirate captain and his crew in difficulty and danger. Men had to stay at the pumps after several shots had pierced the hull. Even after the holes had been patched, the sloop leaked from the many loosened boards and cracks. Wounded men needed to get ashore to rest and recuperate. The fit pirates stayed busy through the night working the sails, manning the helm, and sounding the depth as *Ranger* worked its way north in the dark. Their lives had changed. Strain and exhaustion set upon them. The easy way of life they had grown to appreciate as sea bandits was gone. They still hoped to recover their ship and fortunes, but the months ahead would be full of deprivation and hardship.

✦ CHAPTER 12 ✦

SLAUGHTER IN THE BAY

RANGER, NORTH CAROLINA COASTAL INLET, AUGUST 1722

The disasters at Port Maho and Charlestown bookended an awful half year for Captain Lowther and his followers. They had been beaten by a mob of natives and a merchant ship—hardly the type of actions to instill fear or boost a reputation. Ten months earlier the buccaneers had frolicked on a Caribbean beach, drinking, laughing, and swearing: each trying to utter the most vulgar and offensive oaths to demonstrate their disdain for all forms of authority, even divine. They had been humbled since. Lowther's leadership might have been questioned by some of his men, but the shattered condition of their craft and crew was too great a challenge for anyone else to step forward. The pirate captain accepted the responsibility of his mistakes and the burden of recovering the company's fortunes.

Lowther looked for the closest haven where he could moor *Ranger* and restore the company's situation. The nearest appreciable settlement where he might be able to procure naval stores was the village of Beaufort, near Cape Lookout, over 220 miles distant. He may have worried about sailing that far and having to pass over Frying Pan Shoals with a leaky sloop. More likely, he turned *Ranger* into one of the inlets west of Cape Fear: Lockwood's Folly, Shallotte, or Little River.[1]

The sea bandits found a secluded cove behind the cover of a barrier island, then anchored *Ranger* close to a sandy beach. They needed to keep the sloop from sinking too deep if it took on more water. The healthy men went aloft to unbend the sails for use as tents onshore, where they brought the wounded to recuperate. Lowther had the crew careen the ship to do a more thorough job of repairing the damaged and leaky hull. Once they got the sloop over on its side, they discovered the extent of work required to make her seaworthy again—far more than they had hoped. Lowther understood the problem. It would take weeks, months, to get *Ranger* and its crew back to sea. A merchant ship could stay in port for that long, but a pirate company could sustain itself on the open water only by plundering what it needed from the ships it seized. Henry Smith, the forced carpenter, had likely died or gotten off the sloop somewhere along the way, leaving no one skilled in repairing a vessel. The pirate captain directed his men to begin work while he tallied all the supplies and materials needed to repair *Ranger*.

NEWGATE PRISON, LONDON, SEPTEMBER 13, 1722

Bail having been posted on his behalf, John Massey walked out of Newgate Prison and into the arms of his wife (or betrothed), Mary, and his relatives Isaac and Edmund Massey. The family had arranged with two local weavers to put up money as surety for his future appearance at the Old Bailey. His bail had become urgent after June 28, when a commission of oyer and terminer returned an indictment against him "for Piracy on the High Seas." Once a High Court of the Admiralty tribunal could be convened, Massey would be put on trial for his life.[2]

Outside the prison, his relatives reasoned with him about his circumstances. The charges and the powers lined up against him left no hope for him other than to flee Britain and make a new life somewhere beyond the reach of the law. His reaction baffled them. The former army officer refused to jump bail—he remained determined to plead his case in court. Friends and relations tried to convince him that he was doomed if he stood trial. He did not disagree but felt duty-bound to face the court and explain himself to his accusers and the public. He wanted to confess his crimes because it would give him the opportunity to express his rationale for the actions he had taken in the Gambia. Listening to his convoluted logic, his loved ones could only shake their heads and conclude that he must be "in some Measure disturb'd in his Head."[3]

Massey's relations could not comprehend how someone could be so quixotic and care so little about the threat of hanging. They failed to see that Massey had already accepted that his life was forfeit and his reputation destroyed. All that mattered to him was preserving what little dignity still attached to his name, and proving to the world that he could face death like a soldier. Acting the scoundrel and running away just to spare his life would shred his last hope to preserve some degree of honor. He would never consider it.

The family gave up any thought of saving Massey from trial and advised the bondsmen that they could redeem their sureties. A short while later, John Massey returned to Newgate, where he would wait months for the next session of the High Court of the Admiralty.[4]

Massey had unfortunate timing. Had he been incarcerated at Newgate a year earlier, he might have earned a reprieve. Lady Mary Wortley Montagu, wife of the former ambassador to the Ottoman Empire, had returned from Constantinople on a mission to educate the kingdom on the lifesaving advantages of smallpox inoculation. In 1721 she obtained permission to run a trial at Newgate Prison, since it was experiencing a smallpox outbreak. For the test she selected seven condemned prisoners who agreed to undergo ingrafting in exchange for pardons if the procedure or the disease did not kill them first. All seven of her subjects happily survived the experiment and walked out of Newgate as free men.[5]

Massey was not destined to replicate the salvation of these seven pardoned men, nor would the men of his former pirate company. Over the next twelve months, he and nearly all the rovers would face a reckoning for their crimes on the high seas.

FANCY AND ROSE, THE TRIANGLES OFF FRENCH GUIANA, OCTOBER 1722

Ned Low led his company of buccaneers into protected waters within a cluster of three islands known as the Triangles, a short distance from the steamy shore of the French colony. The islands off the South American coast would later gain notoriety as the site of the French penal colony Devil's Island. The pirates had been through an eventful cruise since leaving Newfoundland in July. They had passed through the Azores, Madeira, the Canaries, and the Cape Verde Islands, capturing numerous fishing vessels and merchant ships along the way. Low kept a French ship as a consort but later burned it in favor of a Portuguese pink, a type of square-rigged ship with a narrow stern that he named the *Rose*. He had also kept a sloop as a tender, but a crew of mostly forced men had taken it over and fled while in the Cape Verde Islands.

The cutthroat band had practiced some cruelty as they passed through the Portuguese and Spanish island chains. Before burning the French ship, Low had its Portuguese cook bound to the main mast because he thought him to be a "greazy Fellow" who might "fry well" as the ship went up in flames. Days later, a couple of Catholic friars became the objects of some amusement after the galley they were aboard fell into Low's hands. The sea bandits tied up and haltered the two with a noose. The crew tossed the lines over the foreyard, then hauled the two friars up by the neck. The unfortunate victims dangled on the verge of death until the pirates dropped them onto the deck like sacks of flour. Low's men were not done. They yanked the two victims back into the rigging and dropped them again. "This they repeated several Times out of Sport."[6]

The sheen on the pirates' burnished arrogance came off when they sailed for Brazil and ran into a hurricane off the South American mainland. For five days "the Sea ran Mountains high." The pink and schooner took on water, and the men bailed night and day with buckets and pumps to keep afloat. Despite their strain and effort, they could not keep up with the raging waves that washed over the decks and threatened to capsize them. Out of desperation the buccaneers threw water casks, barrels of provisions, even a few guns overboard to keep the vessels buoyant against the pummeling waves. Philip Ashton, a forced man, observed how "such mighty Hectors as they were, in a clear Sky and a fair Gale," became mortified when "a fierce Wind and a boisterous Sea sunk their Spirits to a Cowardly dejection." The men who had openly defied the Almighty and taken pleasure in others' terror shriveled in the face of death. "In this time of Extremity, the Poor Wretches had no where to go for Help! For they were at open Defiance with their Maker, & they could have but little comfort in the thoughts of their Agreement with Hell . . . you might plainly see the inward Horror and Anguish of their Minds, visible in their Countenances." Luckily for the crews of the *Fancy* and *Rose*, they were able to keep both vessels above the surface until the storm passed.[7]

The mishaps continued as the pirates sheltered in French Guiana. Low decided to clean the bottoms of his small fleet at the Triangles, even though the corsairs could not stay there for long because there was no source of fresh water and no soft-gradient beach among the small rocky islands. To save time, they chose an expedient method of putting *Rose* on a parliament heel instead of beaching it for a proper careen. The process known as boot topping involved tipping the pink to one side, thereby exposing part of the hull that would normally be underwater. Inside the craft, the crew shifted barrels, trunks, and guns to one side to start it leaning. Low ordered a number of men, many of them forced, to climb the shrouds up to the topmasts to tip it farther onto its side. Philip Ashton climbed all the way to the maintop-gallant yard, along with several others, until their weight at that height started *Rose* tipping. At that moment, everything fell apart. The captain and quartermaster misjudged the number of men to send aloft. The pink started pitching more and more to its side in several fathoms of water. Too late, the men realized that no one had thought to shutter the underside portholes. The moment the openings tipped down to the ocean's surface, water flooded in. The added weight heeled the pink over. The yards and masts splashed into the water, sending Ashton and his mates scurrying up the shrouds in the opposite direction toward the ship's elevated hull. Low and the ship's doctor saved themselves by climbing out the cabin window against the incoming ocean water. The water surged in and the hull settled lower. Soon, Ashton and the others had to crawl and splash back to the topmast yards that still stood above the surface, because the other ends of the yards had hit the bottom. Ashton, a poor swimmer, was saved only when his cousin, Joseph Libbey, pulled him into a launch. Two other men were not as fortunate.[8]

Just like Lowther, Edward Low had lost a vessel while trying to clean it. The pirate captain had no choice but to put his entire company "to the Number of 100, as vile Rogues as ever ended their Lives at Tyburn," aboard one craft, in this case the schooner *Fancy*. Low had more worries than just cramped quarters. The buccaneers had dumped some of their potable water during the hurricane, and more casks sank with the *Rose*. Now dangerously short on fresh water, Low set course for Tobago, the nearest deserted island where he could safely water.

The company had given up the idea of raiding the Brazilian coast. Low and his men agreed that once they took care of their water shortage, they would spend the cool-season months roving the West Indies and revisiting some of the littorals they had preyed upon months earlier. This plan would put him on a path with a Royal Navy ship and an old friend.

RANGER, NORTH CAROLINA COASTAL INLET, WINTER 1722–23

The pirate company gathered around their captain in the sloop's lower deck, where they sheltered from the chill. The preceding months had reduced them to near desperation, forcing the rovers to hunt wild hogs or poach livestock from the few farms within walking distance, though stealing was not a far stretch for men accustomed to robbery at sea. In the warmer months they had lived in tents or slapped-together shelters made from pine logs, but the onset of winter chased them onto the sloop to escape the cold. Pirate crews had notoriously high turnover. With no surgeon to care for them, the men died from dysentery, syphilis, or wounds. Others, especially forced men, deserted near ports or habitations. Lowther's crew had dwindled from the forty-five men he had off the Delaware cape in May to a minimal count—barely more than a merchant vessel. He still had several hearty men, including some holdovers from the Gambia. They would have to do. Huddled on *Ranger*'s deck, they listened as Captain Lowther explained their situation. They were short on provisions, rum, usable powder, tools, and naval stores, but the captain thought the sloop was stable enough to stand out to sea. Lowther proposed that the company leave the North Carolina coast and head south to the warmer waters of the Caribbean. With any luck, he suggested, they could make up their shortfall in provisions and sailors by taking a few prizes on the way. The crew voiced their hearty assent as soon as Lowther put the idea up for a vote.[9]

A short time later, the crew raised anchor and *Ranger* slipped out to the Atlantic. Lowther told the quartermaster to set a course south. The pirates might have planned a stopover in the Bahamas to pick up fresh provisions and water, but their ultimate destination was the western Caribbean. *Ranger* and the pirate company had set their sights on the logwood ships coming in and out of the bay that they had stalked the previous winter.

RANGER, AT SEA, GULF OF HONDURAS, MARCH 10, 1723

Ever since the lookout had called out the sail, Lowther had kept his spyglass on the distant sloop. The white sails stood above a low, dark hull gliding over the shimmering western Caribbean. He observed the sloop as it turned toward *Ranger* rather than flee. He and his company were pirates: they should be the aggressors. Given the dilapidated condition of his own sloop and his diminished crew, Lowther had to consider the consequences of tangling with another vessel that approached so confidently. He weighed the risk against their need to take a prize. He decided to attack. He ordered the helmsman to maintain a course to get closer to the strange sloop. As the two vessels drew near, Lowther called his crew to ready for action. Powder, shot, muskets, and cutlasses were brought up to the deck. The captain began making judgments on how to maneuver. The situation suddenly changed when the other sloop ran up a black flag and hove to. Another pirate! Lowther sailed closer to the other sloop to exchange hails with a brother in crime.[10]

"Hoy, *Ranger*!"

Lowther and his crew looked at each other, stunned by the hail from an unfamiliar vessel. "Aye, tis *Ranger*, and who be it that greets us?" A cheer went up when Capt. Edward Low replied. Nine months after parting, Lowther and Low had found each other.

Old shipmates embraced each other, occasioned by the generous consumption of spirits. Stories and tall tales of adventures and misadventures bounced back and forth between the excited buccaneers, sometimes sobered by the names of other brethren who had died since their last time together. Low's men mentioned that they had taken over a sloop in Grenada, and Low had given the schooner *Fancy* to Francis Spriggs, Lowther's former shipmate on the *Gambia Castle*. Both came close to disaster on January 30, when they went after two ships off Cartagena, and one turned out to be a navy frigate. HMS *Mermaid* chased the schooner and sloop until Low and Spriggs separated. *Mermaid* stayed after Low's sloop. Caught leeward of the ship-rigged frigate, the pirate sloop, named *Fortune*, could not outrun its pursuer. The corsairs escaped only when someone pointed to nearby shoals. Luckily for the sea rovers, *Fortune* cleared the shoals, and *Mermaid* ran aground. *Fortune* and *Fancy* had reunited off Utila Island in early March. Low, now a pirate admiral in his own right, got rid of *Fancy* and gave Spriggs a sloop he had recently taken from the bay.[11]

After the passage of four to five weeks, Low's men could laugh about their near brush with HMS *Mermaid*. Someone more perceptive might have observed that this was Low's second encounter with a navy station ship in six months; yet, no one seemed to remark about the navy's increased activity.

Lowther and Low conferred on more-serious matters while their respective crews celebrated. Lowther must have felt a sense of personal angst by the changed circumstances between himself and Low. When they first met, he commanded a fine, well-stocked galley-frigate and Low a pathetic little boat. Now he and his men were the beggars, and Low's sloop was the one filled with provisions and a chestful of valuables. There had been tension between the two corsairs a year earlier, but Low extended respect and friendship to his mentor. The one-time pirate admiral mentioned that his sloop was hardly seaworthy, and his company was so reduced in number that their prospects for supporting themselves looked grim. Low offered that Lowther and *Ranger* could join his fleet until they could capture more forced men and a suitable replacement for the damaged sloop. Lowther accepted, and the two sloops steered to the inner bay.

After rounding the Zapadilla Keys, the pirate sloops turned north toward the Belize River, the primary spot where the baymen brought their inventory of logwood. The baymen led a shiftless lifestyle, as described by one ship's captain: "The Wood-Cutters are generally a rude drunken Crew, some of which have been Pirates, and most of them Sailors; their chief Delight is in drinking." During the dry season the baymen went upriver to cut and trim logwood, then ferried the timbers down the river when the creeks ran high. Merchant captains arriving at the mouth of the river usually fired a gun that would draw the baymen to their ships from the upriver habitations. For £5 (Jamaica money), the captains could buy a ton of logwood or barter 40s worth of rum for the same inventory. The favorable exchange rates attracted plenty of merchant ships who could sell the valuable dyewood to textile mills in England for handsome profits.[12]

Steering north past Patience Brother Island, the Virgins, and Bawdy Point, the buccaneers ran into a Rhode Island sloop belonging to Capt. Jeremiah Clark coming out. The two corsairs took Clark's sloop with no effort and directed him to return with them to the aptly named anchorage, Rogue's Point. Inside the anchorage, they found several merchant vessels clustered together at anchor and a ten-gun Spanish ship just setting sail. There could be no good reason for a Spanish ship to be lurking in the bay. Low threw out Spanish colors on *Fortune* to deceive the Spaniard. The trick worked. *Fortune* and *Ranger* came up to the unsuspecting Spaniard, then ran up their black flags and ran out their guns. A moment later they fired a broadside to demonstrate their superior firepower. The Spaniard, a guardacosta sent to raid the British logwood operations, could see that Low and Lowther had him outgunned and outmanned. The Spanish captain meekly lowered his sails and his ensign, hoping for favorable treatment from the buccaneers.[13]

The pirates went through the routine of receiving hostages from the guardacosta and sending a well-armed party aboard the Spanish ship. The boarding party disarmed the crew of sixty to seventy men and bunched them on the deck as they rifled the vessel. It was an unusually rich haul of valuables. The pirates could see that the guardacosta men had spent a busy morning looting the logwood sloops. The surprise came when the pirates opened the hatch to the hold and discovered merchant captains Norton, Medbury, Esther, and Spofford, among others, crouched in the dark. The merchant captains explained that the Spaniards were hauling them back to a Spanish port, where they were to be held ransom for the value of their logwood. Members of the boarding party returned to *Fortune* to report the discovery to Low and Lowther.

The pirates discussed the finding among themselves. Holding other mariners for ransom was nothing new for men on the account: Low had done it himself only a few months earlier. This situation appeared different to the pirates. These were Spaniards holding Englishmen captive. It called for a harsh reaction. The idea of putting the guardacostas to the sword surfaced. Heretofore, Lowther had not crossed over from piracy to murder, though Low and his crew had already put captured men to death. Lowther's thoughts on deliberate killing were not recorded, but "the Resolution pass'd to kill all the Company."[14]

The pirates quietly picked up "Swords, Cutlashes, Poll-Axes and Pistols" so as not to alarm the Spaniards. More armed men rowed over to the Spanish ship. The buccaneers checked their muskets and pistols to ensure they were properly charged. When all was ready on both vessels, the armed men gathered around the hostages on *Fortune* and the helpless crew on the guardacosta ship. At a nod from Low, the corsairs started hacking. Axes crushed skulls. Cutlasses thrust into bodies. Shots blew brains out. Men cried and screamed. Any Spaniard who tried to resist was shot and then eviscerated. A few jumped down to the hold but were dragged out and dispatched. The butchery went on. Lust-crazed corsairs slashed away at the bodies of groaning men and the corpses of those already dead. Seven Spaniards threw themselves overboard to get clear of "the Rage of those Merciless Men." A few buccaneers jumped into a canoe to chase them down in the water, smashing their heads with swords and axes. In a matter of minutes, rivulets of racing blood, severed limbs, and dozens of dismembered Spaniards had turned the decks of *Fortune* and the guardacosta ship into human slaughterhouses. The stench of gashed entrails and spent gunpowder filled the pirates' nostrils. Several moments went by before the adrenaline pulsing through their veins slowed enough for them to return to their senses.[15]

The sea bandits wasted no time on remorse. They proceeded to empty the Spanish ship of all valuables and supplies. Low freed the merchant captains, but it was no reprieve from robbery. The two pirate crews ransacked the merchant ships, stealing anything the Spaniards had overlooked. They found Benjamin Wickham, the mate of Clark's sloop, in bed with smallpox. The disease did not deter John Walters, one of Low's corsairs, from forcing Wickham aboard a pirate sloop. Apparently, the need for skilled mariners outweighed fear of the pox.[16]

The looting went into the evening. Some of the crew members, fatigued by the killing and pilfering, took their leisure onshore. Under a canopy of mangrove and pines, the pirates relaxed next to a campfire, drinking and reveling. The merry scene was suddenly disturbed by a rustling in the forest vegetation. One of the Spaniards who had made it ashore stumbled out of the brush and into the flickering firelight. Wounded and exhausted, the Spaniard had given up hope of surviving in the wilderness on his own and pleaded for mercy.

"For God's sake, give me quarters," he begged.

One of the pirates grabbed his musket and jumped to his feet. "I'll give you quarters, presently," he said. The corsair forced the Spaniard to his knees and shoved the muzzle of his firelock into the man's mouth. Pulling the trigger, he sent a bullet down the victim's throat.[17]

Lowther and Low eventually finished cleaning out their prizes. They turned over the sloops to their rightful captains, presumably with their cargoes of logwood still intact. However, they kept one captain's sloop and gave him the guardacosta ship in exchange. Lowther's company jumped from *Ranger* to Clark's sloop, considering it in better shape. Lowther named his new sloop *Fortune's Free Gift*, possibly as a compliment to Low's generosity. Charles Harris, the former mate on the merchant ship *Greyhound*, took command of his own vessel about this time. Harris called his sloop *Ranger*, which may have been Lowther's old command, though there is no direct evidence to link the identity of the sloops. After cross-leveling his sloops and crews, Low ordered his pirate fleet out of the bay, with the prize vessels following. He allowed the merchantmen to sail on their own, with a stern warning to head straight to New York and not to make any move toward Jamaica to alert the station ships. He'd had enough of Royal Navy ships after HMS *Mermaid* had nearly run him down.[18]

George Lowther sailed out of the Bay of Honduras in concert with his former protégé, accepting Low's senior position. It might have been difficult to swallow the reversed statures, but Low had proven himself to be a more productive pirate

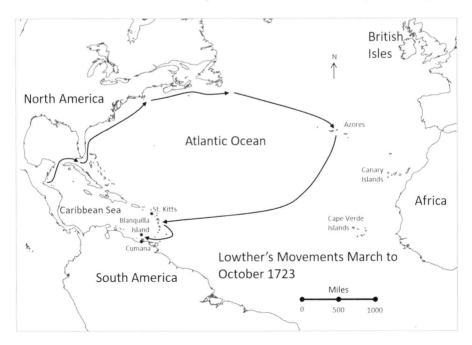

North Atlantic. Lowther's movements, March to October 1723.

British sailor with his hammock and kit. *Gabriel Bray, courtesy of Royal Museums Greenwich*

British fourth-rate ship of the line. *Pearson Scott Foresman, Wikimedia Foundation*

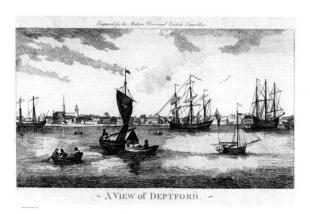

Eighteenth-century view of the Thames River, showing the Deptford naval yard. *Royal Museums Greenwich*

Capt. Edward Vernon, Lowther's skipper and later naval commander in the West Indies. *Charles Philips, courtesy of Royal Museums Greenwich*

Sailors aloft, standing on the horses while reefing topsails. *W. J. Huggins, courtesy of Royal Museums Greenwich*

Navy seamen sounding the ocean's depth. *Antoine Léon Morel-Fation, Wikimedia Commons*

Photo of the gun deck on an Age of Sail replica ship. *Mariordo, Wikimedia Commons*

Lady Mary Wortley Montagu. *Godfrey Kneller, courtesy of Yale Center for British Art*

James Brydges, 1st Duke of Chandos and patron of the Royal African Company. *Michael Dahl, Wikimedia Foundation*

Constantinople's harbor as Lowther may have seen it. *Thomas Allom and Robert Walsh, courtesy of Snell Library, Northeastern University*

Royal African Company coat of arms. *Cakelot1, Wikimedia Commons*

Painting of a Royal Navy galley-frigate similar to the *Gambia Castle*. *Willem Van de Velde the Younger, courtesy of Royal Museums Greenwich*

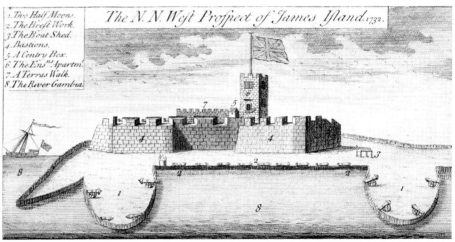

Illustration of Fort James in the Gambia River. *Francis Moore, from* Travels into the Inlands of Africa, 1738

Drawing of a British brigantine. *Boon, courtesy of National Maritime Museum*

Pirates confronting a merchant captain aboard his vessel. *George Alfred Avison, from* Lonely Ships and Lonely Seas

Pirates burning a Spanish ship. *Howard Pyle, from* Collier's Weekly

Portrait of a buccaneer. *From Howard Pyle's* Book of Pirates

Drawing of pirate captain George Lowther at Port Maho. *Toms, courtesy of Library of Congress*

Capt. GEORGE LOWTHER and his Company at Port Mayo *in the Gulph of Matique.*

Crew members breaming a vessel on careen. *Gabriel Bray, courtesy of Royal Museums Greenwich*

Portrait of Chaloner Ogle when he served as Admiral Vernon's deputy and successor. *Unknown artist, courtesy of Royal Museums Greenwich*

THE "SWALLOW" AND "ROBERTS" THE PIRATE.

"SWALLOW." Warship, 672 Tons.　Launched 1703, Blackwall.　Heaviest Gun, 24 Pdr.

HMS *Swallow* in action against Bartholomew Roberts's pirates, 1722. *Charles Dixon, Wikimedia Commons*

To the Merchants of Boston this View of the LIGHT HOUSE is most humbly presented. By their Humble Serv.t W.m Burgis

Drawing of a sloop outside Boston, showing its raked mast and rigging. *William Burgis, courtesy of Library of Congress*

Eighteenth-century prisoner languishing in Newgate Prison. *Wellcome Images, Wikimedia Commons*

British frigate similar to HMS *Greyhound* firing a salute. *Willem Ven de Velde the Younger, courtesy of National Gallery of Art*

Top left: Drawing of pirate captain
Edward Low weathering a hurricane.
*Charles Johnson, courtesy of Library of
Congress*

Top right: Portrait of a buccaneer. *Walter
Appleton Clark, from* Scribner's Magazine

Left: Pirate hanging at Wapping. *Robert
Page Dodd, courtesy of Royal Museums
Greenwich*

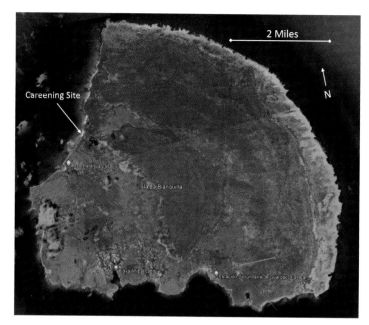

Astronaut photo of Blanquilla Island, showing the beach where Lowther careened his sloop. *Photo from Earth Science and Remote Sensing Unit, NASA Johnson Space Center*

Forlorn pirate marooned on a desolate island. *From Howard Pyle's* Book of Pirates

Painting of the British attack on Porto Bello's Iron Fort, showing HMS *Burford* in the foreground. *George Chambers, courtesy of Royal Museums Greenwich*

View of Port Royal and Kingston Harbor.
Wellcome Images, Wikimedia Commons

Maj. Gen. Thomas
Wentworth, commander of
the West Indies expedition's
land forces. *Allan Ramsay and
Alexander Van Waecken,
courtesy of William L. Clements
Library*

Trading card depicting George Lowther's suicide on Blanco Island. *George S. Harris &
Sons, courtesy of Metropolitan Museum of Art*

Castillo overlooking the entrance to Santiago's harbor. *Hyppolyte de Saint-Rambert, Wikimedia Commons*

Ruins of Porto Bello's Castillo San Jerónimo overlooking the harbor. *Mariordo, Wikimedia Commons*

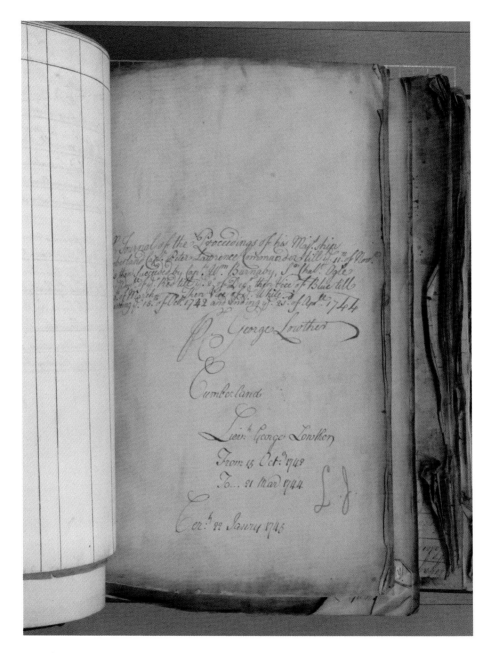

Page from George Lowther's lieutenant's log. *Courtesy of Royal Museums Greenwich*

leader. Lowther bore responsibility for losing one flagship and having another torn to pieces by a merchant brigantine, leaving his company little to show for months of roving. Low had lost a pink through carelessness and courted disaster several times. Despite his recklessness, he and his crew had survived and thrived through rash decisions and multiple errors in judgment. He had earned a reputation for ruthless behavior but was establishing one for enjoying good luck.

With warmer weather on the way, the pirates, a migratory species of mariner, turned their bows northward. The buccaneers set their sights on the North American coast and Grand Banks, where plenty of merchant ships waited for the plucking and hundreds of fishermen cruised in small shallops ready to be forced onto the account.

Low took his fleet up to the Yucatán Passage, then decided to patrol near Cabo San Antonio at the western end of Cuba. It was an excellent lair for pirates. Any traffic leaving the western Caribbean for North America or Europe had to bend around the cape, helped by the current that pushed eastward along the northern coast of Cuba. However, the winds on the coast remained easterly. Low could position his ships north of the cape and pounce from a windward position on any merchant ship leaving the Caribbean. In early May, he made a large haul from the holds of a half-dozen merchantmen and stripped a thousand pistoles from their passengers. Some of the merchant sailors and passengers had been reluctant to divulge the location of their stashes, but the sea bandits used a cruel technique to extract the information they wanted. Placing lighted candles between the victim's fingers, the pirates let the flames burn down to the flesh, by which time the innocents screamed out where they had hidden their valuables. This torture technique, possibly learned from Turkish privateers, would be used again by Lowther's company.[19]

At some point, Lowther separated himself from Low's minifleet to sail ahead to New England and Newfoundland. He either wearied of following Low's company or felt some urgency to get north to plunder more supplies and beef up his crew with more forced men. In late May he was east of Cape Cod when he took a ship coming into Salem, Massachusetts. In contrast, Low worked his way northward at a more deliberate pace, snatching sixteen vessels and personally abusing New England men along the way. His fleet was still southeast of the Delaware capes in early June when he got word that navy station ships from Virginia, New York, and Boston had sortied to hunt for him. Apparently, Lowther, in his passage northward, had alerted colonial governors and navy captains to another season of piratical depredations off their coast, and they had reacted with more vigor than in previous years. Lowther may have tripped the alarm, but it would be Low's company that would endure the consequences.[20]

CHAPTER 13

A TIME FOR RECKONING

FORTUNE AND *RANGER*, AT SEA OFF BLOCK ISLAND, DAWN, JUNE 10, 1723

Edward Low's small pirate fleet had enjoyed a good run of ship seizures on their way north. Low had bragged to the captain of the *Hopeful Betty*, one of his victims, that he had accumulated £60–£80,000 of specie in his chest, presumably before he had sliced off the captain's ears. The buccaneers still itched for more as morning twilight revealed a large square-rigged ship 4 to 5 miles distant. Called up to the deck by the lookout, Ned Low watched the ship tack away—a prey trying to run. Both *Fortune* and *Ranger* raised their sails and gave chase.[1]

Sailing three hours against a light wind out of the west-northwest, the nimbler sloops gained on the ship. Closing to less than a mile, the sloops put up their black ensigns and fired a warning shot over the ship, but the prey refused to yield. After another thirty minutes, Low decided to escalate the intimidation. The black ensigns came down, replaced by bright-red flags. The *jolie rouge* (jolly roger) communicated a vessel's intent to fight and, perhaps, give no quarters to any mariners who did not heave to, at once. The threat failed to halt the square-rigger. Oddly, the prey came about with a shift of the wind from the southwest.[2]

Low in *Fortune* and Charles Harris in *Ranger* opened fire with full broadsides. They edged closer to the large ship, blasting away with their guns. They discovered the ship's identity only when they came abreast, and the prey ship ran out ten guns. A moment later, HMS *Greyhound* unleashed a broadside "with round and grape Shott."[3]

Capt. Peter Solgard, Captain Waldron's replacement on *Greyhound*, had used the same trick that Capt. Chaloner Ogle had used against Bartholomew Roberts's ships. Rather than chase a pirate, he let the pirate chase him. Solgard opposed two sloops that between them had as many guns as *Greyhound* and a few more men than his 130-man crew, but he still liked his odds. Discipline, experience, and sound naval tactics counted for more than the pirates' ferocity. Once the sea rovers absorbed a few broadsides, the lead sloop drew off to fall astern of the frigate, followed by the second. *Greyhound* came about to stay with them. Smoke and flame billowed from the sides of the three vessels, pierced by streaks of reddened shot. Catching glimpses of his adversaries through the sulfurous cloud, Solgard noticed the sloops using their oars. The slight breeze did not provide enough speed, so the pirates had resorted to rowing to get away. The navy captain was not about to let go of the bandits. "We left off Firing and turn'd all hands to Rowing." By 2:30 p.m., *Greyhound* had caught up with the sloops. Seeing they could not outrow the navy ship, the two sloops "clap'd on a Wind" to take advantage of their ability to sail upwind. *Greyhound* turned into the light breeze and worked its way between the pirate sloops. Firing starboard and port guns, *Greyhound* "ply'd them warmly with small and grape Shot." The superior gun handling of the navy gunners and matrosses proved decisive. Their fire knocked down *Ranger*'s mainsail. Solgard had perceived that the damaged sloop had put up the stiffest opposition, and he assumed that the infamous Low captained *Ranger*. He drew next to the helpless sloop to finish her off with a close-in broadside when Charles Harris lowered his ensign and begged for quarter. In the meantime, Admiral Low deserted his consort and fled.[4]

Greyhound accepted *Ranger*'s surrender, though not all the buccaneers were agreeable. Before Solgard's men could board the sloop, "one of the forwardest of the Pirates . . . clapt a Pistol to his head and shot out his own Brains." The navy sailors, once aboard *Ranger*, found four or five dead pirates and took forty-five more prisoner, eight Black men among them. In contrast, *Greyhound* did not lose a single man in the hours-long duel, further evidence that pirates were "a contemptible enemy." Captain Solgard secured *Ranger*, then steered to Newport, where he delivered his prize to the port and his prisoners to the gaol.[5]

After abandoning *Ranger*, Ned Low held course for the Grand Banks, hoping to link up with George Lowther's sloop. His hastiness had brought disaster to his pirate company, though it would be Harris's crew that would suffer the pain. The loss of his consort did nothing to slow his determination to wreak more havoc on the seas, nor did it deter him from abusing his victims. Two days after his narrow escape from justice, Low captured a whaling sloop and beheaded the master. The incident heralded a new, more demented phase in Low's psychosis, where murder and cruelty would become the only solace for his rage against the world.[6]

FORTUNE'S FREE GIFT AT SEA, SOUTHEAST OF NEWFOUNDLAND, JUNE 28, 1723

Captain Lowther and his crew of twenty patrolled the North Atlantic, circling among Cape Race, the Grand Banks, and the Flemish Cap. The air temperatures were mild, the waters frigid. This close to the summer solstice, the crew had more than eighteen hours of daylight to search for victims, though the frequent and dense fogs left them with nothing to do for days at a time other than watch droplets fall from their sails. Still, Lowther and other buccaneers liked to cruise these seas. The fisheries served as a magnet for pirates in search of plunder and forced men. Lowther also fancied these waters because ships coming from Europe used the westbound current skirting Newfoundland's eastern coast, while the prevailing westerlies allowed him to wait for them in a windward position. The day being clear, the lookout soon called his attention to a sail on the eastern horizon. The schooner *Swift*, John Hood master, did not live up to its moniker and fell an easy prey to Lowther's sloop. After securing hostages, the buccaneers rummaged through the schooner and made a delightful discovery. *Swift*'s hold contained forty barrels of salted beef—enough to keep Lowther's crew fed for months. The large haul of provisions made up for the lean months wasted on the Carolina shore the previous year. The pirates spent hours lifting the barrels out of *Swift*'s hold and transferring the loot to *Fortune's Free Gift*. They also pilfered the merchant seamen's private belongings and absconded with any beer, wine, or rum found on board. Lowther was still not finished with Captain Hood's crew. The pirates forced three of Hood's men onto their sloop: Jonathan Deloe, Andrew Hunter, and Henry Hunter. Without further ceremony, Lowther allowed *Swift* to sail on to its home port of Boston.[7]

Fortune's Free Gift continued raiding the Grand Banks and Newfoundland's shores, targeting mostly fishing craft "but none of any great account." Lowther had better luck when he trolled farther east of Newfoundland. On July 5 a brigantine sailing from Dover, the *John and Elizabeth*, came into view. The heavily laden square-rigger had no chance to outrun or dodge the pirates' agile sloop and surrendered quietly. The master, Richard Stanny; his mate, John Mountgomery; and one of their sailors, William Martindale, gave testimony about their experience with Lowther's company after they reached Boston. "These Deponents testify and say, That in their passage from Dover to Boston, They were taken . . . by a pirate sloop, Commanded by one George Lowther, Manned with about Twenty Men, having Seven Guns Mounted; the said Pirates broke open the Hatches of the said Brigantine, and took out of her divers Goods and Merchandizes, and having so Robbed the said Brigantine, and Plundered the Company, they did by Force & Violence carry away Two of the said Brigantines Company on board the said Pirate, Namely, Ralph Kendale of Sunderland, in the County of Durham, and Henry Watson of Dover, aforesaid, and very barbarously Whipt & Beat the said Kendale & Watson." Lowther released the remaining crew of the *John and Elizabeth* to continue their voyage, displaying no more hostility beyond what

Watson and Kendale endured. The incident showed that Lowther and his men could keep their aggression in check, but it was never far beneath the surface. The instant that Watson and Kendale had showed a lack of cooperation, the handspikes and cutlasses came out.[8]

Lowther and his crew could chalk up July 5 as a productive day, unaware of events taking place in London that foreshadowed a fate that many of them would share.

COURT OF THE ADMIRALTY, OLD BAILEY, LONDON, JULY 5, 1723

John Massey, onetime army officer and former partner of George Lowther, entered the courtroom and strode to the dock. Far from cringing under the glare of the judge and jurors, he stood tall and erect in full view of the court. Massey had been anticipating this moment since the time he cast loose from the *Gambia Castle/Delivery* twenty-two months earlier—not that he entertained any optimism about the trial's outcome; rather, this was his moment to address the public and let the world hear of the cruel circumstances that forced him into mutiny.

The advocate general began the proceedings by reading the indictment against John Massey and George Lowther (in absentia). "1. For Piratically seizing the Ship called the Gamboa Castle with the Goods in the same to the value of about 10,000 belonging to the Royal African Company. 2. For Piratically seizing a Brigantine belonging to Boston in New England and taking several Good out of her. 3. For Piratically seizing a French sloop of an unknown Name and taking Wine and Brandy & Money about 80 out of her." The court first deposed Capt. Charles Russell, who testified that Lowther had precipitated the mutiny on *Gambia Castle* by refusing to "stay in the Country." Lowther took over the ship, Russell explained, while he and Colonel Whitney had conferred with the king of Barra at Gillifree (Jufureh). Alexander Thompson, the lone mariner who had left *Delivery* with Massey, attested to Massey's participation in the mutiny and ship seizures in the West Indies. The advocate then entered into evidence the petition to the king written off Barbados in 1721, and the letter to the Royal African Company from January 1722. They showed the documents to the jurors and pointed to the handwriting to confirm that they were written by Massey. After that, the prosecution rested.[9]

John Massey, standing with a "Soldier-like . . . Air and Deportment," faced the jury and began his long-awaited defense. He made no effort to dispute the facts presented or any part of the prosecution's case: an acquittal was not his objective. Massey directed his soliloquy more to the British nation, seeking recognition that he had acted honorably and justly, if not strictly in accordance with the law. He launched into "a very long Rambling Speech" shot full of grievances and self-justifications. His speech, given at length and with sincerity, lacked coherence. He tried to convince the court and the audience that the poor treatment of his soldiers and the need to save them from the fatal illnesses sweeping through their ranks justified his extreme action. Although people witnessing the testimony managed to piece together his roundabout logic, "His Defence consisted of so man[y] wild Excursions, and minute and trifling Circumstances . . . it had near tir'd the Patience of the Court." The judge, though annoyed by the tedious and convoluted speech, indulged Massey, perhaps realizing that he was watching the last, pathetic attempt of a condemned soul trying to retrieve some semblance of dignity from the ruins of his sad life. At long last, Massey ended his oration, then produced the certificate from Governor Lawes commending him for his efforts to chase after George Lowther.[10]

To support his defense, Massey called two character witnesses, his near relations who had bailed him out of Newgate and encouraged him to flee. The Rev. Edmund Massey testified first. A noted cleric, Edmund Massey had acquired a reputation as a fine preacher after giving sermons at several famous venues, including St. Paul's, where he used the pulpit to rail against the dangerous and sinful practice of smallpox inoculation. The reverend spoke truthfully, which meant his testimony did little to help Captain Massey. "[I] had known him these 23 Years and had scarce known him do one reasonable Action in any thing of Moment." Isaac Massey, an apothecary specializing in the sale of "Oyl of Mustard," spoke next, questioning the wisdom of the Royal African Company for giving command to such "a strange and half-witted Man." At that point, Massey closed his case, relieving the judge and jurors from enduring any more of his wearisome defense.[11]

Massey had delivered his long-winded address to the court in the hope of earning respect. What he got was pity. The jurors returned a verdict of guilty on all counts but appended a request that the court look upon him as an "Object of Mercy & Compassion." An observer watching the trial on behalf of the lords justices, Henry Penrice, agreed with the jurors. "His Behaviour during the whole Course of his Tryal & Defence . . . showed him not to be in his right senses." The court ignored the request and sentenced him to be hanged—mutiny and piracy would earn no reprieve.[12]

The Old Bailey in London was not the only place to hold trials for piracy that month.

COURT OF THE ADMIRALTY, TOWN HOUSE, NEWPORT, RHODE ISLAND, JULY 10, 1723

Gov. William Dummer of Massachusetts Bay, Gov. Samuel Cranston of Rhode Island, and the seven other "esquires" of the Court of the Admiralty commanded silence among the assembled spectators "upon pain of imprisonment" while they read their commission under the Act for the More Effectual Suppression of Piracy. After swearing in the members of the court and ordering the prisoners and witnesses to appear, the court adjourned. The next day, thirty-six of the prisoners taken off the sloop *Ranger* appeared before the court and the appointed judge, John Menzies, to plead not guilty. The eight Black men on the pirate sloop apparently had been claimed by the Royal Navy and sold back into bondage. The advocate general, John Valentine, opened the case against the thirty-six with a broad condemnation of pirates, styling them *Hostes humani Generis*, enemies of all mankind. "These unhappy men," he proclaimed, "satiated with the number and notoriety of their crimes, had filled up the measure of their guilt." Sensitive that some officials had scandalously insinuated that pirates had at one time found an outlet for their plunder in the colony, Valentine averred "that such flagitious persons, find as little countenance and shelter, and as much justice at Rhode Island, as in any other part of his Majesty's dominions." With that off his chest, Valentine began calling witnesses and presenting the case against the accused.[13]

Over the next three days, the court parsed the hardened buccaneers from the unfortunate men held aboard *Ranger* before its capture. The accused pleaded not guilty and asserted they were forced men, a valid claim. Only John Brown (the taller man of that name), Thomas Hugett, and William Reed remained from Massey's company of mutineers who had signed the articles in the Gambia. Everyone else, Capt. Charles Harris included, had been forced aboard a pirate vessel at some point. The fact that nearly the entire crew of *Ranger* consisted of "forced men" testifies to the seductive lure of the lazy, self-indulgent, and dissolute pirate lifestyle. Too many mariners chose to enjoy easy living off the misery of innocent merchantmen in lieu of the rigorous discipline of honest work. Depositions by *Greyhound's* officers and recent victims taken by Low and Harris pointed to men in the dock who had harnessed themselves with pistols and cutlasses aboard *Ranger*. The witnesses also picked out men who had been held as captives and took no active part in the crew's piracies. Thomas Mumford, the Native American captured by Low thirteen months earlier, and Joseph Sweetser, who had been taken off *Rebecca*, were acquitted, along with six others. The court condemned the other twenty-eight to be hanged, though two sentences were remitted.[14]

On July 19, members of the admiralty court and colonial officials gathered at Gravelly Point, a small promontory in Newport's harbor, where gallows had been erected "within the flux and reflux of the sea." An important jurisdictional issue dictated the tidal location. The colonial government had authority above the high-water mark— below it, the Admiralty held sway. While Governor Cranston directed the day's somber proceedings, a morbidly fascinated throng of onlookers crowded along the edge of the harbor or sat offshore in small boats to witness one of the largest mass executions in American history. At noon the sad procession marched from the gaol to Gravelly Point under a heavy guard. The large escort had been ordered because three of the condemned men had slipped their irons two days earlier and escaped, only to be recaptured on the "out Skirts of the Town." The prisoners came to a halt in the shadow of *Ranger's* Old Roger, affixed to a corner of the gallows. The dark-blue ensign displayed the image of a skeleton in its center, holding an hourglass in one hand and, in the other, a dart piercing a heart with three drops falling from it. Some of *Ranger's* crew may have ruefully recalled their previous boasts that "they would live and die under it." For two hours the executioners bound, haltered, and dropped the condemned men, several at a time.

As soon as one man finished his "hempen dance" and stilled at the end of the rope, the next man in line took his place on the gallows. Because the condemned hung partially in the tide, death did not come quickly. Even the most-hardened observers grimaced at the spectacle. "Never was there a more doleful sight in all this land. . . . And oh! How awful the Noise of their dying moans."[15]

Rev. Cotton Mather, the famed Boston theologian, followed the dolorous event with a sermon based on a passage in Job: "We will this day Mark the Way that Wicked Men have trodden." Mather had particular distaste for pirates who lived in contempt of the old Puritan moral fortitude he cherished. He held them up to the audience as examples of impious men who "find their Lusts perpetually Enslaving of them." In a long-winded message, he cautioned the congregation to avoid the paths of temptation and damnation that had produced the horrific scene just witnessed. "The Way that Wicked Men have trodden, has newly terminated in a Tragical Execution of Death, on such a Number of Criminals, as our sorrowful Eyes have never before seen together, with hands clapped at them, hissed out of their Place." Mather's sermon, powerful as it may have been, likely did not haunt the minds of the people as much as the final lament left by John FitzGerald, one of the recently hanged men.[16]

> To mortal Men that daily live in Wickedness and Sin;
> This dying Counsel I do give, hoping you will begin
> To serve the Lord in Time of Youth his Precepts for to keep
> To serve Him so in Spirit and Truth, that you may mercy reap.
>
> In Youthful blooming Years was I, when I that Practice took;
> Of perpetrating Piracy, for filthy gain did look.
> To wickedness we all were bent, our Lusts for to fulfil;
> To rob at Sea was our Intent, and perpetrate all Ill.
>
> I pray the Lord preserve you all and keep you from this End;
> O let Fitz-Gerald's great downfall onto your welfare tend.
> I to let the Lord my Soul bequeath, accept thereof I pray,
> My Body to the Earth bequeath, dear Friend, adieu for aye.[17]

FORTUNE AND FORTUNE'S FREE GIFT, NORTH ATLANTIC, EAST OF CAPE BRETON, MID-JULY 1723

Low and the crew of *Fortune* had worked their way to the Grand Banks after the fight with HMS *Greyhound*, as evidenced by the string of mutilations, shootings, and beheadings left in their wake. Off Cape Breton, Low attacked a French fishing fleet and abused several sailors. "At his hand; they cut off some of their Ears and

Noses and treated them with all the Barbarity imaginable." When one French captain asked Low to leave him something after he had pilfered his wine and brandy, Low pretended to oblige. He "accordingly brought up two Pistols, presenting one at his Bowels, he told him there was one for his Wine, and Discharg'd it; and there says he (presenting the other at his Head in the same manner) is one for your Brandy, which said, he discharg'd that also."[18]

Either by prior arrangement or similar patrolling schemes, Low and Lowther discovered each other in the North Atlantic and worked in concert between Nova Scotia and Newfoundland. Ships out of Placentia and Canso spread word of their joint onslaught. "Low the Pyrate had taken upwards of 20 French Vessels. . . . They have taken several English Vessels and Boats on the Banks, Whipt some Men to Death. . . . Lowder the Pyrate had also been upon the Banks." Witnesses gave confused reports about which buccaneer captain was responsible for accosting different merchant vessels. One report speculated that Low had died, because the pirate captain they had seen [Lowther] "is a lusty Man," whereas Low was known to be "a little Man." The treatment of captured mariners provided a better means of separating Lowther's depredations from Low's. "The next vessel they took was one of Capt. Robinson's, whom they divested of their Arms, Ammunition, and Silver Buckels, and then dismiss'd them."[19]

Rumors and hysteria skipped around the Atlantic Seaboard like smoothed stones pitched over a pond. Residents of Block Island issued an alarm after they thought they had been visited by Lowther's sloop. A report from Salem claimed that Low's sloop had been captured near Canso and that Low had died of wounds. A contrary rumor claimed that Low had been taken near Cape Sables. A sloop arriving in Philadelphia spread word that Lowther had gone to Cape Fear to careen his sloop. The excitement kept the navy station ships busy. After dropping off the prisoners taken from *Ranger*, HMS *Greyhound* cruised east in pursuit of Low and later encountered HMS *Seahorse*, the station ship out of Boston. HMS *Solebay* also patrolled from Newfoundland.[20]

The navy frigates returned to port without spotting either Low or Lowther. However, word of their activity reached the ears of the two pirate captains. Both pirate companies decided to leave the Grand Banks before they ran afoul of the Royal Navy: no one wanted to end up like Charles Harris and his crew. Besides, with summer coming to an end, time had come to migrate south. Lowther and Low made plans to sail for the Azores to harass Portuguese shipping.

Before leaving the North Atlantic, Lowther seized the *Baily*, a Virginia ship bound for London. The buccaneers "plunder'd him of all his fresh Provisions, Arms, and Powder, and wantonly thrown over-board a new Cable valued at [£70 1s]." With his men busy emptying *Baily* of its goods, Lowther asked the merchantman's skipper, Captain Graves, "to take a Glass with him," likely from Graves's own stock. Graves obliged the request. He may have been grateful that his captor was being hospitable instead of slicing off his ears as Low would have done. Lowther seemed in good spirits, full of confidence. Then again, he may have been mindful of Harris's recent capture and how precarious a pirate's life could be. "After flourishing his Sword several times over his Head," Lowther turned to Graves to make a bold statement. "I make no doubt, but you expect to see me make my exit at Execution-Dock; but by G— I never will, for if I should be over-power'd, here is that shall End me." Lowther then drew a pistol from his girdle and held it up for Graves to see. This act of bravado seemed to proclaim his defiance of the law and refusal to submit to a hanging, but it might also have a shown a bit of inner trepidation, a hint of worry about where his path was leading. Pirate captains usually concentrated on their next ship seizure, while their men seldom looked beyond their next drink. Most buccaneers avoided thinking too much about the future—there were no favorable long-term prospects. While he ruled his sloop and regaled Captain Graves with his fine cloths and swagger, Lowther could brandish his pistol and pretend to make light of his death. In a few months he would face the harsh reality of choosing the noose or the pistol, a dilemma he would find terrifying.[21]

NEWGATE PRISON, LONDON, JULY 26, 1723

The procession left Newgate Prison in the late afternoon, led by a marshal on horseback who carried a miniature silver oar that symbolized the authority of the Admiralty. A mourning coach followed, carrying Rev. Nicholson of St. Sepulchre's, a second clergyman (most likely the chaplain of Newgate Prison), and John Massey. All headed to Execution Dock in Wapping to keep an appointment dictated by the Court of the Admiralty.[22]

After Massey's trial and sentencing, Mary Massey, his wife, had sent a heart-wrenching letter to the lords justices begging for mercy for her husband—no reply. She posted another letter to the Earl of Cadogan, then master-general of the ordnance, asking him to intervene with the regency on her husband's behalf. She pleaded with the earl that if her condemned husband was executed, she would become "a Deplorable Object of Misery & Sorrow . . . and be reduced to unspeakable Want." Her letter went unanswered. Massey himself sent a petition for reprieve to the lords justices, but to no avail. Despite the calls for mercy from jurors and the public, the regents held firm—no reprieve. Politically, the lords inclined toward strict measures against pirates and mutineers. The merchant class still pressured the government to take more action to clear pirates from the seas. Because of their depredations, shippers had to pay higher insurance premiums and put more guns on their ships, all of it adding to costs. The Royal African Company and the Duke of Chandos still resented the humiliating loss from Massey's mutiny in the Gambia, and their influence could be felt in Whitehall. As pathetic a pirate as John Massey might have been, his demise could not excite enough sympathy among the lords justices to overlook his crimes. His sentence would be carried out.[23]

Massey's 2.5-mile journey began on Newgate Street, passed St. Paul's Cathedral, then threaded through central London. The condemned man kept his composure on his final ride as he had since his conviction, something that impressed the prison chaplain. For a brief stretch his coach traveled Leadenhall Street, where the Royal African Company Court of Assistants and clerical staff stared out the windows at his passing coach. Massey pointed to the Africa House and remarked, "They have used me severely, but I pray God prosper and bless them in all their undertakings." The coach finally came to a halt on Wapping Street, next to stairs leading down to Execution Dock.[24]

By custom, the condemned were allowed a few words. Massey, looking grave and penitent, turned toward his wife, his relatives, and the numerous onlookers to deliver a short, prepared speech.

> Good People, I Beg of you to pray for my departing Soul; I likewise pray God to forgive all the Evidences that swore against me, as I do from my Heart: I challenge all the World to say, I ever did a dishonourable Act, or any Thing unlike a Gentleman, but what might be common to all young Fellows in this Age; but this was surely a rash Action, for I never design'd or intended to turn Pirate, and I am very sorry for it, and I wish it was in my Power to make Amends to the Honourable *African* Company for what they have lost by my Means. I likewise declare upon the Words of a dying Man, that I never once thought of molesting his Grace the Duke of *Chandos,* altho' it has been maliciously reported, that I always went with two loaded Pistols to dispatch his Grace. As for the Duke, I was always while living devoted to his Services, for his good Offices done unto me; and I humbly beg Almighty God, that he would be pleased to shower down his Blessings upon his good Family. Good People, once more I beg of you to pray for my departing Soul. I desire my dying Words may be printed, as for the Truth and Sincerity of them, I Sign them, as a Man departing this World.

When he finished, Massey asked the coachman of the hearse to close his casket without letting his wife or relatives see his corpse.[25]

At the appointed time of 7:00 p.m., John Massey descended the steps to the riverfront, where gallows stood half submerged by the briny tide and nauseating sewerage. The hangman helped Massey step onto a small platform attached to the vertical beam, then looped the condemned man's head inside a noose suspended only a short space below the gallows' cross-member. Massey said a final prayer, "Courage attending him to the last moment." The hangman then shoved him off the platform, letting him drop a couple of feet into the water. The combination of the short rope and high tide ensured that Massey dangled half-suspended in the Thames for several minutes before the tightening noose gradually choked out his life.[26]

CHAPTER 14

BLANCO ISLAND

FORTUNE'S FREE GIFT AND MERRY CHRISTMAS, AT SEA OFF THE AZORES, AUGUST 1723

The Azores stand out from the Atlantic like a handful of emeralds cast on its surface. Ancient evergreen forests, pastureland, and verdant fields of heather cover the volcanic island chain from Corvo in the northwest to Sao Pedro, 380 miles southeast. The archipelago, standing 1,000 miles west of Portugal, had been discovered and settled over the preceding 280 years by Portuguese and Flemish colonists, attracted by the mild subtropical temperatures and rich soil. Active trade with Europe and an absence of navy station ships made the Azores a lucrative stopover for pirates heading south from the North Atlantic.

After their rampage off the Grand Banks, Lowther and Low set their sights on the Portuguese islands, though Low would not make the passage in *Fortune*. Prior to leaving Newfoundland, Low had swapped his sloop for a larger captured ship. He had a habit of switching his flag to a new vessel every few months, much like a long-haul coachman switching teams of horses. Perhaps mindful that he and Harris had been outgunned by HMS *Greyhound*, Low cut more gunports into the hull and mounted the square-rigger with thirty-four guns. He raised his black flag on the maintop masthead and renamed the ship *Merry Christmas*—his affrontery knew no bounds. The two pirate companies enjoyed a quick, easy sail from the Grand Banks on an east-southeast course. Pushed along by the Gulf Stream and catching the prevailing westerlies on a broad reach, Lowther in *Fortune's Free Gift* and Low in *Merry Christmas* arrived in the Azores after a few days' sail. The two buccaneer vessels steered for the central grouping of islands: Faial, Pico, Sao Jorge,

Gracioso, and Terceira. The island cluster offered them several ambush sites on the lee sides of the islands or in protected coves where they could pounce on merchant vessels meandering through the shipping channels.[1]

Capt. Elias Wild, sailing a brigantine owned by a Portuguese nobleman, became the first merchant to fall into the pirates' snare. Wild's ship endured the standard pilfering of its cargo until Low noticed that half of its crew were English and the other half Portuguese. Out of some perceived offense or simply for amusement (with Low it really did not matter), he ordered all the Portuguese strung up by the yardarm. He showed more leniency with the Englishmen, setting them adrift in their longboat and then burning their brigantine.

The sea robbers set a virtual blockade of Faial and its port city, Horta. Several more merchant vessels got caught in their clutches, affording Low more opportunities to unleash his savagery. Lowther, Low's former mentor, observed a disturbing trend in his partner's demented behavior. By custom, buccaneers inflicted abuse and torment to compel captured mariners to join their companies or to forcibly extract any valuables their victims tried to withhold. Low no longer needed a reason to torture or kill. As Cotton Mather had predicted, his impiety had improved to malignity. He and his men made "Mischief their Sport, Cruelty their Delight, and Damning of Souls their constant Employment . . . their Anger had much the same Effect for both were usually gratified with the Cries and Groans of their Prisoners; so that they almost as often murthered a Man from the Excess of good Humour, as out of Passion and Resentment." Others worried about the level of brutality Low meted out. Members of the crew, a hardened lot in their own right, could see that the random torture of prisoners was becoming excessive and potentially counterproductive. Buccaneers preferred to have their prey surrender. If merchant captains feared getting maimed, the pirates might encounter more resistance.[2]

The pirates' blockade and torment of their victims terrified the citizens and port officials of Horta. By the time Lowther and Low left Faial to prowl farther east, the sight of any British vessel caused panic. Capt. Philip Tillingheast, a merchant out of Newport, Rhode Island, tried to enter the harbor shortly after the sea bandits had left. Instead of a welcome, he received a salvo from the fort. He lowered his sails and came ashore to show he had no ill intent, but the Portuguese still threw him in jail. Only after examining his bills of lading and correspondence did they release him.[3]

The pirate sloop and frigate proceeded to the waters off Sao Miguel, looking to intercept merchant ships coming into Ponta Delgada, the Azores' largest city. They soon found a fourteen-gun London-built ship standing in the road. Rather than risk either *Fortune's Free Gift* or *Merry Christmas* in an exchange of salvos, the buccaneers sent boarding parties in their longboats to sneak up to the ship and overwhelm its crew. The attack nearly failed. Captain Thompson, the ship's master, spotted the approaching boats and called his crew to arms. He had enough men to drive off the attackers, but his crew lacked the fighting spirit to do battle with bloodthirsty pirates. Some of the merchantmen may have entertained a notion of joining Low's or Lowther's companies. Thompson was forced to relent. His frustration turned to horror when familiar faces climbed over the gunwales to seize control of his ship. The same cutthroats had captured him a year earlier in the same location, when he commanded the *Rose* pink, which Low took over as his flagship. Ferried over to *Merry Christmas*, Thompson endured another painful audience with Ned Low. The sea bandits chopped his ears off close to his skull, then burnt his new ship, a penalty for daring to resist. Maimed and financially ruined, Thompson was set aboard his longboat and released. A Portuguese bark became the next victim. Either Low had become more relaxed or Lowther made the capture, because the crew suffered no further harm other than having their clothes slashed by the buccaneers. The pirates turned the Portuguese crew loose in their longboat, then burned the bark.[4]

The pirates had swept through the Azores scooping up prey like baleen whales attacking a ball of krill. After clearing merchant traffic from the island chain, Low wanted to drop south to the Canary and Cape Verde Islands before raiding the Guinea coast. Lowther had different thoughts. His time in the Gambia left him with no desire for African shores. He also may have had his fill of Low's company. They were pirates with different agendas. Lowther wanted to survive as a sea rover and take what he needed from merchant ships to sustain the easy lifestyle. Low, on the other hand, seemed bent on revenge against the whole world for the perceived wrongs he had suffered in his turbulent life. The two companies decided to part, Lowther for the West Indies and Low toward Africa. They split amicably and possibly agreed on a rendezvous later in the year in the Bay of Honduras, where they had enjoyed past success. *Fortune's Free Gift* bore south to the thirtieth parallel, then caught the easterly trade winds for a southwest run to the Lesser Antilles.

Low and *Merry Christmas* worked the eastern Atlantic on their way south, taking a Liverpool merchant in the Cape Verde Islands. He had more success off the coast of Sierra Leone when *Merry Christmas* captured a twelve-gun ship, the *Delight*, which had once been in Royal Navy service. The pirates knocked down the interior bulkheads and mounted four more guns to turn the ship back into a frigate. Low put sixty men aboard to crew his new consort and gave command to Francis Spriggs, the quartermaster of *Merry Christmas*. Spriggs had once commanded Low's old schooner, *Fancy*, in the West Indies but reverted to quartermaster when Low reshuffled his pirate fleet in March. Some resentment may have lingered, and a recent dispute with Low may have put Spriggs in a bad temper. He deserted Low two days later and sailed on his own for the West Indies. Low would eventually steer for the West Indies himself, a month later.[5]

FORTUNE'S FREE GIFT, AT SEA OFF THE WINDWARD ISLANDS, EARLY SEPTEMBER 1723

The passage to the Windward Islands stressed *Fortune's Free Gift*'s crew more than Lowther may have anticipated. When he left the Azores, he was well stocked with provisions and loot, but the pirate company had fallen on lean times in the weeks since. The sloop did not have nearly the storage capacity that *Delivery* had the last time

Lowther had crossed the ocean, and *Fortune's Free Gift* carried more men than it had in June. The additional head count of forced men and those who had signed the articles depleted the stores more quickly than the captain may have calculated. The most urgent shortage would have been fresh water, which likely directed Lowther to make landfall at a place where he knew he could refill his water barrels—Rupert's Bay, Dominica. With a replenished water supply, Lowther went roving for more necessities: rum, medical supplies, canvas, cordage, etc. By this time, even the salted beef stolen from *Swift* in June may have been running out. Lowther turned back east to troll the sea-lanes windward of Dominica and ran across a "Martinico Man." A day or two of plundering the local vessel did much to relieve the sloop's supply shortage.[6]

Lowther headed southeast, reversing the course he had taken in 1721. He lowered sails when he fixed the sloop's position on the same latitude as Barbados and a day or so east of the island. *Fortune's Free Gift* stood astride the sea-lane running between Africa and the West Indies, a great spot to jump on westbound victims. Any New England ship turning on the latitude for Barbados could also fall into its trap, like the *Charles* did in 1721. Lowther sent an observer aloft and waited. On the morning of September 14, the lookout called the crew's attention to a sail coming over the eastern horizon. Studying the galley through his spyglass, the pirate captain gauged it to be a "Guiney Man" carrying a cargo of slaves. When the ship drew close enough, the pirates yanked up the mainsail, jibs, and course. They let the galley know their intent by raising their black flag to the masthead and filling the weather deck with armed men, figuring it would intimidate the prey into surrendering. It did not. The slave galley came about and fled.[7]

Capt. John Wickstead, master of the *Princess*, could escape in only one direction—eastward. In that latitude, winds came out of the northeast or east 90 percent of the time, which meant he had to clap on a wind. Wickstead knew that put him at a disadvantage. The fore-and-aft-rigged pirate sloop could sail a point closer to the wind and advance more on each tack than his square-rigger. He could only hope to maintain his lead until nightfall, then use the dark to elude his pursuer.

Lowther kept on the slave ship's stern, tacking back and forth to contain the prey to his windward. The crew had to swing the mainsail boom from port to starboard and back each time the quartermaster turned the rudder to the opposite tack. The hours drifted by, but *Fortune's Free Gift* steadily closed the distance. By late afternoon the sea bandits had *Princess* in gun range. Lowther would have avoided firing a bow chaser at the prey ship, because the gun's recoil would impede the sloop's momentum. In a chase to windward, a pursuing vessel would normally discharge port guns on a starboard tack or vice versa. Pirates usually fired the first volley off the prey's bow or over its sails, hoping the merchantman would come to. *Princess* kept fleeing. The next salvos targeted the galley. The chase ended at 8:00 p.m., when *Fortune's Free Gift* drew alongside and presented its guns broadside to *Princess*. Wickstead knew that the pirate had him outgunned and outmanned for a close sea battle. He struck his sails and ensign.[8]

The grueling process of robbery began with Lowther compelling the merchant crew "to hoist out their boat." Lowther sent some of his own men back to *Princess* in the longboat, who "sett a sentry" on the galley. The boat returned to *Fortune's Free Gift* with several hostages from the merchant crew. The ordeal lasted throughout the next day, "during which time they ransackt and plundered" *Princess*. Lowther and his veterans from the *Gambia Castle* knew enough about slave ships to figure the *Princess* had a stash of purchase money. Nicholas Lewis, Lowther's quartermaster, had recently come over from Ned Low's crew and knew a trick to find out where the crew may have hidden it. The pirates secured Goldsmith Blowers, the second mate, and John Crawford, the ship's surgeon, then tied down their hands. The mate and surgeon watched in terror as the pirates slid matches between their fingers and lit them. The matches burned down, the flesh singed, and searing pain shot through their systems. A few minutes later, the buccaneers got their hands on 54 ounces of gold dust, which soon went into the company chest. Lowther's crew helped themselves to "all their Gun Powder the remnant of their Cargo and Small Arms with two quarter Deck Guns and two Swivell Guns with the Gunner's and Boatswain's Stores the ship Colours and several Things more that the said Pirates thought fit for their purpose." Next, the pirates went below deck to relieve *Princess* of its primary cargo—thirteen enslaved Africans. They added one "Priviledge Slave" (a slave held aboard ship to perform menial tasks) to the haul of human cargo and stuck them into the sloop's hold.[9]

Lowther presided over a final ceremony in the despoiling of the *Princess* galley. He and his corsairs, wearing their finery stolen from other mariners, held up cups of rum and wine to the crew of the slave ship, then beckoned them to join the company. The repugnant service on the slaver coupled with the attraction of the pirates' carefree existence convinced five men to throw their allegiance to the black ensign. In past seizures, few men had come aboard Lowther's vessel voluntarily, and most forced men joined the company only after days of alternating enticements and beatings. The pirates discovered that recruiting from one slaver was easier than pulling men off a half-dozen fishing vessels. The five new men still did not satisfy Lowther's manpower requirements: he needed men with particular skills. William Gibbons, the surgeon's mate, and James Sedgwick, carpenter's mate, were detained by force on the sloop. After adding seven men to his crew, Lowther put one man aboard *Princess*. Andrew Leveiux (Andre Levieux?), a French sailor, had been captured off Newfoundland. Lowther released him either after taking pity on the Frenchman or finding it too difficult to communicate with him—a rare act of compassion for a pirate captain.

Sometime on September 16, the pirates turned *Princess* loose with its reduced crew and empty cargo hold. Captain Wickstead steered straight for Barbados and dropped anchor in Carlisle Bay on September 18. He, Blowers, Crawford, and Benjamin Flint, the ship's boatswain, went to the government house to swear out a deposition about their ordeal before Nicholas Hammond, the island's deputy secretary. The officials could take no action against the reported pirate attack because the Royal Navy station ship assigned to Barbados, the fifth-rate HMS *Lynn*, was moored in New York Harbor at the time.[10]

FORTUNE'S FREE GIFT, BLANQUILLA ISLAND, OFF TIERRA FIRME, LATE SEPTEMBER 1723

The long chase of the *Princess* may have bothered Captain Lowther. He thought that his sloop should have closed on the slave galley more quickly. Too many barnacles and too much seaweed, plus other sludge clinging to the hull, must have reduced its speed. *Fortune's Free Gift* needed a cleaning. The presence of a carpenter's mate may have persuaded the pirate captain that the time had come for some ship's maintenance. Lowther searched his charts for a secluded bay or island where he could put the sloop on careen. That meant he had to leave the busy sea-lanes and bear west into the southern Caribbean. He bypassed the Grenadines and Tobago, the fictional setting for Daniel Defoe's *Robinson Crusoe*. Just as well. HMS *Winchilsea* had surprised Capt. John Fenn and his crew while they were careening their ship there in April. Not wanting to get too close to the Dutch Antilles, Lowther selected Blanquilla Island, off the coast of what is now Venezuela. Pirates sometimes used the island because of its seclusion and the lack of sea hazards along its shore.[11]

Blanco Island sits at 11°50' north latitude, 58 miles from Isla Margarita and 83 miles north of Punta de Araya, on the South American coast. Flat and sterile, the island has a shape resembling a quarter slice of pie with a curved northeastern coast. The island covers 25 square miles, with its long dimensions reaching roughly 6 miles north–south and east–west. Short white embankments bound nearly the entire shoreline, but the island is surrounded by a soft sandy bottom. At the time, the vegetation consisted of acacia and lignum vitae trees interspersed with prickly pear cacti. It held no human habitations, perhaps because it had no significant bays in which to anchor ships. On the protected, western side, a couple of shallow indentions in the shoreline provided beaches suitable for careening. A freshwater spring could be found just a few yards from the beach, near the midpoint of the western shore. Lowther anchored his sloop close to this beach, above a white oozy seafloor.[12]

The crew and newly forced men went to work lifting the sakers and minions out of the sloop and ferrying them to the island, though they apparently left at least one bow chaser on the weather deck. The water, rum, and gunpowder barrels came ashore along with some of the heavier stores. The men unbent the sails and spread them out over the beach as canopies where Lowther and his senior pirates lounged under the shade, sipping their drinks. Once *Fortune's Free Gift* had been lightened, the crew used lines to careen it on its side. James Sedgwick, the carpenter taken off the *Princess*, supervised the forced men as they went through the unpleasant task of breaming and sealing the hull with the stinking mix of tar and brimstone. Meanwhile, Lowther let the old hands roam the island to hunt down the messes of green iguanas that infested the island—fresh meat for supper! A few days later, the men righted *Fortune's Free Gift*, then careened it on the other side to resume the breaming process. It took several days to finish cleaning and repairing both sides of the hull, but Lowther and his men may have decided to relax on Blanco Island for a few extra days, given the ready supply of fresh meat and fresh water. Even pirates could enjoy time away from the sea.[13]

SLOOP *EAGLE*, AT SEA OFF BLANQUILLA ISLAND, OCTOBER 5, 1723

Capt. Walter Moore, master of the slave ship *Eagle*, piloted his sloop from St. Kitts toward Cumana on the Spanish mainland. The sloop belonged to the South Sea Company, a stock company formed to service Britain's war debt at the end of the War of the Spanish Succession. The company also had a secondary source of income. The British government awarded exclusive rights to the South Sea Company to sell the slaves and goods to Spain's West Indies possessions under the asiento, further boosting the firm's financial prospects. The lucrative trade rights and annual debt payment from the government attracted numerous investors from Britain's upper classes. In 1720 the share price ballooned tenfold before bursting, financially ruining many and giving the company a reputation almost as unsavory as the pirates'.[14]

The asiento, besides stimulating speculators, had cracked an opening into Spain's colonial markets that British merchants tried to turn into a full-sized rupture. The South Sea Company abused its limited trading rights by selling contraband goods off its slave ships and exceeding the navio permiso's allowable tonnage, several times over. Even though *Eagle* was an asiento vessel, Captain Moore did not sail directly from Africa to a Spanish port but stopped at St. Kitts first. The company had recently installed a factor on the island who facilitated loading bale goods and foodstuffs on the sloop to market out of its hold while it offloaded its authorized slave cargo in a Spanish port. From St. Kitts, Moore charted a course almost due south to Cumana. The unusual route outside the normal sea-lanes took *Eagle* past the western side of Blanquilla Island.[15]

Days out from St. Kitts, the cry of a lookout interrupted *Eagle*'s routine progress toward Cumana. The sharp-eyed observer had spotted the bare mast of a sloop anchored near the shore of Blanco Island. Captain Moore suspected trouble, "knowing that Island to be a place where Traders do not Commonly use, it being Uninhabited." He assumed he had run across a pirate, but upon closer observation he found that the sloop "just Careened with her Sails unbent and her Great Gunns on Shore." Merchants usually avoided pirates: just not helpless ones. Moore approached the island cove to challenge the suspicious sloop. *Eagle* hoisted its colors and fired a shot at the sloop "to oblige her to Show her Colours."[16]

The sighting of *Eagle* set off panic aboard *Fortune's Free Gift*: no guns, no sails, and no way to escape. Lowther knew he had to bluff his way out of the emergency. He responded to *Eagle*'s challenge by ordering his men to run up the flag they had recently taken off *Princess*. The nervous buccaneers fired their gun to warn off the menacing merchant sloop as soon as the cross of St. George fluttered from their topmast head. The sea bandits held their breath, waiting for *Eagle*'s reaction. Curses echoed across the deck when they saw the merchant sloop continue to bear down on them. Lowther shouted orders to his crew to cut their anchor cables and use the lines to haul their stern onto the beach. It was a purely defensive move. Lowther wanted *Fortune's Free Gift* in the shallows, where his opponent might either run aground or draw off. He also may have tried to face his bow gun against *Eagle* in a desperate effort to hold off potential boarders.

Moore countered by bringing his sloop "to an Anchor a thwart their harse." With broadside against bow gun, the fight was short lived. *Eagle*'s crew "engaged them [the pirates] untill they call'd for Quarters and Struck."[17]

The pirate crew gave up rather than let *Eagle* blast them to pieces. The forced men stood on deck, hoping for deliverance from their captors, while Lowther and thirteen of his hardened men tried to escape. The buccaneers scurried below deck, then dashed to the stern. One by one, the corsairs jumped out the cabin window into a few feet of water, then splashed their way to the beach. The fleeing pirates, dripping in their wet clothes, collected whatever weapons, powder, bottles, or other necessities they could find on the beach and then retreated into the scrub. Lowther probably halted the moment he felt concealed. He needed to see what *Eagle*'s crew would do before he could decide his next move. Peering through the foliage, Lowther and his fugitive band watched the merchant seamen board *Fortune's Free Gift* and take captive everyone remaining on the sloop. They continued spying as the mariners secured the sloop and worked it free from the shallows. Hearts sank when Lowther and his loyal followers realized that *Fortune's Free Gift* had become a prize.

Captain Moore and his men rejoiced once they anchored the sloop in deeper water. The news only got better when they inspected *Fortune's Free Gift* and discovered its hold full of enslaved Africans removed from *Princess*. The Admiralty would claim the prize and its valuable slave cargo, but *Eagle*'s crew would still be entitled to a handsome payout. Moore's crew took their captives aboard *Eagle* for later disposition. The merchantmen did not have time to sort the sea bandits from the forced men, so all of them got tossed into the hold with the slaves. A few inquiries with some of the cooperative captives confirmed that Moore and his men had taken the vessel commanded by the notorious George Lowther. Every ship's captain on the African coast knew and hated the man who had led a mutiny on a slave ship and terrorized the sea-lanes for over two years. With the pirate sloop floating in deeper water, Moore turned his attention to the escaped buccaneers and their infamous leader. He ordered a skeleton crew to watch the two sloops, then organized a strong shore party to hunt down Lowther and his remaining crew.

The pirates onshore had kept an eye on the two sloops to see what the merchantmen were about. Their curiosity turned to fright when they sighted a boat coming ashore with twenty-five heavily armed men. Lowther and his followers turned from the shoreline and fled deeper into the brush. They had some muskets, some pistols, a powder flask or two, a few canteens, and almost nothing to eat—not nearly enough to make a stand, and precious little to avoid capture.

Some of Moore's armed men stood guard at the beach while the majority pushed into the ramble in pursuit of the corsairs. Roles had reversed. Merchant mariners had turned stalkers and pirates had become prey. The fugitives in their desperation could outpace their pursuers but left tracks in the soft soil. They could pause for just a few minutes before Moore's men caught up with them. Lowther's gang began fracturing. Young and nimble pirates deserted the older and slower ones. Even the swift could run for only a few miles before reaching the far shore. After that, each man had to dodge the armed hunters on his own.

For five days, Captain Moore combed Blanco Island. Time favored the pursuers. The pirates could not stop long enough to eat, and Moore's men guarded the only freshwater spring. Each morning the armed patrols set out to cover a different part of the island and follow the footprints in the sand. The men on the run exhausted themselves trying to stay ahead of the hunters while draining their water, rum, or whatever they carried to drink. Five of Lowther's men collapsed or got cornered by the patrols, then got dragged back to the beach. The fugitives grew weaker each day.

Though the hunters had time on their side, it did not favor Captain Moore, whose asiento sloop had a cargo of slaves to deliver. Moore had to call off the search after five days. On October 10, *Eagle* and *Fortune's Free Gift* weighed anchor.

Lowther and his eight remaining crew stood along the shoreline with mixed emotions, watching the sails slowly dip below the southern horizon. All felt relieved that they had escaped capture and the inevitable hanging that their fellow pirates would suffer. Yet, their relief was offset by the realization that they were now marooned on a deserted island with no way off. They were alive, but for how long?

CHAPTER 15

A PIRATE'S FATE

EAGLE AND FORTUNE'S FREE GIFT, CUMANA, TIERRA FIRME, MID-OCTOBER 1723

Capt. Walter Moore steered his two sloops into the Rio de Manzanares, where the asiento vessel tied up under the watchful guns of Castillo Santa Maria de la Cabeza. The castillo's guns and those of two other fortifications would normally be used to drive off British ships and other *piratas*, but the sloops moored peacefully in the Spanish port. Moore walked to the castillo and got ushered into an audience with Juan de la Tornera Sota, the governor of Cumana and captain general of the province of Nueva Andalucía.

Tornera's duties included rigorous enforcement of the trade embargo against foreign merchants; however, the asiento vessel had been granted access by treaty. As a Spanish officer, he had to permit the foreigner to dock, though he was merely expected to tolerate its slave transactions. Yet, Tornera eagerly greeted the Englishman. He fully expected Moore to arrive with a healthy purse of *pesos de ochoa* and to spread the silver generously among the port's officials. The citizens of Cumana, tired of the overpriced goods coming off the galleons from Spain, welcomed the asiento sloop with equal enthusiasm.

The interview with Captain Moore went better than Tornera had expected. Besides the cargo of slaves to be auctioned and the hold full of illicit goods to be sold, the British captain brought in a second sloop, a pirate vessel that he had captured along with twenty-four suspected buccaneers—one less corsair to trouble the coast! The governor posted a sentry on the captured sloop, then convened a court. Tornera showed his gratitude by officially condemning

Fortune's Free Gift and awarding it as a prize to Captain Moore. The certificate from Tornera allowed Moore to maintain possession of the vessel despite its lack of charter or bills of lading. With the governor's blessing, *Eagle* began turning over its slaves to the auctioneers while local merchants went below deck to barter for its contraband goods.[1]

Captain General Tornera then attended to some unfinished business. The asiento sloop had left nine pirates on Blanco Island, and it was up to Spanish officials to kill or capture the ones who had eluded Captain Moore. He commissioned a local sloop and recruited twenty-five hands to man it. The Spanish sloop left Cumana and set course for the small island 97 miles north of the port.

BLANCO ISLAND, LATE OCTOBER 1723

The fugitive pirates were alive but hardly living. With few firearms and fewer supplies, George Lowther and his men were stuck on Blanco Island with no boat to get off and, without tools, no possibility of clapping one together. Stranded, they had to survive hand to mouth. The band collected near the beach, the scene of their disastrous encounter with *Eagle*, where they drank from the only freshwater spring on the miserable arid island. Captain Moore's crew had hauled off all the victuals, though nature provided a ready source of meat: a large population of green iguanas. The isolated men managed to knock the plentiful creatures out of the trees or spear them on the ground with sharpened limbs. At least Lowther and his followers could feed themselves without wasting their gunpowder and shot. The marooned men sat in the sparse shade and baked in the tropical heat, helpless to improve their lot.

In difficult times, sailors look to their captains for solutions. Lowther had few to offer. They could get by in the short term, but their long-term prospects looked no better than those of a stranded mackerel on a tidal flat. What could be done when a man got injured or sick? How long could they survive before madness set in? With nothing but idle time to occupy their thoughts, the men would soon question their poor choices that had led them to this forlorn condition. Lowther knew enough about leadership and human nature to see their biggest threat: despondency. Hope was the only weapon he had to fight it. He likely used it to encourage his followers to keep their spirits up. They had no means to get off Blanco Island on their own, but fortune could still rescue them. Another pirate ship might stop at the island and take them on. They had used Blanco Island; so might another rover. Even if a merchant ship sailed close by, they might pass themselves off as innocent shipwrecked mariners. Then one day, as if to fulfill his promise, a sloop appeared offshore.

The expectant fugitives stared at the sloop drawing near the beach, then noticed that it flew Spanish colors. The brief hopes of rescue vanished the moment they saw heavily armed men transfer from the sloop to a longboat. For a second time, Lowther and his few remaining men fled into the ramble to save themselves from men coming to hunt them. The pirates had outlasted Captain Moore's pursuit a couple of weeks earlier. They knew survival depended on constant movement through the thickest brush to slow down and discourage their pursuers. Desperation was their only advantage. Panting and sweating, Lowther and his men hustled to the remote ends of the island. The stiff branches ripped their clothes to rags, and the cacti thorns stabbed their feet and arms; yet, they had to keep moving.

The pirates did what they had to do to stay ahead of the hunters, but they were weaker this time. Two weeks on the bleak island with no shelter and a diet of roasted iguana had sapped their energy and their spirits. None of them could carry enough water to last in the heat. They could not stay together. The feeble, the injured, and the disheartened had to be left to their fate. The strong and strong-willed shifted for themselves. Each man was soon on his own, listening for any rustling of the leaves and bolting away whenever he heard voices. The pursuit reduced itself to a battle of wills: the pirates' desire to stay alive versus the Spaniards' determination to finish them off. Four of Lowther's crew were not up to the challenge, either run down by the hunters or unable to evade any longer. The Spaniards bound their captives, then dragged them back to the sloop standing just off the beach. The hunt lasted for days until the Spanish captain gave it up, not seeing enough reward for the hot work on Blanco Island. With four pirates locked in the hold, he raised anchor and sailed back to Cumana. Governor Tornera later condemned one of the pirates to prison and sentenced the other three to spend their few remaining days as slaves aboard a Spanish galley.

By Captain Moore's count, Lowther, a cabin boy, and three men were left unaccounted for on Blanco Island. They had either persevered or perished under some bush unnoticed by the Spanish hunters. The marooned handful of pirates did not seem to merit further attention from him or the Spanish authorities. How long would it take for madness or nature to take their course?

Back on the island, Lowther and the other survivors warily searched for any sign of the Spaniards and their sloop. After a day or so of quiet, they drifted back to the freshwater spring. They may have felt relieved that the hunt was over, but only for a moment, before their dire situation clouded their minds. A few miserable wretches abandoned on a barren shore; what could they look forward to? Their brief hope of rescue had turned to a nightmare. They had exhausted themselves to avoid capture, but to what purpose? Had they traded a quick choke under the gallows for a long, excruciating death on the wretched island?

Depression settled over the marooned pirates like a shroud. Lowther felt it. For over two years his name had spread terror from Barbados to Newfoundland while he lived in ease and plenty aboard his own vessel. Now he had nothing to eat but roasted lizards while his own body baked on a deserted island.

DELIGHT, AT SEA OFF HONDURAS, EARLY APRIL 1724

Capt. Francis Spriggs clapped on a wind and steered for the Leeward Islands on a mission of vengeance. While seizing ships and torturing prisoners in the Bay of Honduras, he learned that Capt. Moore's asiento vessel had captured Lowther's sloop on Blanco Island and taken most of the crew prisoner. Spriggs had reportedly served under Lowther on the *Gambia Castle* and thrown in with him when they had mutinied and turned pirate. The senior pirate captain had shown him how to lead a company of lazy, drunken corsairs and still take what they needed to survive from merchant ships on the open water. Spriggs first learned to navigate, find prey, and chase down fleeing brigantines under Lowther's tutelage. Both had shared the harshness and dangers of the sea as well as the easy joviality of living on the account. Spriggs tended more toward Low's habit of abusing prisoners and forced men, but he still held Lowther in high regard—enough so to sail 1,600 miles to avenge his mentor's demise with Moore's death. It was a rare display of loyalty among a caste of mariners who changed ships and leaders more frequently than bathing.[2]

The *Delight* set course for St. Kitts, making an eastward passage similar to the one that Lowther had charted after natives had burned his galley-frigate in 1722. Spriggs figured that Capt. Moore and *Eagle* would return to the island after selling its slaves and contraband goods in Cumana. He hoped to intercept the asiento sloop on its way back, then make an example of Moore for any other captain who might consider attacking a pirate vessel.

Plans for revenge had to be stowed when Spriggs discovered a French man-of-war in his path. He came about and threw out all his sails to make a quick getaway. His flight did not escape the Frenchman's notice, and the warship put up its topsails and gallants to give chase. *Delight* fled westward, but the ship out of Martinique had greater speed running before the wind and gained on the pirates. For a time, Spriggs and his men faced grim prospects until the Frenchman's main topmast cracked, forcing the navy ship to give up its pursuit. The close call convinced Spriggs to abandon his attempt to wreak vengeance on Captain Moore. He turned *Delight* northward and headed to Bermuda.

He was eight weeks too late, anyway.

EAGLE AND FORTUNE'S FREE GIFT, OLD ROAD, ST. KITTS, FEBRUARY 20, 1724

The two sloops created a stir when they moored off the coast of the small British-held island. Besides bringing in a haul of Spanish goods and silver from the mainland, Captain Moore delivered *Fortune's Free Gift* with a hold full of captured pirates and recaptured African slaves for future disposition by the admiralty court. John Hart, governor of the Leeward Islands and a former governor of Maryland, was away on a tour of his new domain, so everyone had to wait a few days before any proceedings could be undertaken. Hart acted quickly after returning to St. Kitts on March 5. He took a deposition from Moore on March 10, then convened a High Court of the Admiralty the next day.[3]

The governor swore in a panel of judges including the lieutenant governor of Montserrat, the council members of St. Kitts, and Capt. Humphrey Orme, commander of HMS *Hector*. The king's solicitor, Thomas Butler, then presented the first indictment against Robert Corp and Henry Wynn, two men who had come off *Princess* in September. The young lads had helped man the longboat when it first ferried over to Lowther's sloop from the slave galley, then remained with the pirate company. Three other men— William Churchill, Abraham Crane, and Richard Hardwell—had jumped from *Princess* to Lowther's crew too, but they were not among the pirates brought back in *Eagle*. Though Corp and Wynn had not committed any piracies since coming aboard *Fortune's Free Gift*, they were charged with deserting *Princess*, joining the pirates, and resisting Captain Moore's *Eagle* when it attacked Lowther's sloop. Corp had no reply other than acknowledging his guilt, but Wynn pleaded not guilty. Solicitor Butler, who had to present his case against Wynn, called William Gibbons, surgeon's mate, and James Sedgwick, carpenter, who testified that Wynn "acted in concert with the said Pirates and was always deemed and esteemed by them as a Volunteer." Moreover, Sedgwick recalled that he had witnessed Wynn sign the pirates' "Articles of Regulation" just three days after being taken aboard their sloop. The court met in private and a short time later returned a unanimous guilty verdict.[4]

The solicitor ordered the remaining prisoners up to the bar: John Churchill, Edward McDonald, Nicholas Lewis, Richard West, Samuel Levercot, Robert White, John Shaw, Andrew Hunter, Jonathan Deloe, Matthew Freebarne, Henry Watson, Roger Grange, Ralph Cander, and Robert Willis. The indictments charged them with "Feloniously and Piratically" taking the ship *Princess*, plundering its goods, taking out of it "Eleven Negro Slaves," and terrorizing Captain Wickstead and his loyal crew members. Nicholas Lewis, Lowther's quartermaster and previously Low's, knew he had numerous witnesses against him and no defense to offer. Richard West had been one of Captain Massey's mutineers in the Gambia. He had over two years of piracy to answer for. Both experienced buccaneers decided to avoid having their long list of crimes aired before the court, and pleaded guilty. The other twelve tried their luck with a not-guilty plea. Gibbons and Sedgwick again pointed their fingers at the men before the bar and declared "all of them of the Number of the pirates who took the said Shipp *Princess*."

Not all the evidence favored the prosecution. A deposition from New York, probably written by John Hood, master of the *Swift*, claimed that Jonathan Deloe and Andrew Hunter had been forced off his schooner in June. When Lowther had taken *Swift*, he had also forced a third man, Henry Hunter, possibly Andrew's brother. No record mentions whether Henry died, was lost, killed, or taken by the Spaniards. The court may have been skeptical of the deposition in Deloe's and

Hunter's defense; after all, most pirates went on the account after being forced aboard a pirate vessel, but Capt. Moore also put in a word on their behalf. When he and his men had boarded *Fortune's Free Gift* at Blanco Island, Deloe and Hunter "did not resist or fly from him but on the Contrary thanked him for their Deliverance." Robert Willis had a witness come forward in his defense. Capt. John Smith, the former mate on the brigantine *Rebecca*, happened to be in St. Kitts and testified that Lowther had forced Willis onto *Ranger* in May 1722. Willis, who had a broken arm at the time, had protested vigorously against staying aboard Lowther's sloop. Smith asked the court to excuse any of Willis's later transgressions, because he was "but a very foolish youth."[5]

Having heard all the evidence, the judges had the court cleared and deliberated among themselves. They acquitted Deloe, Hunter, and Willis but convicted the other nine. The three spared men staggered out of the court into the streets of Old Road, undoubtedly relieved to walk away as free men but traumatized by how close they had come to hanging. The solicitor then called Corp, Wynn, Lewis, West, and the other nine men found guilty up to the bar and presented them to Governor Hart for sentencing. The governor asked each man if he had anything further to say in his defense. All of them hung their heads and declined. Hart proceeded with sentencing. "What now remains for me to do is to pronounce the Judgment the Law has appointed for such Offenders and that Judgment is: that you . . . be carried from hence . . . to the place of Execution where you and each of you are to be hanged by the Neck till you be Dead, Dead, Dead."[6]

After the constable took the condemned back to the gaol, the judges asked for a further audience with Governor Hart to make a request. The members of the court singled out Robert Corp and Henry Wynn as "Objects of His Majesty's Mercy." They reasoned that Corp and Wynn had only consented to join Lowther's crew and not committed any acts of piracy. "And as they are very young. It's uncertain how far the Apprehension of ill-usage might prevail over their Fears to gain their Consent." The governor heard them out but made no decision to pardon either of the two.

The admiralty court also officially condemned *Fortune's Free Gift* and its cargo, including 54 ounces of gold dust and the slaves stolen from *Princess* by Lowther and later retaken by Moore. The salvage laws of the time turned Lowther's sloop over to the island's "receiver of the casual revenue," not the original owner, Capt. Jeremiah Clark, who had to live with his loss. Once the receiver auctioned the sloop and cargo, the proceeds went straight into the Crown's coffers. The enslaved Africans had endured a dizzying and melancholy journey. They had passed through the hands of the South Sea Company, Lowther's pirate crew, the South Sea Company again, the customs officers at St. Kitts, and finally to a West Indies buyer, all without enjoying a moment of freedom. Interestingly, the number of slaves had dwindled over time. Captain Wickstead claimed a loss of fourteen enslaved Africans from *Princess*. Only eleven made it to St. Kitts and just nine to the Crown's receiver.

What happened to the missing five? Did Wickstead overstate his loss? Did some die in the meantime? Did Moore drop three off in Cumana to bribe Governor Tornera or sell them himself? Did a couple of them slip into Governor Hart's possession before the trial? The answer remains hidden within the murky history of colonial-era trade practices.[7]

Seashore at Old Road, St. Kitts, March 20, 1724

The day of execution had arrived. Governor Hart ordered gallows erected against the sparkling backdrop of the Caribbean Sea between the ebb and flow tides. An air of somber dread hung over the gaol where thirteen men waited to have their sentences carried out. The days of profane oaths and disdainful boasts were gone, replaced with feelings of remorse and regret. Even the governor noticed the attitude of the condemned, who "behaved themselves with greater Marks of Sorrow and Contrition than is usually found amongst those wretched sett of People." Nicholas Lewis, a hardened pirate who had spent months witnessing and participating in Ned Low's atrocities, came clean about Low's marauding. He gave lurid accounts of the slaughter of the guardacosta crew in the Bay of Honduras, and an earlier incident in which Low murdered the entire crew of a Portuguese vessel. Finally, on his way to the gallows, Lewis rediscovered his humanity. He declared that Henry Wynn and Henry Watson were no more than forced men and "never Acted in Concert with the Pirates." To reinforce his claim, Lewis revealed that "he had whipt Watson Twenty-Six times but could not prevail with him to Sign their Articles." Standing in the shadow of the noose, Wynn and Watson heard the judges pronounce their pardons. They owed their lives to the seemingly heartless quartermaster who had thrashed them repeatedly aboard *Fortune's Free Gift*.[8]

The remaining eleven men, including Wynn's partner Robert Corp, climbed the short ladders and then swung off when the executioner kicked them off the steps. The knotted ropes around their necks squeezed on their flow of blood and air while their bodies twitched partly submerged in the surf. Death did not come quickly. Relatives or sympathetic observers at these executions were sometimes known to wade out to the dangling men to grasp their legs and tug them down to shorten the ordeal. Less sympathetic witnesses usually hissed or gave a sour look as the condemned men choked.[9]

Governor Hart reported the executions to the Board of Trade and Plantations five days later. Nicholas Lewis's testimony about the wholesale murders of Spanish and Portuguese crews by Edward Low still weighed on his mind. As he noted the successful elimination of George Lowther's company, he lamented Low's continuing freedom, the lone remaining buccaneer he knew of. "A Greater Monster never Infested the Seas," he asserted. Hart suggested offering a pardon and reward to any of Low's associates "who should bring him in alive or Dead." He need not have bothered. Ned Low had already disappeared.[10]

Low left the African coast shortly after Spriggs and the crew of *Delight* had deserted him. Sometime in late 1723 or early 1724, his ship, the *Merry Christmas*, captured a ship out of Martinique. An ensuing argument between Low and his quartermaster precipitated a falling out. Later that night, Low, still fuming over the disagreement, crept up to the quartermaster while he slept and murdered him. For the pirate company, that was enough. The men, who had grown tired of his endless cruelties, removed him from the ship and designated Richard Shipton their new captain. Low and two companions were either marooned or set loose in a small boat. Some accounts suggest he was caught by a French man-of-war and hanged. Other reports claim he went into hiding among the Mosquito Indians. Aside from one or two random and, likely, apocryphal reports, nothing else was heard from Low, a strong indication that he either died or was killed. Considering his murderous and reckless nature, it seems inconceivable that Low could have settled in some out-of-the-way place, idle and quiet.[11]

Edward Low was not the only buccaneer to disappear—it was a fate many shared. The Royal African Company listed the names of forty-nine mutineers from the soldiers and artificers in the Gambia who formed Lowther's pirate company, men such as Robert Pattison, who abandoned his wife; Thomas Tucker, who fled the Gambia with his wife and son; James Sympson, a sergeant; Thomas Bobons, a soldier; and Jeremiah Mersow, a cooper. To this list can be added Lowther, Alexander Thompson, and Francis Spriggs (perhaps), the only identified mutineers from *Gambia Castle*'s crew. Of these fifty-two names, five were known to have been hanged, and Alexander Thompson was pardoned. The rest vanished within the obscure pirate universe.[12]

Without question, most of the unaccounted perished over the course of their pirating careers. Yellow jack, intermittent fevers (malaria), bloody flux (dysentery), and syphilis probably carried off most. The poor understanding of tropical diseases and the dearth of medicines available to sea rovers ensured that corsairs laid low by illness seldom recovered. Several had been killed at Port Maho and Charlestown. Others likely drowned or suffered injuries that proved fatal.

Twelve men who left *Delivery* with John Massey may have lived out their days in Jamaica. Others may have jumped ship and blended into local populations, though no desertions were recorded after Massey's.

Besides the original mutineers, untold numbers of innocent mariners got swept into the buccaneer life as forced or willing men. Some stood by their morals and endured the torment, while many succumbed to the pirates' enticements, leading to a variety of outcomes. The names of thirty-two men brought into Lowther's company, voluntarily or not, have been recorded through depositions at the time of their abduction or their testimony in an admiralty court. Nine were set free or acquitted, twelve died on the gallows, and eleven disappeared, along with the many others whose names were never jotted down.

The numbers tell the terrible story of men caught in the piracy meat grinder. Only a small minority lived to tell of their time on a sea bandit's vessel.

Spriggs and Shipton continued roving for another year before reports of their depredations stopped. Philip Lyne, who had been Spriggs's quartermaster, marauded in his own sloop until October 1725, when he was captured and later hanged. He was among the last pirate captains to scavenge the seas during the prime era of Atlantic piracy. Thomas Anstis had been murdered by his crew in 1723. A mutiny led by forced men killed John Phillips the next year. John Fenn, who had been captured by Captain Orme and HMS *Winchilsea*, was hanged in Antigua and then gibbeted, a procedure where the dead man's corpse is doused in tar and then hung by chains in a prominent spot to serve as a warning to anyone else thinking of robbing at sea.[13]

From 1723 to 1726 the numbers of active pirates fell off dramatically; by some estimates, only two hundred men remained on the account from the 1,500–2,000 who had been active in piracy's heyday. They had made themselves too much of a nuisance, as noted by the commissioner of Trade & Plantations. "The great Depredations made by Pirates . . . has occasioned an excessive Rise in the Rates of Insurance." Britain's merchant class protested the extra expenses they had to bear in arming their ships to protect themselves from the rovers. After King George I's blanket pardon of 1718 failed to bring the pirates to heel, the authorities took more-active measures to combat the villains. The act prohibiting trade with pirates cut into the sea robbers' easy access to supplies and stores from merchants who once transacted with them. The chests of pirate captains could swell with pesos and pounds, but where to spend the coins? The Admiralty had been embarrassed by the near loss of HMS *Greyhound* in Cuba and the charges of private trading from governors such as Nicholas Lawes. The admirals started pressuring naval captains to patrol more actively against the buccaneers, leading to notable successes by Chaloner Ogle, Peter Solgard, and Humphrey Orme. Mariners who once might have been predisposed to go on the account could see that supporting themselves by robbing at sea had become more difficult and dangerous. The visibility of official retribution against captured pirates became discouraging. Mass hangings at Cape Coast Castle, Wapping, Newport, Jamaica, and St. Kitts sucked the wind out of the corsairs' once-bold defiance of the authorities. In the ten-year span from 1716 to 1726, admiralty courts strung up between four hundred and six hundred pirates, something bound to make an impression on anyone sailing the seas.[14]

The famed buccaneers who once terrorized the Atlantic, Benjamin Hornigold, Blackbeard, Howell Davis, Bartholomew Roberts, Calico Jack Rackham, and Ned Low, had met their demise. But what of George Lowther?

When Captain Moore and *Eagle* returned to St. Kitts in February 1724, local authorities learned that the Spanish crew sent by Governor Tornera had left Lowther marooned but still alive on Blanco Island. They dispatched a ship to the island to kill him, find his body, or, if alive, bring him to St. Kitts for trial along with his crew. At first the British hunters could find no evidence of anyone living on the bleak island, then upon further search the pirate "was found dead with his Pistol busted at his Side." The marooned buccaneer had given up hope and blown out his own brains. With the grim discovery, the pirate rampage of the notorious George Lowther had come to its dismal and ignominious end.[15]

CHAPTER 16

PORTO BELLO

PORTO BELLO, PANAMA, NOVEMBER 21, 1739

The news roared through the town like a blast wave. Wealthy families tossed their children and valuables into carriages and wagons. Panicked gentlemen of means jumped on their horses or mules carrying sacks of silver. Anyone with transportation bolted for the roads to Nombre de Dios or the interior. The ordinary citizens resorted to burying their prized possessions and silver in obscure spots in their gardens or nearby woods.

The previous evening, four guardacosta ships had entered Porto Bello with terrifying intelligence—a British fleet was coming. The guardacosta commander, Francisco Abaroa, reported that they had been chased by six British warships coming out of Jamaica. Abaroa told Gov. Francisco Martínez de la Vega Retes that he thought the British were coming to attack Porto Bello. Martínez attempted to organize a defense of the town, though he had few resources at his disposal. A hodgepodge force of garrison soldiers, guardacosta sailors, and militiamen scurried in the dark to reinforce Castillo de Todo Hierro, what the British called the "Iron Fort," guarding the harbor entrance. One of the guardacosta officers, Lt. Juan Francisco Garganta, took command of the Iron Fort from the constable and began preparations to defend Porto Bello. Garganta was not pleased with what he had to hold off a powerful British fleet. Only a handful of the castillo's guns had carriage mounts, and he had enough powder and shot for only sixteen rounds per gun.[1]

Meanwhile, fear gripped the town. Elderly citizens could recall the terror that people felt seventy-one years earlier, when Sir Henry Morgan had sacked Porto Bello and stripped it of all its wealth. When daylight came, nervous residents and officials could see the six British ships of the line standing to the west outside the harbor, held up by a contrary wind. They still had hope. In 1726 an even-larger British fleet had blockaded the port for months before a providential pestilence forced them away. Would this fleet remain outside the harbor too? Their hopes disappeared once the wind changed, and the enemy line of battle steered for the entrance channel.

The lead ship, a huge vessel with three decks lined by guns, maneuvered close to the Iron Fort. The townsfolk standing on rooftops or lining the walls of Porto Bello's fortifications cheered when they saw smoke and shot spew from the Iron Fort's ramparts. They fell silent when the British ship replied with a massive broadside four to five times the size of the castillo's salvo. Even worse, the British guns fired again before the fort could fire its next volley. As smoke clogged the harbor entrance, the Spanish citizens had to rely on the guns' reports to follow the course of the battle. It became apparent that blasts from the British guns overwhelmed the defenders' fire. After thirty minutes the lead British ship drifted away from the Iron Fort but was replaced by a second, then a third. The steady pounding of the British guns continued unabated, while the occasional reports from the castillo became less and less frequent. The battle entered its decisive stage when another triple-decked British ship slid into position close to the Iron Fort. This ship looked more distinctive. A large blue flag fluttered from the foretop masthead, while a more ominous red flag on the maintop masthead seemed to portend death and destruction. The castillo fired a small salvo at the big ship, but the townspeople could sense that it was more like a death rattle than a heavy blow. A moment later, a huge thirty-five-gun broadside shook the harbor and seemed to smother the brave Spanish defenders. The British ships pounded the forlorn castillo with heavy guns for a few more minutes, then went quiet. Through the billowing smoke, a few longboats could be seen rowing toward the Iron Fort, followed by a smattering of small-arms fire. The harbor turned quiet. The light easterly breezes eventually cleared the smoke enough to let the citizens get a good look at the castillo. A collective groan echoed throughout the town. A British union jack waved above Castillo de Todo Hierro, signaling the enemy's triumph.[2]

Porto Bello enjoyed a brief respite. The easterlies kept the British ships clustered near the harbor entrance. Overnight, Spanish officials and the small garrison tried to prepare for the expected onslaught against the town's protective fortifications, Castillos Santiago de la Gloria and San Jerónimo. Everyone who remained in Porto Bello spent an anxious night. As daylight rose, the six British warships became visible standing near the vanquished fort. Citizens jittered from tension as they waited for the climactic battle to begin. Hearts fell when a boat with a white flag affixed to a staff left Castillo Gloria and rowed out to the British squadron. It could only mean surrender.

A few hours went by before the boat returned to shore. Soldiers, townspeople, and Governor Martínez crowded around Ensign Francisco de Medina and one of the governor's representatives who had met with the British admiral. All wanted to learn their fate. Are we surrendered? Are they going to destroy the town? Why did they come here? The two men reassured the frightened populace. The admiral accepted their surrender and promised not to molest the town, its residents, or its Catholic churches. A huge sigh of relief escaped everyone's lips, as if an executioner had lowered his ax. The men explained that the British king had recently declared war against their master King Felipe V. The attack on Porto Bello was the opening blow in the new conflict. It was not unexpected. The two kingdoms had escalated tensions for the past couple of years, and the Royal Navy had been blockading Spain for months. When asked what the British admiral wanted, they replied that he intended to open commerce between Porto Bello and British possessions. His only demands were the removal of the Spanish garrison and the surrender of three guardacosta ships. The British did not intend to occupy the town but would tear down its defenses. Porto Bello would be left defenseless, all the easier for the British to reenter the port whenever they pleased. The governor, the guardacosta officers, and the citizens could live with those terms, a far better result than what they had feared. Someone asked the name of the British admiral, the new master of their town. Medina and the representative answered that he was a British vice admiral named Edward Vernon.[3]

HMS *BURFORD*, PORTO BELLO HARBOR, EARLY DECEMBER 1739

The tedium of diplomatic negotiations, occupation duty, and their concomitant correspondence weighted down Admiral Vernon like mud clumped to his shoes, but he plowed through the minutiae with his customary attention to detail. Sitting in the cabin of his flagship, the seventy-gun *Burford*, Vernon dispatched instructions and directives to his captains and Spanish officials to ensure an orderly administration of his temporary rule over Porto Bello. He had to arrange the release of prisoners taken at the Iron Fort, dispatch a force into the town to halt a riot by the Spanish garrison who were abusing their own countrymen, issue passes for one Spanish sloop and the guardacosta crews to return to Cartagena, demand the release of South Sea Company factors held in Panama City—the list went on and on. The work may have been onerous, but Vernon far preferred his latest command of Britain's Jamaica Station fleet to where he had been six months before.

Since his departure from Jamaica in 1721, Vernon had struggled through a very up-and-down career. When Britain was at war, he had command of a ship. As soon as the conflicts cooled, he went on half pay. He won election to Parliament but sat with the Tories on the wrong side of the house. Known for his irascible temperament, hardened opinions, and caustic speech, Vernon used his seat to castigate the policies of Sir Robert Walpole and the Whig government. He especially railed against Walpole's timid handling of Spanish guardacosta depredations in the West Indies. Needless to say, the Admiralty had denied him a flag command, given his vociferous opposition to the ruling party.

In the run-up to the Anglo-Spanish War of 1739–44, otherwise known as the War of Jenkins' Ear, the merchant class, the Tory Party, and a wing of the Whig Party known as the Patriot Whigs had stoked the flames for military action against Spain, a kingdom they perceived as weak. The prospect of bullying Spain into major trade concessions motivated the bellicose rhetoric of the opposition, Vernon's voice one of the loudest. When the Walpole government's negotiations with Spain failed to reconcile the trade disputes, the government relented and authorized hostilities against Spain. One of the Admiralty's first initiatives was taking offensive action in the West Indies. Overlooking Vernon's political views, the First Lord of the Admiralty, Sir Charles Wager, and the Admiral of the Fleet, Sir John Norris, promoted Captain Vernon all the way to the rank of vice admiral of the blue and gave him the vital command of the Jamaica Station squadron. The elevation of a political opponent surprised most observers, but they had overlooked Vernon's past associations with the senior admirals. Vernon had often served with Wager and Norris, including Wager's Caribbean operation in 1708 and Norris's 1715 mission to the Baltic. Both admirals thought highly of Vernon's seafaring and leadership skills. His frequent speeches scolding the Walpole government to take vigorous action against Spain merely convinced the admirals that Vernon would boldly execute his mission.

In July 1739, Vernon took command of several ships at Portsmouth and sailed to the Caribbean. Upon arriving in Jamaica, he organized a quick strike at Porto Bello, one of the key ports used by the Spanish treasure galleons. Its capture was a British triumph and vaulted Vernon to the status of national hero.

With Porto Bello in his hands, the admiral took steps to maintain cordial relations with its officials while disrupting its usefulness for the Spanish treasure fleet. Vernon had no desire to hold on to Porto Bello—he just wanted it left so he had freedom to bring his ships into the port at his leisure. Vernon had put two of his naval engineers, Capt. Charles Knowles and Capt. Edward Boscawen, to work dismantling the port's defenses. At times the harbor was rocked by huge explosions as another part of Porto Bello's fortifications got blown to pieces. Knowles and Boscawen used 122 barrels of powder out of the Spaniards' stock to mine the ramparts. While the engineers demolished the castillos, shore parties confiscated all the Spanish brass cannons and knocked the trunnions off all the iron ones.

The admiral had other plans in mind "to distress the enemy in their very vitals, to destroy their mines, to seize upon their treasures, to take their ships, to ruin their settlements." However, Vernon needed intelligence on Spanish ports, shipping, fortifications, and guardacostas to carry out his ambitions. Poor knowledge of Spanish shipping practices had already frustrated him. When he first arrived in the Caribbean, he dispatched two ships to La Guaira to locate Spanish galleons, only to have them repulsed by a strong garrison. He knew that the Spaniards conducted a huge fair at Porto Bello when the treasure fleet arrived to pick up Peruvian silver, but he did not know how the Spaniards coordinated the movements of the bullion and the galleons. To get a better picture of his opposition, he turned to the South

Sea Company factors, merchants who had spent years living in Spanish ports across the Caribbean. Once Vernon secured their release from the president of Panama, he interviewed them to learn what they knew about Spain's West Indies possessions. The factors helped him understand more about the fair and the galleons, but he needed more-precise information on Spanish ports, fortifications, shipping channels, and sea hazards to plan a military operation. He would get more-detailed information, but from a totally unexpected source.[4]

During the interviews with the factors, the admiral received a private communication from someone residing in Panama. The precise method of this communication can only be guessed, but Vernon had been approached, and by subtle means. Under the circumstances, it would have most likely arrived as a private letter, delivered in person to Vernon. Any other form or method of conveyance would have been too dangerous. One of the South Sea Company factors, who knew the originator and had an opportunity to meet with the admiral, would have been the natural choice to pass the letter to Vernon. After Vernon dismissed the factors, he sat at his desk and opened the letter. He soon knit his brow. The letter turned out to be a strange proposal, an offer to share intelligence. Intrigued, Vernon read on. His eyes flew open when he read the signature at the bottom of the page: George Lowther.[5]

Vernon certainly knew about Lowther's pirate career, especially given his personal connection with the infamous buccaneer. Lowther's name had been smeared across numerous newspapers and bandied about in countless pubs throughout the Atlantic basin. The admiral would also have heard of Lowther's supposed demise after it had been broadcast in many papers and publicized in Charles Johnson's celebrated *A General History of the Pyrates*. It seemed hard to believe that Lowther could have fooled everybody and lived quietly out of sight for sixteen years. How did he get off Blanco Island, and whose body did the search party discover? Did he murder one of his crew to stage his fake suicide? Did he somehow get off the island while leaving someone behind who shot himself? Lowther never explained. Regardless of how he escaped, Lowther had seized the opportunity that heaven or fortune had presented him when it placed an old acquaintance at the head of a British force who needed his services.

Reading the letter more intently, Vernon saw that Lowther was offering his knowledge and counsel to the Crown in exchange for a favor—a pardon for his past sins. There was a lot to forgive. The admiral resented Lowther's betrayal of his oath as a Royal Navy seaman and despised his acts of mutiny and piracy, which ran counter to his instincts as a sailor, yet the offer enticed him. He knew Lowther and had confidence in his seafaring skills. The old pirate had spent years cruising and living in the Caribbean. Vernon itched to get the type of intelligence that Lowther might be able to provide: sketches of Spanish coastlines, comings and goings of the galleons, details of Spanish fortifications, etc. He decided to pursue Lowther's suggestion.

Before he colluded with an infamous buccaneer, Vernon recalled the factors and inquired about their knowledge of Lowther, or the man whose identity he was known by. The name of George Lowther would not have been safe to use, even in a Spanish port. The factors vouched for the mariner. He had always cooperated with them and acted to advance Britain's welfare. As far as they knew, he was a proper British gentleman who owned property. He was known to have slaves and often used them to cut roads through the woods. Somehow, Lowther had turned his life around and forsaken the pirating lifestyle. More than that, he was living a remarkably domestic life—married with two young daughters. Such a return to a normal existence was nothing short of miraculous. Vernon took the next step.[6]

The admiral continued the secret correspondence. By letter or private messenger, he told Lowther that he would entertain his proposal, though he withheld a final decision. Vernon may have had misgivings. Lowther had cruised the West Indies in his pirating days, but sixteen years had gone by since he had been marooned on Blanco Island. Vernon needed more evidence that he had recent experience journeying through Spanish possessions. The admiral made it clear to the ex-pirate that a pardon would be forthcoming only if he could demonstrate his sincere reformation and prove his worth in service to the king. In the meantime, Vernon promised Lowther safe harbor so long as he cooperated with British interests. He did, however, put Lowther's potential value to a test.

The admiral had designs on the port of Chagres, at the mouth of the river of the same name. The British knew that the guardacostas staged out of Chagres and that the river provided access to Panama's interior. Unfortunately, they had no accurate maps of the coastline between Porto Bello and Chagres, nor did they know how to negotiate the many shoals to enter the harbor safely. Vernon challenged his former shipmate to provide the details they needed to force the harbor entrance and subdue the Spanish defenses. Vernon advised his petitioner that his squadron would soon depart Porto Bello, but he would meet with him personally upon his return to the port. On December 11, 1739, the British Jamaica Station fleet raised anchor and sailed back to Port Royal, Jamaica.

PORTO BELLO HARBOR, MARCH 15, 1740

Sniffing the saltwater air on a moderate and cloudy morning, George Lowther stepped off the dock and into a launch that rowed him out to the sixty-gun HMS *Strafford*, moored in the harbor. As he had done a quarter century earlier, Lowther climbed the ladder onto a British ship of the line, where he would come face to face with Edward Vernon, who had switched his flag from *Burford* while it underwent repairs. This time he came aboard as a fugitive to have an audience with a vice admiral.[7]

Vernon's fleet had slipped back into Porto Bello's harbor to refresh itself after its most recent action. At the beginning of March, the British ships had conducted a reconnaissance of Cartagena de Indias in Vernon's campaign to distress the enemy. For several days, the British had sounded the depths of Cartagena's coast while two bomb ketches pummeled the city with 350 mortar shells, each weighing over 300 pounds. The Spaniards fired back with long-range cannon fire, which merely helped the British pinpoint the number and locations of the city's guns. Vernon, having studied Cartagena's defenses, brought off his fleet and steered for Porto Bello. He would use his time in port to repair his ships and prepare for his next operation, the capture of Chagres. As soon as HMS *Strafford* had dropped anchor, Vernon sent a summons to Lowther.[8]

The reformed buccaneer had eagerly accepted the conditions that Vernon had dictated, delighted that he had a chance to put his past crimes behind him. His eagerness speaks to his motivation. Lowther had achieved something exceedingly rare among pirates: a comfortable living. He had a family, property, and obscurity. His desire to get out from under the cloud of a capital crime is understandable, but why risk the contented life he enjoyed in Panama to come forward? He could have easily stayed incognito and prospered. The world thought he was dead, and no one was looking for him. Why sacrifice anonymity for a pardon? The answer suggests that he had a goal beyond mere survival—redemption.

Escorted into the admiral's cabin, Lowther greeted his former captain. Twenty-two years had passed since the two had seen each other, but Vernon could tell that the man standing before him was the navy seaman he had served with. The exchange was tense. Vernon called the meeting to size up his old shipmate, not to share pleasantries or recall their times aboard HMS *Assistance*. Vernon disapproved Lowther's conduct following his time in the navy and may have communicated his distaste through word and manner. Still, he wanted to learn what Lowther could offer in the way of intelligence and, most importantly, whether he could be depended upon. The admiral demanded to see how well the former pirate had heeded his advice to make himself useful to Britain's war efforts. Lowther rolled out a meticulous chart of the coastline between Porto Bello and Chagres that he had prepared since their correspondence in December. The chart pinpointed landmarks such as Islas Naranjos, Punta Longa Remos, and Punta Brujas that could help ships navigate to the objective. Lowther provided crucial details about the layout of the port, the river's mouth, the position of Castillo San Lorenzo, and the dangerous shoals in the middle of the harbor entrance. Vernon was impressed—his old shipmate had outdone himself. This was the precise intelligence that Vernon needed to plan his attack on the Spanish port. Vernon sensed that Lowther was "a sincere penitent" and that his pledge to serve the king was genuine. No question, Lowther yearned to make amends. Before excusing Lowther, the admiral "promised him to be his intercessor for a pardon." Once the former pirate left *Strafford*, Vernon signaled his captains to attend a meeting to begin planning the attack. Three days later he dispatched Capt. Charles Knowles to take command of the fireship HMS *Success* and lead the fleet into Chagres, using Lowther's chart as a guide. He instructed Knowles, his principal engineer, to assess "how the fort at the mouth of the Chagres can be attack'd." Knowles later confirmed that Lowther's chart and intelligence about Chagres proved "to be very exact."[9]

The British fleet descended on the Spanish port on the afternoon of March 22. Knowles maneuvered HMS *Success*, HMS *Norwich*, another fireship, and three bomb ketches past the Alaja Rocks, which obstructed the mouth of the Chagres River. Henry Morgan had lost five ships on these shoals in 1670. The naval engineer found a suitable location in the road within range of Castillo San Lorenzo, and that evening the bomb ketches began lobbing their massive mortar shells at the Spanish fortification. Vernon warped into the harbor later that night with HMS *Strafford*, *Princess Louisa*, and *Falmouth*. The bomb ketches and the four ships of the line bombarded San Lorenzo in earnest the next morning. By midday on March 24, the Spanish commander, Capt. Juan Carlos Gutiérrez Cevallos, figured his heavily outmatched garrison had taken enough punishment, and he surrendered. The British followed this success by sinking two guardacosta vessels in the river, demolishing the castillo, and emptying the customhouse of its goods, amounting to 4,300 bales of cocoa, Jesuit bark, and Spanish wool.[10]

A beaming Admiral Vernon returned to Porto Bello on April 1, the lucrative haul of Spanish loot having further sweetened his second demolition of an enemy port. While his ships collected in the harbor and refitted, Vernon penned a lengthy report of his activities to Admiral Wager, the First Lord of the Admiralty. The letter gave him an opportunity to boast about the successful reconnaissance of Cartagena, the reduction of Castillo San Lorenzo, and the plundering of Chagres. He discussed routine maintenance issues about his ships and some of his diplomatic gyrations with local Spanish authorities. He also spoke about his personal negotiations with George Lowther. Vernon gave a generous description of Lowther's enthusiasm for serving the king and the value of his potential contribution to the fleet's campaign in the West Indies. The admiral vouched for Lowther on the basis of his experiences while serving with him in the Royal Navy. "I find him capable of doing greater services to his Majesty and know him to be a good seaman and gallant man." He then asked Wager to intervene on Lowther's behalf with the king. "[I] must beg your favour to procure his pardon from our royal master." Vernon handed his correspondence to the captain of a packet boat for rapid transmittal to London, then prepared his squadron for movement back to Jamaica.[11]

NUMBER 10 DOWNING STREET, LONDON, JULY 1, 1740

One by one, ornate carriages pulled up to the official residence of the first lord of the treasury, where the illuminati of British nobility alighted their coaches and entered: the archbishop of Canterbury; the secretary of state, the Duke of Newcastle, the man chiefly responsible for the execution of the war; the Duke of Montagu, who served as the army's master-general of ordnance; Admiral Sir Charles Wager; the Duke of Wilmington, who doubled as the lord president of the council; the lord steward, the Duke of Dorset; the lord chamberlain, the Duke of Grafton; the Duke of Bolton; the Duke of Devonshire; the Earl of Pembroke; and the Earl of Ilay. All were greeted by their host, Sir Robert Walpole, the head of the ruling Whig

Party. Not in attendance was the lord privy seal, John Hervey, who may have been preoccupied by one of his frequent visits to Lady Mary Wortley Montagu's bedchamber. The assembled excellencies, known collectively as the lords justices, had been called together to decide urgent matters in the absence of King George II, who was spending the summer in Hanover. With a war being prosecuted against Spain, the lords justices were empowered to act on issues that otherwise would have been presented to the monarch. Walpole had several matters to debate that required immediate resolution. The kingdom was staging two military expeditions: a naval strike under Admiral Norris against the Spanish fleet sheltering in Ferrol, Spain, and a massive land-sea enterprise under Maj. Gen. Lord Cathcart to seize a crucial Spanish port in the West Indies. Both Norris and Cathcart had made requests for more resources to prepare their expeditions. Also, the king's nineteen-year-old son, the Duke of Cumberland, had volunteered to accompany Admiral Norris. Their excellencies had to make special arrangements to accommodate his royal highness.

Walpole began the meeting by having the minutes of the previous session read and approved. The lords then turned to new business. Before proceeding to Norris's, Cathcart's, and Cumberland's applications, Admiral Wager took the floor to read the latest missives from Edward Vernon, the nation's hero admiral. The news of Chagres's capture put the lords in good humor. They voted to acquaint the admiral "with their Ex.^cies approbation of his Conduct, and to congratulate him upon his Success." Discussion progressed to Vernon's appeal to obtain a royal pardon for George Lowther. For a few moments the most-illustrious and most-powerful politicians in Britain devoted their attention to the case of the former mutineer and buccaneer. If any of the lords objected to his pardon, none made note of it. "The L^rds Justices will recommend to His Majesty His Request of a Pardon for Lowther the Pirate, for the reasons mentioned in his Letter, which their Ex.^cies are persuaded His Majesty will be graciously pleased to grant."[12]

In the name of wartime expediency, the chief nobles in the kingdom had wiped away Lowther's past crimes. The mutiny aboard the *Gambia Castle*, the plundering and firing upon British ships, the torture of prisoners and forced men, and the murder of Spanish guardacostas—all of it was remitted. George Lowther, now a free man, had escaped a likely death sentence. His past crimes had been forgiven. One question remained. Could they also be forgotten?

· CHAPTER 17 ·

CUBA

Capt. Robert Maynard, commander of the twenty-gun HMS *Sheerness*, opened the dispatch from Vice Adm. Edward Vernon only to have his heart sink. Vernon, the Jamaica Station chief and naval forces commander for the largest overseas expedition Great Britain had ever launched, was sending him on an errand.

Two weeks earlier, Rear Adm. Sir Chaloner Ogle had arrived in Jamaica with his reinforcing fleet of twenty-one ships of the line, which bulked up Vernon's armada to fifty warships. Ogle's ships escorted a massive flotilla of transport ships carrying 6,200 British soldiers, the land forces for the expedition. The British regiments linked up with another 3,500 recruits from the North American colonies, who had arrived in Jamaica separately. The expeditionary army had been organized by Maj. Gen. Lord Cathcart but was now under the command of Brig. Gen. Thomas Wentworth after Cathcart, eight other officers, and 484 enlisted men had perished on the long-delayed convoy. The huge West Indies enterprise had been planned by the government of Sir Robert Walpole under the direction of the Duke of Newcastle and Admirals Sir Charles Wager and Sir John Norris. Newcastle targeted at least one of three crucial Spanish ports used by the treasure fleets to haul New World silver back to King Felipe V's treasury: Havana, Vera Cruz, or Cartagena de Indias. The capture of any of them would produce a strategic victory for the nation and abundant spoils. As a naval captain, Maynard would be entitled to a hefty slice of the booty—except he would not be there. He was bound for Porto Bello to nursemaid a trade convoy.[1]

Admiral Vernon wanted to maintain commercial relations with Panama, "As the vent of our manufactures is of so national benefit." He directed *Sheerness* to safeguard the merchant ships from threats en route and while in Porto Bello. Maynard was to ensure that the traders lived up to their pledge not to sell any contraband goods that would be useful to Spain's military. The admiral also admonished Maynard not to do any private commerce with His Majesty's ship. As if the tedious duty was not bad enough, Vernon added another instruction that may have particularly annoyed Maynard. "His Majesty, having, at my request and representation in his favour, been most graciously pleased to grant his royal pardon to Lowther the pirate, you will make use of the best means of privately informing him of the same, and assuring him of a secure retreat on board your ship for his person and family effects, with my advice to him not to neglect so favourable an opportunity to embrace this testimony of royal favour to himself, and manifesting the sincerity of his repentence by his zeal in his Majesty's and his country's service."[2]

Robert Maynard had some experience with pirates. He was serving as a lieutenant aboard HMS *Pearl* in November 1718 when the governor of Virginia received crucial intelligence that Edward Thache, otherwise known as Blackbeard, was moored in a North Carolina sound. *Pearl*'s captain, George Gordon, ordered Maynard to fit out two sloops capable of negotiating the shallow inlets and destroy Blackbeard's company. On November 22, Maynard's sloop, *Jane*, and his escort, *Ranger*, found Blackbeard's *Adventure* at Ocracoke Inlet and attacked. *Jane* drew alongside *Adventure* as the pirate vessel blasted the lightly armed navy sloops with its guns. Seeing *Jane*'s deck cleared of fighters, Blackbeard and ten of his men stormed onto Maynard's sloop, but the lieutenant had a surprise for him. He had hidden twelve of his men below deck, who charged onto the weather deck to fight the pirates hand to hand. In the ensuing melee, the navy seamen "fought like Heroes, Sword in Hand, and they kill'd every one of them that enter'd." Maynard and his men had to shoot the seemingly indomitable Blackbeard five times and slash him with their swords twenty times more before the pirate captain finally collapsed and died. The victorious Maynard sailed back to Hampton, Virginia, on *Adventure* with Blackbeard's severed head hung from the bowsprit.[3]

Sitting in his cabin, Maynard watched Vernon's mighty fleet and 120-plus transport ships sortie from Port Royal on a mission that would take them to Cartagena on the South American mainland, one of the ports used by the fabled Spanish treasure galleons. It took Vernon's mammoth and elongated armada five days to clear the harbor. *Sheerness* weighed anchor with its small mercantile convoy on February 6 and bore away for Porto Bello, aided by a slight wind. Six days later, Maynard moored his frigate outside Porto Bello's harbor. The situation was tricky. Spanish officials and town merchants had agreed to open commerce with Jamaican traders, but the two sides were officially at war, requiring some deft diplomacy to manage the transactions. Relations got off to a poor start when Spanish garrison soldiers attacked a shore party from *Sheerness*, killing one man and taking the rest captive. It took a couple of days for Maynard to intimidate the governor enough to force their release. Maynard shifted *Sheerness* away from Porto Bello to ease tensions. He anchored in the Garrote, a protected harbor 6 miles northeast of Porto Bello, near Bastimentos Island (modern-day Isla Grande).[4]

Commercial negotiations got past the incident, helped by the influence of George Lowther. Thrilled by news of his pardon, Lowther embraced the commercial mission, introduced the Jamaican merchants to local tradesmen, and convinced both parties to overlook national differences in the pursuit of mutual profits. By early May the Jamaican brigs had sold their merchandise and reloaded with Panamanian goods. Lowther, his wife, Mary, and their two young daughters, Sarah and Grace, boarded one of the merchant ships and sailed to the Garrote to link up with *Sheerness*. The convoy weighed anchor on May 9 and sailed for Port Royal. Lowther and his family were out from under the shadow of his past and headed to a new life as British subjects in Jamaica.[5]

HMS *SHEERNESS*, PORT ROYAL, JAMAICA, MAY 21, 1741

The harbor scene shocked and horrified Captain Maynard, his crew, and the passengers aboard the merchant ships, including Lowther. Admiral Vernon's mighty fleet and General Wentworth's powerful expeditionary force had returned from Cartagena shattered and humbled. Spanish admiral Blas de Lezo's six *navios* and a two-thousand-man garrison under the overall command of Viceroy Sebastian de Eslava had rebuffed the massive British force. Worse, yellow jack and scurvy ravaged the ships' crews and regiments, killing over two thousand and sending thousands more to the hospitals in Port Royal and Kingston. The port surgeon had to make emergency requisitions of private homes to provide more beds and later resorted to putting up tents to shelter the vast number of sick. A cloud of disillusion and recrimination hung over Jamaica as land and sea officers struggled to grasp how they could have suffered so terrible a reverse.[6]

Lowther attended Admiral Vernon two days later aboard his flagship, HMS *Princess Caroline*, where he found the admiral in his customary state of issuing directives at the pace of a currency speculator in the Royal Exchange. Vernon interrupted his schedule to greet his old shipmate, this time warmly. Any doubts of Lowther's contrition or willingness to serve had been erased by his intelligence work and Maynard's report of his vital contribution to the recent trade mission. Vernon embraced Lowther "as a bold and resolute Fellow" capable of doing much to further Britain's cause. Lowther found the admiral in surprisingly good spirits, considering the disaster the expeditionary force had suffered at Cartagena. Vernon had already cleared his conscience. "Neither the Guilt, or Blame, is to be laid at my Door," he claimed. He attributed the setback entirely to the land forces and his counterpart, General Wentworth. The forward-looking admiral had since turned his attention to new objectives.[7]

Though a significant portion of his fleet would have to be sent home for repairs, including *Princess Caroline*, Vernon still had freedom of action in the West Indies and outmatched the Spanish squadron of Admiral Rodrigo de Torres harbored in Havana. Vernon expected France to join Spain in the war, and set his sights on the French colony of Saint Domingue, just a few days' sail from Jamaica. Capturing part of King Louis XV's realm would add more luster to his reputation and eliminate a potential threat to Jamaica. Because France was still officially neutral, he could not attack the colony directly, but he reasoned that seizing Santiago de Cuba, across the Windward Passage from Saint Domingue, would allow him to position his fleet and Wentworth's army for a quick strike as soon as word of war with France reached him. First, he had to win over the generals and the governor to the idea. Vernon wrote a letter to Gov. Edward Trelawny asking him to host a joint council of war to open discussions between the admirals and generals about future operations. He began the correspondence by writing a brief introduction for George Lowther, who would deliver the note. Lowther took the letter from Vernon, crossed the bay to Kingston, then hailed a cab to Spanish Town, where the governor resided. After an audience with Governor Trelawny, Lowther returned to *Princess Caroline* and was surprised when Admiral Vernon handed him a commission as a Royal Navy lieutenant. The admiral advised the pardoned pirate that he would serve as a fifth lieutenant on the admiral's flagship and function as a staff officer reporting directly to him.[8]

It was a unique honor. Throughout British history, plenty of pirates had been pardoned and plenty of privateers had been commissioned, but George Lowther was the only one to go from indicted pirate to navy lieutenant.

Three days later, Vernon, Sir Chaloner Ogle, Governor Trelawny, and General Wentworth gathered in Spanish Town, away from the many distractions in Port Royal and Kingston. The admirals were able to steer the council of war in the direction they wanted. The four leaders recognized that the diminished state of the land forces precluded any venture against an objective as challenging as Havana. However, they did approve Vernon's idea of seizing Santiago and using it as a future base of operations. Governor Trelawny encouraged the new undertaking by volunteering the services of a thousand chosen Black men from the island's plantations as a workforce. Though approved, the new initiative against Santiago had to wait until the sailors and soldiers in the hospitals recovered from the bloody flux, scurvy, and yellow fever. It took until mid-June before Vernon could advise the Duke of Newcastle that the general sickness had "greatly abated."[9]

Admirals Vernon and Ogle planned the attack on Santiago, while Wentworth was preoccupied with reconstituting the land force. There was no issue with relative combat power—Santiago had few ships to oppose the powerful British squadron and few troops to battle the British land force. The problem facing the British was getting past the fortresses guarding the entrance to Santiago's harbor, Castillo San Pedro de la Rocha, and Batería Estrella. Built on the face of a cliff, the castillo presented three batteries to the channel opening, stacked like stairsteps from just above the surface to the crest. Estrella occupied a promontory north of San Pedro and covered the narrows farther down the channel. Any attempt to force the harbor entrance had to pass both San Pedro and Estrella, exposing the ships to their guns on a 1,000-yard passage.[10]

Vernon had learned a hard lesson about engaging stone fortresses with his precious ships. At Cartagena he foolishly sent four ships to bombard Castillo San Luis de Bocachica, only to have them retreat with heavy loss. He formulated a rubric to govern future actions against fortifications: "No ships should ever be brought to batter against stone walls unless they are first assured, they can place their ships within less than a musket shot of them." The upper batteries of San Pedro stood 100 and 170 feet above sea level and were difficult to hit from a lower gun deck. Vernon ruled out any attack on the castillo from the sea: the army would have to seize it before the navy forced the channel.[11]

This decision required the expeditionary force to make an amphibious landing on the ironbound south coast of Cuba, windward of Santiago, followed by a landward advance to Castillo San Pedro, but where to land? Intelligence reports pointed to a small cove 11 miles east of the castillo, a site defended by Batería

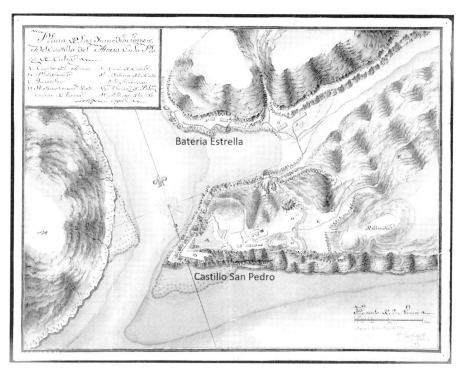

Plano Castillo and Estrella Batería. Eighteenth-century Spanish map of Santiago Harbor entrance, showing Castillo San Pedro and the Estrella Batería to its north. *Courtesy of Archivo General de Indias*

Juragua Chica (modern-day Siboney). The Spaniards had a second artillery battery at another cove, Juragua Grande, 2 miles farther east. Vernon passed over these two sites. He still harbored a grudge about the two weeks during the Cartagena campaign his fleet spent anchored in the open waters of the Caribbean while the army conducted its siege of Castillo San Luis de Bocachica. The strong winds and currents sprung masts, dragged anchor cables, and buffeted his ships. He was not about to put them through the same ordeal in the Windward Passage while the sluggish Wentworth plodded through another siege. Vernon made up his mind to put the army ashore in a protected harbor where his fleet could anchor in calm waters, a decision he made without consulting the generals. The British did not hold another council of war to jointly approve Vernon's plan of attack against Santiago. The generals simply accepted Vernon's logic that the channel entrance could not be forced by the navy, and allowed Vernon to select the best landing site for the army. They would come to regret giving him so much leeway.[12]

HMS *BOYNE*, AT SEA OFF NAVASSA ISLAND, JULY 12, 1741

Only after the fleet and transports had sailed from Jamaica to the westernmost tip of Saint Domingue did Admiral Vernon finally share his plan for the amphibious landing with General Wentworth. The admiral was directing his ships and the convoy to Guantánamo Bay, a harbor he identified as Walthenam, where he would put the army ashore—45 miles east of the castillo. The admiral tried to reassure Wentworth that the planned landing would best serve the operation. "I am fully perswaded [*sic*] that there is no way to begin it with Success but from thence." Vernon's assessment appeared to look only at the naval perspective and failed to consider the challenge the army faced of moving thousands of troops across undeveloped country without any draft animals. To help Wentworth digest the news, the admiral forwarded an intelligence report from John Drake, who gave a glowing account of the army's route to reach Santiago. He described the road to Santiago as "so broad that ten Men may very well go a-breast." Drake's account did little to inspire Wentworth, who summed up the report: "If to be rely'd upon, give[s] us a much better prospect than I expected."[13]

Governor Trelawny had misgivings about Vernon's intentions before the expedition had departed Jamaica. He had written to Wentworth warning about the dangers of landing the army too far from Santiago and forcing the troops to march through rough terrain "perplexed with prickly and intangling shrubs . . . so proper for forming ambuscades." He also wrote to Vernon separately, urging him to reconsider the plan of attack. Vernon took no action on Trelawny's suggestion, though it seems his warnings may have added to Wentworth's misgivings.[14]

Someone else had doubts about landing the army so far from its objective. Lt. George Lowther handed Admiral Vernon a separate operational plan he had devised to reduce Santiago. On his own initiative, Lowther proposed a complex joint attack, using both sea and land forces to overwhelm the Spanish fortresses. He selected the two Juragua coves to land the regiments. Two small Spanish batteries defended the coves, but Lowther planned to use a seventy-gun ship to blast them into submission in a preparatory bombardment. The navy had proven its ability to crush similar coastal batteries during the Cartagena landings. He suggested a quick march from Juragua in the direction of Santiago as a diversion, followed by a sudden change of direction against Castillo San Pedro and Batería Estrella. Lowther observed that the Estrella battery had no defenses from the landward side and could be easily overwhelmed. San Pedro would take more effort to capture. It had guns and two ditches defending its landward (eastern) side. Lowther proposed a simultaneous attack against Castillo San Pedro by Wentworth's army and Vernon's fleet. The army would attempt to penetrate the castillo at its crest while the ships fired broadsides into the lower and middle batteries as they ran up the channel. He figured the garrison could not withstand attacks from land and sea at the same time. Even if the castillo did not fall, once Vernon's ships entered the harbor the fleet could cover the army's march on Santiago. With the port subdued, the British could return to reduce San Pedro at their leisure.[15]

Lowther's proposal is an astonishing document. With no training as a naval officer, he developed a joint plan of attack using the separate capabilities of ground troops and ships to seize a fortified objective. Exercising his knowledge of the coast and a careful study of the Spanish artillery batteries, Lowther identified the weaknesses in the Spanish defense: (1) the Juragua batteries could not prevent an amphibious landing because they could be demolished by naval vessels, (2) the Estrella battery was defenseless on its landward side, (3) without the Estrella battery the channel did not have enough defense in depth to stop fast-moving ships from sailing past Castillo San Pedro and entering the harbor, and (4) San Pedro could be attacked simultaneously from land and sea. Lowther's plan had multiple moving parts with challenging timing issues, but its use of joint capabilities shows a tactical acumen ahead of its time and, apparently, beyond the expertise of the expedition's admirals and generals. The fact that he developed his own proposal shows how intent Lowther was on manifesting his zeal in His Majesty's service. Vernon ignored it.

HMS *BOYNE*, GUANTÁNAMO BAY, NOON, JULY 18, 1741

The admiral supervised the fleet's entry into the expansive bay from the quarterdeck of his new flagship, HMS *Boyne*. The warships and forty-one transports slipped through the narrows and dropped anchor in the protective cover of Walthenam Bay by 6:00 p.m. Once ensconced in the calm waters, the admiral rechristened the bay as Cumberland Harbor in honor of the king's youngest son. Vernon had grown concerned that Wentworth might refuse to land his troops so far from Santiago, so he quickly organized an inland reconnaissance mission with four of his trusted subordinates to allay the general's worries. At five o'clock the next morning, Lt. George Lowther; John Drake, the man who provided intelligence about the countryside; Capt. Thomas Watson, skipper of HMS *Boyne*; and a company of North American marines commanded by Capt. Lawrence Washington (older half brother of George) boarded six longboats and then shoved off for the mouth of St. Ann's River (renamed the Augusta River). The boats entered the river's elongated delta, which stuck into the southwest corner of the bay like a chameleon's tongue. Rowing against the flow, the party snaked upriver 4 miles past salt ponds and estuaries before reaching the lowlands, dominated by squat stands of cedar and gumbo-limbo trees interspersed with mahogany. The narrow river and remote forestland, far from the busy fleshpots of Port Royal and Kingston, exuded the eerie, claustrophobic ambiance of a primordial wilderness closing around the scouting party. The boats meandered another 3 miles through swamps and sloughs before reaching a cataract below a scrubby hill. Lowther, Drake, Watson, and Washington decided to explore the high ground, the first vantage point they had encountered since leaving the bay. The hummock rose to only 50 feet but was part of a ridge that extended northward, rising to a height above 140 feet. The officers climbed to the top and got their first good look at the landscape, a mix of forested lowlands carved by several watercourses, patches of dry savannas, and a distant farm.[16]

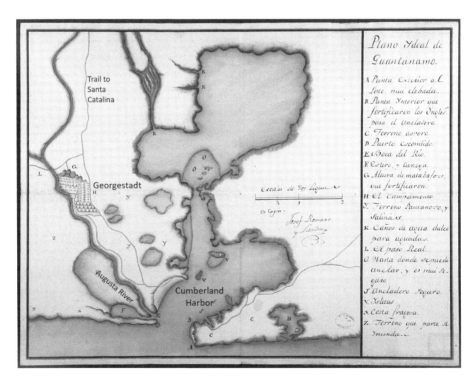

Plano Ydeal de Guantánamo. Eighteenth-century Spanish map of Guantánamo Bay, with the Georgestadt encampment visible on the western side.
Courtesy of Library of Congress

A sudden *crack!* interrupted the scout. One of the American marines crumpled to the ground, wounded by a lurking gunman. Washington's marines chased off the lone Spaniard, who disappeared into the brush. The incident with the Spanish militiaman posed no further threat to the reconnaissance party, but it put the British on notice that the Spaniards were aware of their presence at Guantánamo Bay.

Lowther and Watson returned to *Boyne* that evening to give a positive report of the terrain's suitability for the army's march to Santiago. The admiral scheduled a council of war for the following day, wanting to sell the good news to the generals. He wrote to Wentworth claiming, "I think the Informations so plain and clear, and the Execution so easy . . . that I cannot entertain the least Doubt of Success." The optimistic statement proved that the admiral had almost no conception of how a land force operated. A navy ship, with its hold filled with tons of water, provisions, powder, and ball, could move freely with all it needed to strike an enemy—not so an army.[17]

The July 20 joint council began with tension, then progressed to contention. Wentworth presented a resolution from the generals that listed eight reasons why the army should not undertake a march through the Cuban interior to Santiago. The generals, instead, recommended that the navy break into Santiago's harbor and land the troops at the port. Vernon went into hard-sell mode, as if he was peddling South Sea Company shares at Charing Cross. He produced the letters from Drake, then introduced Lowther and Watson, who had seen the terrain the day before. Noticeably, he did not invite Captain Washington to the council, the one army officer who went on the reconnaissance. The two naval officers vouched for the accuracy of Drake's description and answered the generals' questions about the road and local geography, at least as far as they could see from the hilltop. Vernon then dismissed the notion of using his ships to attack Santiago by bringing in a ship's captain who had recently examined Castillo San Pedro, though from afar.[18]

The generals still were not buying. Without beasts of burden and wagons to haul water, armaments, and provisions, the army could not advance 60 miles through enemy country no matter how wide the road was. Once inland, the troops would be separated from their supply base and limited to what they could hump on their backs. How many 24-pound cannon balls could one man carry?

Vernon countered with a new argument. Cumberland Harbor itself was an important asset and could prove vital as a future base to strike Saint Domingue. North American colonists could be lured to settle there, he suggested, eventually leading to a takeover of the whole of Cuba. The generals, seeing no alternative to the impasse, relented. Wentworth agreed to land the troops and organize a march to Castillo San Pedro and Batería Estrella, "if the approaches to them are found practicable for His Majesty's forces." He also consented to sending a reconnaissance in force to take possession of Santa Catalina (near modern-day Guantánamo), a village on the main road running between Santiago and Baracoa on the island's northern coast. The reconnaissance mission could go forward while the army settled in.[19]

Thanks in part to Lowther's testimony, Vernon got what he wanted: the army would do the work while he moored his ships in a calm bay. The regiments offloaded from the transports over the next three days, eventually occupying an encampment behind the hilly ridge discovered during Lowther's and Watson's reconnaissance. Wentworth named the new camp Georgestadt in honor of the king. The general then issued orders for the reconnaissance in force to explore the way from Georgestadt to the village of Santa Catalina, where they could locate the road to Santiago. Vernon made Drake available as a guide for the party of one hundred North American marines and an equal number of Jamaican load bearers. Drake came with his own personal retinue led by naval Lt. Thomas Sturton, commander of an eight-gun fireship, HMS *Success*. While Sturton safeguarded the guide in the Cuban interior, Vernon ordered Lieutenant Lowther to takeover command of Sturton's small warship. It must have seemed odd to the ex-pirate to have command of a Royal Navy vessel after steering clear of them in his younger days.[20]

On July 27 the American recon force reached Santa Catalina and found two ranches, some cattle pens, and a few hog crawls. The so-called village offered little to sustain an army on a march through the Cuban countryside. Nevertheless, Wentworth sent reinforcements under Lt. Col. James Cochrane to hold onto the advanced post. The troops spent several days scouting their surroundings, searching for provisions and Spanish militia under the command of Capt. Pedro Guerra, who had been harassing them. Sturton and Drake returned to Cumberland Harbor to give accounts of the army's explorations at Santa Catalina. Lowther, who had become a useful staff officer whom Vernon leaned on frequently, escorted Drake back to Santa Catalina on August 5 for the purpose of guiding the army to Santiago. The march was never made.[21]

The expedition's senior leaders lived in separate realities. The admirals, gleaning every testimonial and report, envisioned a highway, wide and level, extending from Guantánamo Bay to Santiago. All the generals could see was a winding path through woods and parched savannas, cut in several places by rivers and gullies. Wentworth surveyed the terrain himself and declared the route unsuitable for hauling the army's provisions and ordnance. Vernon countered with a specious argument that the army could make a rapid march with a thousand picked troops and a thousand Jamaican load bearers to surprise the San Pedro garrison, despite having firm intelligence that the governor of Santiago had already learned of their entry into Guantánamo Bay within twenty-four hours of the landing. Wentworth asked the admirals to release several hundred American marines who were backfilling missing sailors on the warships, but Vernon refused. He claimed the fleet needed the Americans on their ships in case the Spanish fleet in Havana approached. Vernon then suggested that the army could march on Santiago without the Americans, and when they reached the city, he could reinforce Wentworth by landing the Americans at Juragua, the landing site that Lowther had recommended. Vernon's suggestion reveals how close-minded his thinking had become. He used the possibility of landing troops at Juragua to counter Wentworth's request, but he refused to consider the Juragua coves, as Lowther had, as possible landing sites for Wentworth's entire force. The senior leaders eventually tired of exchanging nasty correspondence and agreed to meet at a joint council of war to settle on a course of action.[22]

HMS *VESUVIUS*, CUMBERLAND HARBOR, 8:00 A.M., AUGUST 13, 1741

The admirals and generals climbed aboard the eight-gun fireship, each side intent on convincing the other to submit to their point of view. The leadership of the expedition immediately fractured between the two services. The generals, forearmed with their own testimonials about the impracticability of a land march to Santiago, sank the admiral's proposal by declaring "we cannot march anybody of Troops further into the Country, without exposing them to certain Ruin." The admirals reciprocated by burying any thought of using their ships to break into Santiago's harbor. Vernon refused to consider any option other than a landward advance and assault. Unable to budge Wentworth and his subordinates, the temperamental admiral refused to sign any joint resolution and stormed out of the council. The admirals returned to their flagships and the generals to their camp.[23]

Wentworth penned a letter to the Duke of Newcastle the next day to complain about Vernon's pigheadedness. "Being altogether unacquainted with the land service, he looks to the end without considering the means." Vernon's report to Newcastle at the end of the month included copies of all the resolutions and correspondence passing between the two services, as he started building his case with the secretary of state to blame the land forces for the inaction in Cuba. To bolster his case, he dispatched Lowther in the sloop *Triton* on August 22 to scout the coast between Cumberland Harbor and Castillo San Pedro and verify the absence of any suitable anchorage. Lowther surveyed the shoreline to the Juragua coves, then returned as bad weather set in. He confirmed that "the whole Coast is an Iron-bound Shore, and steep too in all Parts." Lowther's mission to prove that no suitable anchorages existed on the southern Cuban coast provides a clue to Admiral Vernon's thinking. The army wanted a landing site closer to Santiago where longboats could come ashore, but Vernon attached a further condition that the troops could be landed only in protected waters, where he could anchor his ships out of the winds and currents of the Windward Passage.[24]

With the admirals and generals at loggerheads, the force sat idle, and the troops grew uneasy. One officer complained, "Our inactive situation is very melancholy as well as useless." They had nothing to do but sit in camp and get sick. "Our men are very sickly and die fast, more from want of necessaries than the inclemency of the climate, I fear. Some die by their own excesses in drink. Fluxes are the reigning disorders among them."[25]

Lowther may have suffered his own disillusions. He had moved his family out of Panama and joined the Royal Navy with the goal of restoring his reputation. The campaign to capture Santiago was key to his purpose. He needed to be part of a triumph to expunge the stain of wickedness still attached to his name. That was looking less likely. More troubling, he could see that his patron and superior, Admiral Vernon, bore much of the responsibility for the sad state of the expedition. When he had returned from his excursion to Santa Catalina, Lowther admitted that Vernon's plan for an inland march was hopeless. Worse, Vernon's obstruction and intransigence stood in the way of other sensible options. Lowther had been a dutiful subordinate. He had given testimony at Vernon's behest and done his bidding, but he could not help questioning the fitness of the man he worked for.[26]

CUMBERLAND HARBOR, SEPTEMBER 14, 1741

Bands of clouds scudded southward. The waves slapped the coastline more fiercely and higher up on the shore. Water in the bay lifted the ships higher and anchor cables strained. A hard gale with driving rain blew through and then cleared. Looking east, sailors could see more dark clouds piling high. Sir Chaloner Ogle knew what the signs portended. He had seen the same thing before in 1722. His ship HMS *Swallow* had been anchored at Port Royal when a violent hurricane hit Jamaica and nearly destroyed the port. Lowther had been in the West Indies long enough to recognize the approach of a hurricane too. At 5:00 p.m. the storm hit with full fury. Dense clouds and a deluge of rain darkened the bay, pierced by flashes of lightning. Crew members scurried aloft to strike the topmasts and yards. Others lowered a sheet anchor and wrapped its cable around the bitts, upright oak timbers attached to beams. The winds and rains hit their peak in the evening. During the gale, the crew had to splice one of the anchor cables that had parted from the strain. *Boyne* and the other ships rode out the storm in the bay, but the troops at the Santa Catalina outpost had more trouble with inland flooding. The rivers rose 20 feet and washed away six sentries. Several Jamaicans staying at the advanced camp had to climb into the trees to escape drowning.[27]

The hurricane passed the next day, though it took several more for the rivers to drain. The expeditionary force and Vernon's fleet felt relieved to have withstood the storm; however, it took a few weeks for the greatest threat to manifest itself. The swollen creeks, soaked vegetation, and numerous puddles provided ideal breeding grounds for the *Aedes anopheles* mosquitoes, carriers of the *Plasmodium falciparum* parasite. Swarms of adult mosquitoes in October led to the emergence of intermittent fevers (malaria). By early November, Wentworth warned Admiral Vernon that 1,500 soldiers in camp had fallen ill. "The Distempers they Labour under is universally Agues and Fevers." He went on to describe the impact on the force. "Our Duty Men are scarcely sufficient for the ordinary guards." On November 6 the army's surgeon general advised that "a contagious Epidemia which reigns among the soldiers may in a very short time spread throughout the whole army."

The surgeons urged the general to embark the army on the transports to remove them from the hostile climate. On November 27 the transports stood out to sea for Jamaica. Vernon lingered at Cumberland Harbor until December 6, when he weighed anchor. The mighty British expeditionary force was, once again, compelled to retreat from Spanish territory, this time after barely firing a shot.[28]

The army and the fleet felt awful about the humiliating retreat, though each service blamed the other for the miscarriage. Lowther felt particularly perturbed at the poor result. He had invested his hopes in the British expedition and his trust in Admiral Vernon. He lost both. Back in Jamaica, he would find a way to revive his hopes, but his abandoned faith in the admiral would lead him to take a drastic step.

CHAPTER 18

PANAMA

KINGSTON, JAMAICA, JANUARY 5, 1742

HMS *Boyne* finally returned to port on a clear January afternoon, the kind of dry, balmy day that delighted Jamaica's English residents. Once the ship moored, George Lowther and his servant, John Roberts (or Rogers), had the chance to slip ashore and savor some family time. Lowther reunited with his wife and daughters—he had been gone for six months. The joy of seeing his loved ones certainly lifted his spirits, though the failure of the Santiago enterprise weighed on his mind. The nation expected more from the hugely expensive expedition, and so did he. The lieutenant barely had time to embrace his family before duty and an opportunity drew him away from domestic life.[1]

While they were in Cuba, word had reached the generals and admirals that the Duke of Newcastle was sending them a three-thousand-man reinforcement, giving the foundering British expedition one more chance to achieve something notable.[2]

The troops coming from Britain would find themselves caught in the middle of a huge tug-of-war between the land and sea officers over the future of the enterprise, a struggle that Lieutenant Lowther saw firsthand. Wentworth, his subordinates, and Governor Trelawny still focused on seizing some part of the Spanish West Indies, as their orders from the king directed. Because of the depleted strength of the original regiments, any campaign required an infusion of fresh troops. The inbound convoy would give the expeditionary force just what it needed to tackle a worthwhile objective. Vernon had other ideas. He considered British naval supremacy in the West Indies as the ultimate military goal, and the seizure of a Spanish port as nothing more than a distraction and a diversion of resources.

With Admiral Torres's fleet in Havana and a French squadron potentially coming to Saint Domingue, he thought the three thousand men could perform no greater service than beefing up the crews of his ships. After leaving Cuba, Vernon, with Lowther by his side, cruised south of Hispaniola for a month in the hope of intercepting the inbound convoy and converting the army's soldiers into Royal Navy crewmen. Only the steadfast refusal of the army officers on the convoy to obey orders from anyone other than General Wentworth spared the reinforcements from being purloined by the obdurate admiral.[3]

Besides squirming at the sight of the admiral's mulish behavior, Lowther had come to see Vernon as an obstruction to the expeditionary force's mission and his personal goals. If he wanted to redeem his name by way of a British victory, he would have to channel his energy through a different sponsor. When he learned that the senior leaders had scheduled a joint council for January 8 to consider how to utilize Newcastle's reinforcement, he decided to submit a campaign proposal of his own, not through his commanding officer but directly to the council. It was a bold act. Lowther knew that Vernon was reluctant to consider any further land operations. Upsetting his boss could have severe repercussions for the lieutenant, who owed his pardon to the admiral's favor. Despite his fears, Lowther drafted a plan to seize control of a vital Spanish port that he knew intimately: Panama.

For months, the generals, admirals, and Governor Trelawny had kicked around numerous designs: capture Vera Cruz, seize Campeche on the Yucatán Peninsula, occupy Ruatan Island off the coast of Honduras, stir a revolt among the Mosquito Indians, and conquer Panama. The last was a favored project of the governor. The trail between Panama (Ciudad Panamá) and Porto Bello provided a crucial link in the transport of Peruvian silver to Spain. Henry Morgan had sacked the city in 1671, then left it to the Spaniards. Securing the isthmus for King George, however, would do more than disrupt the treasure flow; it would give Britain a vital port on the Pacific Ocean. Everyone could see the benefit, just not the means to obtain it. Once the army landed on the Caribbean coast, the soldiers would have to negotiate mountain passes, march through thick jungles, and cross a river to reach Panama. Hauling the ordnance seemed impossible, and the march column would be exposed to ambuscades along its route should the Spaniards mount even slight opposition. The task looked insurmountable, until George Lowther crafted a scheme that would show the council how it could be done.

Creating an operational plan was only the first concern: Lowther also had to get his proposal in front of the council without going through his superior officer. Lowther reached out to Governor Trelawny with his idea, knowing of the governor's interest in Panama. He also found an unexpected friend in General Wentworth. Lowther first came to the general's attention while briefing joint councils of war about conditions in Cuba and the West Indies. Vernon had used his lieutenant's testimony to push the navy's agenda; nevertheless, Wentworth seemed to value Lowther's opinions. The general may have learned that the ex-pirate had privately expressed his doubts of Vernon's idea of marching the army from Guantánamo to Santiago. When an October council had been called to consider operations outside Cuba, Wentworth asked for Lowther's attendance because "he is capable of giving us usefull Intelligence, not only as to this Island but of other parts belonging to the King of Spain's Dominions." Lowther later cemented his relationship with Wentworth by giving him a peek at his proposal for capturing Santiago, which Vernon had ignored. The general, outraged by the revelation, complained to London, "The scheme of attacking St. Jago from the sea, and landing our troops near to it, was given to Mr. Vernon . . . which he suppressed. . . . I can not but think in my conscience, (if he had any meaning at all, in landing us where he did) it was to destroy the Land Forces, and by their miscarriage to cast an odium on the Ministry." Lowther's new friends helped him secure a hearing in the council to present his Panama proposal.[4]

COUNCIL OF WAR, SPANISH TOWN, JAMAICA, JANUARY 8, 1742

Recently promoted Maj. Gen. Thomas Wentworth, and his deputy, Brig. Gen. John Guise, joined Vernon, Ogle, and Trelawny at the governor's estate to barter and argue over the expedition's future operations. Admiral Vernon started the meeting by proposing that the senior general-grade officer (himself) should be able to cast a deciding vote whenever the council was evenly divided, a blatant attempt

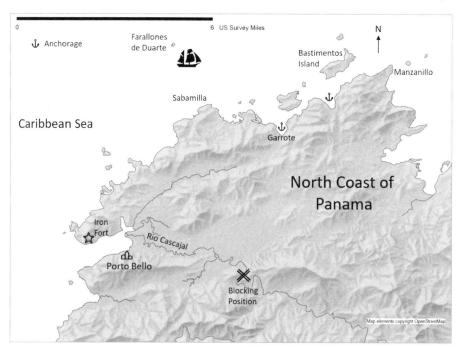

Porto Bello. Panama coast near Porto Bello.

to impose his will on the council. The generals and governor voted down the self-serving motion. Next, the council invited three officers to discuss their ideas for taking or disrupting parts of New Spain (Central America and Mexico). The morning session adjourned without any of the suggestions looking workable.[5]

The senior officers ushered Lowther into the council when it resumed in the afternoon. The naval lieutenant held their attention as he read the details of his operational plan. Just as he had done with his strategy for Santiago, Lowther pieced together an intricate scheme with multiple, simultaneous moving parts. He recommended that the army land at Porto Bello, a sensible suggestion given that the port was defenseless. The landing would be followed with a rapid march by infantrymen over the mountains to the town of Cruzes, on the upper reaches of the Chagres River. Lowther explained that the men needed to carry rations to last only five days. At Cruzes the troops could seize boats and mules to cross the river and advance to Panama. To get the ordnance and supplies inland, Lowther planned a second force of Mosquito Indians and navy seamen, augmented by Jamaican Black men, to ferry the artillery and provisions up the Chagres River. The two forces would unite at Cruzes, where the ordnance and baggage could be loaded onto wagons drawn by mule teams. The army would then have an easy march from Cruzes to the objective.[6]

Lowther emphasized that his plan depended on the element of surprise. He warned the council that once Spanish authorities learned of the British invasion, they would clear the boats and mules from Cruzes and bring troops from Panama to impede the army's march. However, Lowther added an ingenious stratagem to prevent an alarm from reaching the interior. He pointed to the Garrote, a protected harbor near Bastimentos Island. A modest force of five hundred troops could land at the Garrote before the main force disembarked at Porto Bello. The advanced party could then march 4 miles south to the mountain passes that crossed from the Rio Cascajal valley to the headwaters of a northern tributary of the Chagres River. Securing the passes would enable the advanced party to intercept any Spanish troops fleeing Porto Bello and anyone trying to spread alarm to the authorities in Panama. This part of the plan would allow the main force to move undetected from Porto Bello to Cruzes and snatch the boats and mules before the Spaniards could react. Even if the British force was discovered on approach, the boats would not be destroyed, because the alcalde of Cruzes resided in Panama. Knowing the Spaniards, Lowther assured the officers that no one would burn the boats without the alcalde's orders.

It had been nearly a year since Lowther had left Porto Bello. He cautioned that the Spaniards could have rebuilt their defenses since then. To ensure that the British had a good picture of the situation on the isthmus, Lowther volunteered to lead a spying mission to Porto Bello. He proposed sailing in a sloop posing as a trader, possibly with other merchant ships. A navy frigate could escort the convoy, much as HMS *Sheerness* had when it picked him up the previous year. Once the sloop moored in Porto Bello, Lowther could go ashore to scout the Spanish defenses and locate sympathetic residents to serve as guides for the advanced party's march to the passes. Meanwhile the frigate could patrol east of the port to cut off Porto Bello's communications and secure the Garrote for the advance party's landing and linkup with the guides.

Lowther's plan, with its intricate details and clever solutions to difficult problems, fascinated the senior leaders. They queried him closely. "Is it wise that a man-of-war go with those traders to Porto Bello that are ready to sail?"

"By all means," he replied.

"Is it better for you to return to Jamaica or stay about Porto Bello, or where else till our fleet arrives on that coast?"

"It's better to return to Jamaica, because if the Spaniards should have any reinforcement, or notice of our coming, the expedition might sail. Then the expense attending our coming on that coast with the fleet will be useless."

"Will the Mosquito men be of use and wherein?"

"Certainly, they'll help by knowing how the river sets, carrying the artillery up the Chagres, and one hundred of them can go ahead as a vanguard."

"Is the road proper or fit to carry the artillery from Cruzes to Panama?"

"The road is paved and broad enough for ten to eleven miles from Cruzes through a fine savannah. After that there are several roads leading to Panama."

"How many troops will it take for the expedition to succeed and what else will you need to support it?"

"At least 3,000 soldiers are required. In addition, we'll need 500 Negroes and 400 Mosquito men. I ought to have an advance of £500 to procure guides and intelligence, plus another £400 in goods and £100 worth of liquor."[7]

The meeting abruptly ended before any vote could be taken, because General Guise, Wentworth's deputy, grew too ill to continue. The other four leaders reconvened the next day. General Wentworth immediately declared "that Lieut. Lowther's scheme is the most practicable of any yet offered." The council fell in line for "putting the said scheme speedily in execution . . . [and] to advance £500 to Lieut. Lowther." They further approved a £1,500 expenditure to win the cooperation of the Mosquito Indians.[8]

The reformed pirate had pulled it off. He got the expeditionary force moving toward a new objective with a plan attached to his name. His deft maneuvering behind the scenes may have alienated his superior, Admiral Vernon, but the other senior leaders had shown their support for the junior officer, and Vernon had gone along.

The admiral did not reveal his true feelings until a council held in Kingston on January 20. After reading an intelligence abstract about the possibility of France joining Spain in the war, Vernon and Ogle posed a question about whether the

British forces should not prioritize an attack against Saint Domingue over other ventures. The governor and Wentworth held firm to the Panama operation. The admirals switched to a different tactic. If they could not torpedo Lowther's plan outright, they might be able to starve it of resources. Vernon and Ogle noted that Admiral Torres had a comparable fleet in Havana. They questioned the council whether the army had enough men to launch the Panama attack and backfill the fleet's complement of sailors to confront Torres, and, if there were not sufficient men for both missions, should not fully crewing the warships be the first priority? Wentworth, who had come to suspect that Vernon was trying to evade executing Lowther's plan, had to delay his answer until after he could consult with his subordinates. The generals conceded that they did not have enough men, but they put the onus back on the admirals. They demanded that any troops sent aboard the warships be made available for land operations, in which case their numbers would suffice to capture Panama.[9]

The showdown came at a council meeting a few days later. The generals stated that the Panama mission was the only viable option and that it could be launched, so long as Vernon agreed to provide nine hundred sailors for the Chagres River force and land the soldiers serving on the warships when asked to do so by the army. The army's attempt to pin him down to a specific commitment incensed the volatile admiral, who "broke out into very scurrilous language" before he stomped off . . . for a time. Vernon had to relent. He knew better than to allow Wentworth to saddle him with the blame for canceling the Panama mission. After cooling off, he returned to the council and signed the resolution authorizing the Panama operation.[10]

HMS *EXPERIMENT*, OFF SALT PAN HILL, JAMAICA, EVENING, FEBRUARY 4, 1742

Capt. Henry Dennis, skipper of the twenty-four-gun frigate *Experiment*, scanned the waters around Manatee Bay after clearing Port Royal and the keys off Rack Point. All he could see was the sloop *Triton*. The shore boats were gone. The moderate winds were predictably easterly and the sky a bit hazy. *Experiment* could cruise safely off the south coast of Jamaica. The time had come to retire to the quiet of his cabin and open his sealed orders. His curiosity had been gnawing at him since Admiral Vernon's envelope had come to him two days earlier, along with instructions to escort *Triton* wherever it needed to go. That was another mystery. Why was the admiral's tender going to sea, where was it going, and why was it under the command of the admiral's lieutenant? He ripped open the envelope to get his answers—Lieutenant Lowther was heading to Porto Bello to spy on the Spaniards.[11]

The admiral, in his usual fashion, laid out thorough guidance to Captain Dennis. *Experiment* would sail at Lowther's direction to the vicinity of Bastimentos Island, near Porto Bello, and render what assistance the lieutenant required to support his reconnaissance and the recruiting of guides for the army's advance party. The admiral directed Dennis to subsist the guides on the frigate until the main force arrived. He gave *Experiment* a secondary mission of interdicting any communications coming in or going out of Porto Bello. Once Lowther obtained his intelligence, the sloop *Triton* would return to Jamaica to inform General Wentworth about the situation in Porto Bello for the upcoming invasion. One small change from Lowther's initial plan: the lieutenant would remain with the guides aboard *Experiment* rather than return with *Triton*. Finally, the admiral constrained Dennis "to keep cruising in such stations, as we may be sure of not missing you" when the ships carrying the advance party arrived on the coast. A failed linkup would have fatal consequences for the mission. To emphasize the point, Vernon warned Dennis that he either stayed near the rendezvous point or he would "answer the contrary at your utmost peril."[12]

TRITON AND HMS *EXPERIMENT*, AT SEA OFF THE COAST OF PANAMA, 9:00 A.M., FEBRUARY 10, 1742

It must have seemed like old times for Lieutenant Lowther. After marking the San Blas Islands to their southwest, he and Captain Dennis spotted three sails to their west. Dennis ordered his topsails unreefed to give chase. It took the British frigate and Lowther's sloop an hour to run down the unidentified brig and sloops. As soon as *Experiment* fired a warning shot, the three vessels hove to. They turned out to be British merchants returning from the Garrote to Jamaica. The news pleased Lowther. The presence of British merchant traffic would give him perfect cover for his spy mission.[13]

Triton took the lead as the British vessels steered for Bastimentos Island. Lowther piloted the small convoy past Manzanillo Point, then threaded the channel between the mainland and the island. The two British vessels anchored in Bastimentos Harbor that evening. They slid 2 miles farther southwest into the Garrote the next morning, where they found Dutch and French merchantmen. Lowther's plan was working: the British would arouse no suspicion moored in the Garrote.

PORTO BELLO, FEBRUARY 13–14, 1742

Appearing carefree and nonchalant, George Lowther strolled the streets of Porto Bello. He could not hide his identity. People in town knew him and were aware that he had left for Jamaica with a British merchant convoy the year before. What the townspeople did not suspect was that he had become a serving Royal Navy officer. Trying not to draw too much attention, he looked across the harbor to the Iron Fort—it lay in ruins. The bastions of Castillos Gloria and San Jerónimo were still crumbled. He did not see guns mounted at the castillos or any evidence of new batteries around the port. Spanish soldiers milled around the governor's residence, but only a modest garrison. The port was as defenseless as Vernon left it two years earlier.[14]

Lowther proceeded to the next task in his spy mission, which likely took him back to the Garrote. He knocked on doors of people he knew, friends who were inclined to welcome a British regime in Panama and could be trusted to hold a confidence. Meeting privately, he poured generous cups from the liquor ration he carried, and spoke in hushed tones. The £500 advanced by General Wentworth helped him make a persuasive argument with amenable residents. He needed men familiar with the shortest paths from the Garrote to the mountain passes and was willing to pay handsomely for anyone willing to take the risk. On February 16, Lowther climbed aboard HMS *Experiment* with two locals, Cayetano Rodríguez and Pedro de Caudillo (or Castillo). Captain Dennis kept the two men aboard and arranged to feed them while the ship waited for the linkup with Admiral Vernon.[15]

The guides were set, and *Experiment* was on station. The time had come to alert the main body in Jamaica that all was ready for the invasion. Lowther penned a report to General Wentworth, assuring him that the expedition could proceed. Porto Bello, he wrote, "is quite defenceless, & the ennemy neither alarmed or apprehensive." Lowther handed the letter to his second officer on *Triton*, who would deliver it to the general in Jamaica. *Experiment* and *Triton* weighed anchor and left Bastimentos heading east. Captain Dennis escorted the sloop as far as the San Blas Islands before turning it loose.[16]

KINGSTON, JAMAICA, MARCH 9, 1742

Frustrations continued to plague General Wentworth, most of them involving manpower. Even with the reinforcements from Britain, the army had shrunk to only 5,841 enlisted men. The number available for the upcoming campaign quickly dropped as the new arrivals "in a short time moulder away." By early February, 1,963 had fallen ill. Vernon, who put the needs of the fleet above all else, sucked up nearly 1,900 soldiers to fill his crew complements. Wentworth despaired of getting them back. He complained to Newcastle, "I can have no dependence on the Land Forces, when once embark'd on the King's ships." Only 2,022 enlisted men were left to board the transports for the Panama landing, a thousand fewer than Lowther recommended. The transports raised another issue. Once the navy finished impressing mariners from the island, the merchant captains barely had any men to crew their ships. The general turned to Governor Trelawny for help. A new regiment was formed from some of the island's independent companies. Five hundred of them would compose the advance party destined to land in the Garrote. The governor had more trouble rounding up enough free and enslaved Jamaican Black men to ferry the trains up the Chagres River. Fortunately, a sufficient body was collected by the beginning of March. Then Vernon left—not for Porto Bello, but for Cartagena.[17]

An intelligence report had alarmed the British. Several Spanish ships were supposedly headed to Cartagena with reinforcements for the garrison. An emergency council of war voted to have Vernon sortie with six ships to intercept the Spanish convoy, taking hundreds of soldiers serving on the ships with him. With Vernon sailing separately from the transports, Wentworth worried that he would never see those troops again. The Panama mission could still proceed with Admiral Ogle using the remaining warships to escort Wentworth to Porto Bello. The general, the transports, and Ogle's squadron finally left Port Royal on March 9. Far from feeling relieved that the invasion force was underway, the general was beset by uneasiness. Once at sea, the army was dependent on the navy to get them ashore, something that troubled him more than the enemy's dispositions.[18]

HMS *EXPERIMENT*, AT SEA OFF BASTIMENTOS, 2:00 P.M., MARCH 10, 1742

A shout from the lookout at the masthead alerted Captain Dennis and Lieutenant Lowther to a large boat coming from Porto Bello and passing between Sabamilla Point and the Farallones de Duarte. Dennis sent out his launch with an armed party, led by his lieutenant. Three hours later the launch pulled alongside, with nine prisoners taken off the boat. The Spaniards had just come from the governor of Porto Bello with a packet of letters addressed to Sebastian de Eslava and Melchor de Navarrette, the viceroy and governor in Cartagena. Lowther examined the letters, getting further confirmation that the port had no inkling of British designs on Panama. His plan to catch the Spaniards by surprise seemed to be holding. *Experiment* had come out of the Garrote nearly a week earlier to cruise the coast north and east of Porto Bello and to be in good position for the linkup. Lowther had brought a third guide, Francisco Garrindo, aboard the frigate, and all appeared ready to guide the advance party after the linkup, an event that seemed overdue. They stayed off Sabamilla until the nineteenth, when they chased an unidentified sail into Bastimentos Harbor. The brigantine turned out to be British. Captain Dennis released the nine Spanish prisoners and sent them back to Porto Bello in the launch, apparently assured by Lowther that the prisoners could alert the governor only that a British frigate had intercepted his letters.[19]

Releasing the prisoners proved that Lowther still felt good about achieving surprise. What began to unsettle him was the delay in the main body's arrival. The dry season had only another few weeks to run. After that, the rains would make any march through the Panamanian jungle difficult and dangerous. *Experiment* lingered in Bastimentos Harbor until March 25, then sailed out to the Farallones de Duarte and anchored, hoping to get an early sighting of Vernon's fleet when it came on the coast. Lowther and Dennis could do nothing more than wait.

HMS *GRAFTON*, AT SEA OFF CARTAGENA DE INDIAS, MARCH 9–25, 1742

Since the moment they had departed Port Royal, Maj. George Lestanquet could see the tenseness in his commander, General Wentworth. A close friend of the general, the major had come to Jamaica with the reinforcement convoy to join

Wentworth's command. He remained by the general's side and usually dined with him as they sailed aboard HMS *Grafton*. Lestanquet observed how anxious and vexed Wentworth had been because of the time lost preparing the army for departure, but his demeanor had not eased once the convoy got underway. Admiral Ogle was steering the convoy to Cartagena to join Vernon rather than bearing directly for Porto Bello—more time lost. A few days out, the convoy seemed to "tack & stand again for the Land of Jamaica." Lestanquet noted, "The Gen'l does not like the proceedings." Wentworth's attitude brightened on March 15, when Admiral Ogle joined him on *Grafton* and passed Lowther's report revealing that Porto Bello was unaware and virtually undefended. At least Lowther's part of the operation had gone smoothly.[20]

Major Lestanquet's moment of disquiet came once he and the general boarded HMS *Kent* to have a conversation with Governor Trelawny. The major conversed with a civilian, William Beckford, who was familiar with the Panamanian countryside. Beckford felt confident that the army could take Panama if they could reach the city before the April rains. When Lestanquet asked what to expect on the way to the objective, he learned that the army faced six days of marching through "very woody" terrain. The British Army had well-developed exercises to confront enemies in the open farmlands of Europe and trained to fire and maneuver in compact formations, tactics that Lestanquet understood would be impossible to execute in a jungle. When the major remarked about how dangerous such a march would be, Beckford replied that Henry Morgan and his band of buccaneers had done it in 1671. Lestanquet dismissed Beckford's advice as coming from "one very ignorant of the Rules & practice of War." The discussion gave the army officer more appreciation for Lowther's insistence on surprise. "It is possible to Succeed if the Ennemy be not upon their Guard," he wrote, "but if they are we shall be almost destroy'd."[21]

The two army officers continued fretting until midday of the twenty-fifth, when the convoy spotted the coast of the Spanish mainland near Cartagena de Indias.

HMS *BOYNE*, AT SEA OFF CARTAGENA DE INDIAS, NOON, MARCH 25, 1742

The sortie to intercept the Spanish reinforcements had been a waste of time: no Spanish ships were in Cartagena. The spurious intelligence report of a Spanish reinforcement had sent Admiral Vernon on a wild-goose chase. Because of it, his six warships had been buffeted and tattered by the relentless Caribbean winds and waves for weeks. HMS *Worcester* and his own flagship, HMS *Boyne*, had each sprung masts since arriving. The idea of opposing Admiral Torres with his ships in such poor condition filled him with dread. He fumed to himself that he should have stayed in Port Royal until Wentworth got his act together. Now he had to wait for the tardy convoy while his ships needed to get to a harbor for rest and refit. At least the intelligence was good. He had reports that Lowther had made it into Bastimentos Harbor, and the mission to recruit the Mosquito Indians was going well. A lookout's call interrupted his thoughts and brought the admiral onto the deck of his flagship. Peering through the sunlit haze, he caught sight of forty-two sails approaching Cartagena from the north, Admiral Ogle's squadron with Wentworth's transports in tow.[22]

Vernon ordered his six warships to weigh anchor, then instructed the unified fleet to sail immediately for Porto Bello, not giving Ogle's squadron and Wentworth's transports a breather from their two-week passage. The following morning the admiral prepared for the next critical step in the operation, the linkup with HMS *Experiment*. At 9:30 a.m., *Boyne* raised a signal for HMS *Montague*'s captain, William Chambers, to come aboard to confer with the admiral. Vernon told Chambers to sail ahead of the fleet and "to endeavor to fall in Between the point Sembloes [Punta de San Blas] and Bastimentoes and to look out for the Experiment." To complete the linkup, *Montague* was ordered "to Bring him into the fleet."[23]

Montague caught fresh northeasterly gales and bore away for Bastimentos. By 6:00 p.m., Chambers was well ahead of the fleet, though he could still see their sails in the fading light. He stayed under sail during the night, though he changed direction to the northwest, apparently to stay well clear of the Panamanian coast in the dark. At midnight he shifted to the east, then steered southwest under full sail at dawn on March 27. Chambers made landfall by midmorning, but his navigation had been off. He had overshot Porto Bello by a dozen miles and missed *Experiment*. Inexplicably, Chambers failed to tack back to Bastimentos to fulfill his mission. Instead, he wasted the afternoon chasing a merchant vessel farther west, until he discovered it was a trader out of Curacao. Not until 9:00 p.m. did he start tacking eastward, then west-northwest around midnight, and eastward again the next morning—too late to effect the linkup.[24]

HMS *BOYNE*, AT SEA BETWEEN PORTO BELLO AND CARTAGENA, MARCH 27, 1742

Admiral Vernon felt the warm glow of power and satisfaction with his fleet and the army's transports sailing under his direction. The plan to attack Panama had not been his—it had been Lowther's. The decision to approve the plan had not been his—it had been the generals'. The time had come to put his stamp on the proceedings, and, while at sea, he had unfettered authority. He organized the fleet into two lines of battle, comprising his and Admiral Ogle's ships. The transports would follow the warships. With strong following northeasterly winds, the entire fleet put up sail for a speedy run to Porto Bello. He then notified the ships' captains of his intent to "go into the harbour of Porto Bello in line of battle."[25]

On board HMS *Grafton*, all should have seemed in order from Wentworth's point of view. Lowther was standing by in Bastimentos, the Mosquito Indians were coming to Chagres, and the expedition was bearing down rapidly on the Panamanian isthmus—too rapidly for General Wentworth's taste. Wentworth knew that the expedition was getting close to the coast, and he wanted to make last-minute arrangements for debarking the troops before making landfall. The advance party was loaded onto dedicated transports for the linkup, but the main force was jumbled among the other transports, and some key leaders had died while at sea. The general also worried that the fleet, moving quickly with the wind, might reach Porto Bello before the advance party could land and secure the mountain passes behind the town. He sent a message to Vernon via the *Grafton*'s commander, nudging him about moving too hastily. "I presume you will either lay by or come to an anchor . . . that sufficient time be given for . . . holding a Council." The boat returned a short time later with Vernon's reply.[26]

The admiral reassured the general that he had sent HMS *Montague* ahead to locate *Experiment*, Lowther, and the guides. Then he dropped a bombshell. "But if we do not meet with them, we must not lye in the sea, and I shall carry the whole fleet directly into Porto Bello." He dismissed any concern about missing the linkup, by arguing that the troops could be landed at Porto Bello and reach the mountain passes just as quickly as they could from the Garrote. Regardless, Vernon held no interest in arguing the point. "There can be no occasion for calling a council of war till we are quietly anchored in the harbour." Vernon had made up his mind—he wanted his ships in Porto Bello by nightfall the next day and would tolerate no delay.[27]

Vernon's dismissive response left Wentworth aghast. He paced his cabin, muttering about the admiral's interference in the operation: "The enemy will be alarmed. . . . It's contrary to the scheme we agreed upon. . . . We shall miscarry!" Major Lestanquet, in typical British understated fashion, recorded the general's feelings: "The Genl. very much out of humour." That night, Wentworth took a boat over to HMS *Kent* to confer with Governor Trelawny, who was equally disgusted by Vernon's behavior. The two leaders vented their frustrations to each other but recognized that they were powerless to stop Vernon while the force was at sea. The Panama expedition was Vernon's operation now. At dawn the warships and transports unreefed their sails and bore away for Porto Bello, propelled by strong northeasterly gales.[28]

HMS *EXPERIMENT*, AT ANCHOR NEAR THE FARALLONES DE DUARTE, 1:30 P.M., MARCH 28, 1742

For three days the lookout had scanned the ocean from his perch in the foremast top armor, only to report no sightings. The prevailing winds had brought rains and squalls from the east, but no British ships. Captain Dennis had anchored *Experiment* somewhat west of the entrance into the Garrote, rather than position the frigate windward of Bastimentos Island. He and Lieutenant Lowther may have considered the waters off Sabamilla Point as the safest place to spot Vernon's ships in case the fleet approached the coast west of the intended linkup point. By this time, the two naval officers must have been especially anxious. The linkup was overdue, and the campaign season in Panama was running short. Where were Vernon and Wentworth?

At last, the lookout cried, "Sails, to the east-northeast!" The officers pulled out their spyglasses to get a better look. They could make out a large flotilla of ships under full sail running toward Porto Bello: Vernon's fleet. The crew scrambled to effect the linkup. Brawny sailors strained against the capstan to lift the anchor while seamen went aloft to unreef the sails. In a half hour, they "stood out to the N'ard." Dennis got the frigate underway, but Vernon's fleet was moving so rapidly that they did not have a chance to tack windward to meet them at the channel entrance to the Garrote. *Boyne* was passing around the farallones by the time *Experiment* could get within hailing distance. Vernon shouted to Captain Dennis to have his frigate follow his line of battle into Porto Bello, effectively annulling the linkup and advance party landing. Hearing the instructions from the deck of *Experiment*, it became Lowther's turn to feel aghast. He watched helplessly as *Experiment* fell in with Vernon's line of battle and turned the headland into Porto Bello's harbor.[29]

GOVERNOR'S RESIDENCE, PORTO BELLO, 4:30 P.M., MARCH 28, 1742

A runner burst into the office of Lt. Col. Juan Colomo, governor of Porto Bello, with alarming news. The British fleet that had been spotted earlier in the day had turned toward the harbor entrance in line of battle, as if they intended to attack. The presence of the fleet outside the port had not excited the governor earlier in the day. British warships had come and gone into Porto Bello before. He went to the castillo walls and saw British warships nearing the ruins of the Iron Fort and dozens of other ships outside the harbor, waiting to enter. The frightening sight startled him. The British were staging a full-scale invasion! Colomo collected his regular soldiers, about eighty in number, and bolted for the interior. Another three hundred militiamen joined him at the mountain passes, where he blocked the road to Panama, the same location Lowther had intended to occupy with the British advance party.[30]

HMS *BOYNE*, PORTO BELLO, 5:00 P.M., MARCH 28, 1742

HMS *Boyne* dropped anchor just off the Iron Fort, or what was left of it. Vernon, examining the town from the forecastle, noticed citizens "flying from the town." He assumed they were ordinary townsfolk, terrified that the British were coming to sack Porto Bello. Actually, he may have been observing Colonel Colomo and his forces leaving for the mountain passes. The admiral sent an officer ashore to stop the panic. The officer returned to *Boyne* with a delegation of town officials to meet with the British senior leaders, who had gathered aboard the admiral's flagship. Wentworth, Trelawny, and the regimental commanders joined Vernon and Ogle in reassuring the people that they had nothing to fear so long as they behaved properly and did not oppose the British forces. The Spanish officials welcomed the promises from the council that they could "continue peaceably in their possessions."

Vernon then asked them where the governor was. He was taken aback by their answer. Colomo and eighty regular soldiers had already fled into the mountains, they said, likely on their way to Panama. The land officers heard the reply too, while flashing angry glances to each other.[31]

General Wentworth called a council of his subordinates aboard HMS *Grafton* on March 30. The general requested that Lieutenant Lowther attend the meeting to apprise the army officers of the situation in the Panamanian interior. Though no record of their meeting exists, Vernon called Lowther to his cabin, likely to relay the army's request. It afforded Lowther his first opportunity to speak privately with his superior since he left Jamaica in February and since the admiral had overturned his precisely planned scheme—he could not let the moment pass. Lowther confronted Vernon. Why did he cancel the linkup? The plan depended on achieving surprise; how could he throw it away by barging into Porto Bello as if he was Drake attacking Cadiz?[32]

Lowther's candor and presumption triggered one of Vernon's volcanic tirades. Who did he think he was to question an admiral? Vernon scorched him for disloyalty. Had it not been for his personal intervention, Vernon reminded him, he would be hanged for the contemptible pirate he was. The admiral belittled and berated Lowther, perhaps getting a bit of payback against the man who cooked up the Panama operation that he had opposed.

Lowther stood before the admiral and absorbed the invective. He had suffered the rage of a superior once before in the Gambia, precipitating a mutiny on his part. He knew better than to repeat that mistake. Shouted out of the admiral's cabin under a cascade of oaths and deprecations, Lowther took a boat over to *Grafton* to join the land officers. Major Lestanquet chanced upon him in the *Grafton*'s wardroom later that day. His diary entry captured the naval lieutenant's sentiments hours after his brutal audience with Vernon. "Mr. Lowther incensed against the [vice admiral] for abusing him in an ungentlemanlike manner."[33]

The Panama operation that Lowther had conceived and scouted was officially aborted on March 31, when land and sea officers assembled aboard *Boyne* for a joint council of war. This time, Admiral Vernon was the recipient of a fait accompli. Wentworth handed the admiral a resolution signed by the senior army officers, listing the difficulties of proceeding against Panama. The resolution drew particular attention to the failure to interdict Governor Colomo's withdrawal and prevent an alarm from reaching Panama. The resolution concluded, "We think it is for His Majesty's Service to lay aside that Enterprise." Wentworth backed up his subordinates: there would be no landing of troops at Porto Bello. In a letter to Newcastle, he pinned responsibility for the unwelcome end of the operation on Vernon for canceling the linkup with Lowther and his reckless entry into the harbor. "That extraordinary step made by Mr. Vernon . . . would have disappointed the whole scheme" had they gone forward. Governor Trelawny stepped forward to read aloud a letter he had composed for the Duke of Newcastle, excoriating Vernon as "being the Cause of all of our disappointments." Just as Lowther had done the day before, Vernon stood and endured the condemnation. Major Lestanquet observed, "The Adml. sayes not a Word. Much discomposed."[34]

SLOOP *TRITON*, PORTO BELLO, APRIL 14, 1742

At Lieutenant Lowther's command, the sloop tender's crew weighed anchor and then raised the mainsail, square course, and jib. *Triton* caught the northeasterly breeze blowing down the length of Porto Bello's harbor and fell in convoy behind HMS *Experiment* and the sloop *Endeavour*. Admiral Vernon was dispatching them on a diplomatic mission to solicit the help of local Indians in driving the Spaniards out of the Isthmus of Darien. The short sail to Darien was nothing more than a minor diversion in the British-Spanish conflict, which suited Lowther just fine. Now terrified by his superior's frequent displays of wrath, he welcomed the chance to get away from his domineering presence.[35]

A misty rain fell as the former pirate surveyed the harbor, mirroring the somber mood that prevailed aboard the fleet and transports. The port, once jammed with British ships, was rapidly emptying. Trelawny had sailed. Wentworth had left. The soldiers, the Jamaicans, and the last of the transports were departing. HMS *Boyne's* crew were bending on their sails and would leave the next day. The British expeditionary forces trickled out of Porto Bello, and, with them, the last chance to accomplish something noteworthy in the West Indies. The farcical attempt to capture Panama never achieved so much as a landing. The troops were going back to Jamaica without having fired a shot.

None left with greater regret than George Lowther. His bold design of conquest and his hopes for a glorious victory had been dashed. For all his clever planning and daring reconnaissance, he earned nothing beyond a humiliating rebuke from Admiral Vernon, his superior, patron, and the chief architect of his scheme's downfall. Lowther had to swallow the bitter realization that his efforts to restore dignity to his name had failed as miserably as John Massey's sad pleas for respect from an unforgiving court. His only solace: at least, he would not hang.

CHAPTER 19

RETURN TO BRITAIN

SLOOP *TRITON*, BAY OF CALEDONIA, ISTHMUS OF DARIEN, 5:00 P.M., APRIL 21, 1742

An empty, morbid atmosphere hung over the water as Lowther's *Triton*, the sloop *Endeavour*, and HMS *Experiment* entered the gloomy bay. Both Spanish and Scottish colonies had been planted here then vanished—ventures attended with heavy loss of life. Despite the passage of nearly two and a half centuries of discovery and settlement, the bay bore little evidence of any European presence. It seemed ridiculous that Britain would come to such a forsaken place for assistance in its fight with Spain, but Lowther had orders from Admiral Vernon to cultivate an alliance with the local Indians.

For the previous five days, the three British vessels had crept down the Darien coast, sounding the depths of the channel behind the barrier islands until they reached the bay and measured 14 fathoms above a muddy bottom. Captain Dennis, finding the harbor suitable, ordered them to drop anchor. *Endeavour* fired a gun to signal their arrival to the natives, the Guna people. They lived a safe distance from the shore to give themselves a buffer against Spanish or pirate-raiding parties. The next morning, Captain Pauncheo, the local chief, came aboard with a contingent of his villagers to initiate commerce and negotiations with the visiting Britons.[1]

The diplomatic mission lasted four days, a leisurely time for the crews but a bit more tense for the officers. Dennis and Lowther secured the natives' cooperation in driving the Spaniards from the isthmus. To cement their pledge, Captain Pauncheo's brother and son, plus two other Indians, boarded *Experiment* to sail for

Jamaica, where they would remain as hostages. In exchange, Captain Dennis gave the Indians six muskets, 10 pounds of shot, and half a barrel of powder—hardly enough to mount an insurrection.[2]

The three British vessels unmoored and weighed anchor on the morning of April 25; however, *Experiment* took most of the day to clear the harbor after getting stuck on a rocky shelf. Luckily, it was the only mishap on their return voyage. They fared better than the rest of the British ships.

SLOOP *TRITON*, PORT ROYAL, JAMAICA, 10:00 P.M., MAY 8, 1742

Where was Vernon? Where was Ogle? Where was Wentworth? What happened to all their ships and transports? Port Royal Harbor was nearly empty. Lowther had been delayed in Darien while the rest of the fleet and transports had left Porto Bello for Jamaica. The convoy had a two-week head start, but he and Captain Dennis found only seven warships and one storeship in port. Vernon's fleet and the transports were missing. The answer to the mystery came by a land courier a few days later. The expedition's ships had been pushed westward by strong winds and made landfall at the lee end of Jamaica. Unable to struggle eastward against the current, Vernon's ships remained stuck in Withywood Bay. Their predicament may have reminded Lowther of his own difficulties sailing east from Port Maho against the Caribbean easterlies in 1722.[3]

Vernon eventually returned to Port Royal in late June after being forced to travel overland. Once back in port, he and the other leaders held another joint council of war at Governor Trelawny's residence in Spanish Town. Because of the expedition's depleted resources, the admirals and generals could advance only one offensive operation, the occupation of Ruatan Island. The uninhabited island off the coast of Honduras had little to offer other than as a stopping place favored by pirates. Edward Low had stayed there in 1723 before linking up with Lowther in the Bay of Honduras. The British leaders thought that a garrison on the island might protect the logwood operations in the Bay of Honduras and provide a base to foment unrest among Guatemalan natives.[4]

The council had an assignment for Lowther too. They were sending him and Captain Dennis back to Darien, this time with enough muskets and ammunition to arm two hundred natives. However, the expectations were more realistic. Vernon had already noted, "These Indians seem an innocent inoffensive people, but do not promise for being of a very enterprising genius." The British wanted only their cooperation "to intercept all packets of letters coming or going between Carthagena, Panama or Porto Bello." Given the trackless forests and mountains of the Darien isthmus, there would have been no courier traffic to interdict.[5]

Lowther, who may have worried about his standing with Vernon after their falling out in Porto Bello, was reassured that the admiral still held him in high enough regard to entrust with another mission. Vernon had recently commended him to the Duke of Newcastle. "I think he has an hearty good will to serve his Majesty faithfully and diligently." Lowther was also esteemed by General Wentworth, but for different reasons. Wentworth wrote Newcastle's undersecretary, asking for an official inquiry into the "causes of our ill success," and he wanted Lieutenant Lowther brought to London to give testimony. "I believe him to be better acquainted with ye coast of New-Spain than any Englishman," Wentworth claimed, "and has been more particularly employ'd by Mr. Vernon than any officer in the navy." After recommending Lowther to the duke, the general begged the undersecretary to keep his suggestion of recalling Lowther a secret, "least [sic] some evil should betide him."[6]

With the approbation of the admirals and generals, Lowther left Port Royal in *Triton* on July 9, along with Captain Dennis in *Experiment*, bound for the southernmost corner of the Caribbean. The British sloop and frigate had an uneventful voyage. They reached the Bay of Caledonia on July 25, then spent twelve days trading with the Indians while plying them with the liquor that Lowther brought from Jamaica. Captain Pauncheo and Captain Janey, a chief from another local tribe, split the firelocks and ammunition, and each offered up two youths to return to Port Royal "as hostages of their fidelity." After cruising between Bastimentos and Cartagena, the two British vessels returned to Port Royal on September 9. Lowther's mission could be counted as a success, but of little import.[7]

PORT ROYAL, JAMAICA, 4:00 P.M., SEPTEMBER 23, 1742

HMS *Gibraltar*, a twenty-gun Royal Navy frigate, announced its entry into the harbor with a rousing fifteen-gun salute to Admiral Vernon's flagship, HMS *Boyne*. The arrival of a navy ship from Britain did not normally excite much notice, except that this one carried long-awaited instructions from London. Earlier in the year, Sir Robert Walpole, Britain's longest-serving prime minister, was forced to step down from office, obliging his Whig government to reorganize under the nominal leadership of Lord Carteret. Sir Charles Wager was out as First Lord of the Admiralty, replaced by Lord Winchilsea. The Duke of Newcastle remained secretary of state and kept responsibility for handling the war with Spain, although his attitude about the West Indies expedition had changed. After successive failures at Cartagena, Cuba, and Panama, Newcastle and the British public had lost enthusiasm for offensive operations in the Caribbean. There would be no more attempts to capture part of Spain's New World empire. The duke instructed Vernon to turn over command of the Jamaica Station fleet to Admiral Ogle and return to Britain in *Boyne*. Ogle would still have a sizable, though slimmed-down, squadron at his command to annoy Spanish commerce. He was also charged with safeguarding Jamaica from Admiral Torres's fleet, which had shown little inclination to venture out of Havana's harbor. Newcastle also recalled General Wentworth and dissolved the expeditionary army. The Americans and a few surviving veterans of the old regiments would go home, but the majority of British soldiers were dispersed to the warships to plus up their crews.[8]

Admiral Vernon's recall left Lowther without his original sponsor and the man who had commissioned him in the Royal Navy. It could have been a serious blow to his future. Fortunately for the ex-pirate, he had already established his reputation as a valuable staff officer and the individual most knowledgeable of the Spanish West Indies. General Wentworth's hoped-for board of inquiry would not be formed, leaving no reason for bringing Lowther to London to testify about the miscarriages in Cuba and Panama. On October 15, Lowther transferred from HMS *Boyne* to HMS *Cumberland* as a fifth lieutenant on Sir Chaloner Ogle's flagship. "This Day I rece'd my Commission for ye Cumberland," he recorded in his lieutenant's log. Four days later, every ship in Port Royal saluted Admiral Vernon and the *Boyne* with seventeen guns, as the vice admiral departed Jamaica for the final time. General Wentworth and the transports left three weeks later, closing one of the worst chapters in Britain's military history.[9]

There would be no further naval campaigns to help the lieutenant restore luster to his name, but Lowther still had an eye for enterprise, this time of a mercantile nature. Before the convoys sailed from Port Royal, he sold his pay tickets and his lieutenant's log for his time on *Boyne* to John Whiting, master of the transport ship *Weston*. Turning in his tickets and log was a condition for a lieutenant to receive his pay for the time he had served on a ship when it was paid off. Whiting paid Lowther in cash for the rights to his pay that he would collect once *Weston* reached London. Sadly, Whiting lost Lowther's log on the homeward passage, though he was still able to recoup his investment from the Admiralty. Lowther took the £90, less Whiting's discount, and invested in a partnership with John Young, a resident of Jamaica. Lowther never described the type of business that he and Young launched—sugar plantation, shipping venture, rental housing, or some other scheme, but he considered the partnership a major part of his estate.[10]

The business venture may have given Lowther a welcome diversion from the desultory duties of a fifth lieutenant on the admiral's flagship. Most of his log entries recorded routine ship maintenance and supply duties, such as "Empld. In Scraping of masts and Blacking yards and Taking in Ballast" or "Came on bd. [board] 30 Firkins of Butter & 12 Casks of Pease." He also noted the comings and goings of the ships of the line, frigates, and sloops dispatched by Admiral Ogle to harass Spanish shipping. Gone were the days of planning major operations, attending councils of war, and scouting Spanish defenses. *Cumberland* remained stuck in port for the next fourteen months.[11]

Word of King George's declaration of war against the French king finally stirred Admiral Ogle from Port Royal. On June 3, 1744, he sortied with five ships, including *Cumberland*. The squadron struggled against strong easterly gales and currents, not reaching the south coast of Hispaniola until July 5, where Ogle intended to intercept French ships coming in and out of Saint Domingue. The British ships had hardly gotten on station before they started buckling under the strain of steady winds: two had to be sent back. By July 18, *Cumberland*'s masts had loosened, its shrouds had snapped, and its hull began leaking. The admiral called the mission off and returned to port himself, "not hav[ing] the good Fortune to see any of the Enemies ships or vessels during my Cruise." *Cumberland* sortied again in September with HMS *Falmouth* and *Assistance*, Lowther's old ship, but they had only a brief chase of two French warships that managed to elude them. *Cumberland* then moored at Port Royal until spring of 1745.[12]

Lieutenant Lowther changed ships again when Vice Adm. Thomas Davers assumed command of the Jamaica Station fleet from Vice Admiral Ogle. On March 31, 1745, he was discharged from *Cumberland*, then recommissioned two days later as a fifth lieutenant on Admiral Davers's flagship, HMS *Cornwall*. Lowther's tenure under Davers was short lived. That summer he submitted a request for a leave of absence to return to Britain, citing "reasons of great Consequence to him." Davers did not share the nature of Lowther's personal business, but he was satisfied with the lieutenant's explanation. Lowther promised to return to the West Indies as soon as he settled his private affairs in London, assuming the Admiralty approved his return to service. The admiral discharged Lowther and gave him and his family berths on HMS *Prince of Orange*, which was shepherding a convoy of merchant ships back to Britain. The ship left Port Royal on August 6.[13]

HMS *PRINCE OF ORANGE*, THE DOWNS, ENGLAND, NOON, OCTOBER 21, 1745

Riding abeam of the westerlies in rainy, squally weather, HMS *Prince of Orange* pulled into the Downs, an anchorage 3 miles off Deal and the flat Kentish countryside where several of His Majesty's ships already lay at anchor. Among them stood the ninety-gun HMS *Royal George*, flying the white ensign of Admiral of the White Edward Vernon. Lieutenant Lowther watched as *Prince of Orange* heralded its return to English waters with a seventeen-gun salute to his former commander. His thoughts may have drifted back to the time he and Vernon had anchored in the Downs for several weeks aboard HMS *Assistance*. Over the next several days, *Prince of Orange* moved up the coast and entered the Thames, finally mooring at Longreach on October 28. The crew spent the next week unloading its guns and preparing the ship for scheduled maintenance.[14]

The interlude afforded Lowther and his family an opportunity to debark and begin a new life in London. For the first time in nearly a quarter century, George Lowther set foot on British soil, an exceedingly rare event for an ex-pirate. The family set up residence within the parish of St. Martin-in-the-Fields in Westminster. While his wife and daughters settled in, Lowther attended to his personal business. Unfortunately, Lowther left no clues as to the nature of his pressing affairs, although several possibilities exist: an issue involving his Jamaican partnership, a matter concerning his larger English family, or something related to his royal pardon. It remains a mystery.

At some point, Lowther appears to have resolved his personal affairs, allowing him to request passage on a ship going to Jamaica so he could resume duty aboard Admiral Davers's flagship. Before he could ship out, his past caught up with him. The Royal African Company still operated, though as a shell of its former self, having abandoned its slave trade in 1731. Yet, institutions have long memories. Some of the elders among the Court of Assistants might have wondered how George Lowther could enjoy a navy salary when his partner in crime, John Massey, had been hanged. The 1st Duke of Chandos had died the year before, and his son, who had inherited the duke's massive debts, could have expressed his resentment about the presence of someone who had absconded with part of his father's investments. Insurance and maritime interests, who had suffered heavily from sea depredations, may have challenged the Royal Navy for keeping a notorious pirate on its commissioned rolls. Regardless of the source of antipathy, the Admiralty decided that Lowther's return to HMS *Cornwall* was "not agreeable to the Establishment." The move effectively ended Lowther's naval career. He would stay in London and live on his lieutenant's half pay.[15]

Lowther was not the only one whose Royal Navy career ended abruptly. Shortly after Lowther's arrival in London, Admiral Vernon became irritated by the Admiralty's refusal to name him as the commander in chief of the North Sea Fleet, even though he held sway over the ships protecting the coast. In a huff, he requested to be relieved rather than continue without the title and trappings he thought he deserved. The matter might have ended with a change of assignment, but Vernon could not restrain his tongue or his pen. In early 1746, two pamphlets circulated with verbatim texts of Vernon's acrimonious correspondence with the Lords Commissioners of the Admiralty, *A Specimen of Naked Truth from a British Sailor* and *Some Seasonable Advice from an Honest Sailor*. When an admiralty board confronted him about the leak, Vernon refused to cooperate. On April 11, 1746, the board advised him that the king "had been pleased to direct their lordships to strike his name out of the list of flag officers." With his naval career over, Vernon returned to parliament and continued his outspoken ways until his death on October 30, 1757. The British nation later honored him with a monument in Westminster Abbey, the failures in the West Indies never having tarnished his reputation or his popularity.[16]

ST. MARTIN-IN-THE-FIELDS PARISH, LONDON, OCTOBER 20, 1746

After surviving for decades in the febrile and malarial tropics, George Lowther's "lusty" constitution ebbed away under the onslaught of an unspecified illness contracted while in England's temperate climate. The naval lieutenant, facing his approaching death, took time to set his financial affairs in order by writing his will. "I, George Lowther lieutenant in his Majesty's Royal Navy," he began, "being of sound and disposing mind and memory thanks be to God do declare and pronounce this to be my true last will and Testament." The next sentence, though standard verbiage for a will, reads in sharp contrast to Lowther's irreligious pirating days. "I recommend my soul into the Hands of Almighty God hoping for Redemption through the Words of our blessed Saviour." Lowther likely found comfort that the redemption he failed to earn in his service to the king could still come to him through divine grace. He named his wife, Mary, his executrix, then left her his half of the "produce of the Effects and Merchandise" of the Jamaican partnership with John Young. He stipulated that his two underage daughters, Sarah and Grace, would inherit his "moiety" upon the death of their mother. He made a specific bequest of £10 to Ann Hand, wife of Patrick Hand, a tailor from the same parish. He also bequeathed to Patrick a silver watch chain and seal (a souvenir from his days as a sea bandit?). All the rest of his estate he left to Mary Lowther.[17]

George Lowther, the man who had dodged death in the Gambia, on the sea, and at Blanco Island, passed away a few days after preparing his will. He was buried in the cemetery of St. James Paddington on October 25, 1746. Regrettably, the graveyard has since been built over, erasing Lowther's final resting place. Mary Lowther proved his will two days after the funeral.[18]

What can be gathered from a life so singular as that of George Lowther? Excising the years 1721–23 from his history, we see a picture of a capable, dutiful mariner, entrepreneur, family man, and naval officer. From his humble beginnings, he advanced his station in British society and accumulated some modest wealth. Yet, in the three years sandwiched within those periods of respectability, we find a man engaged in wickedness who sowed pain, suffering, and tragedy across the Atlantic basin. How can we explain this paradoxical behavior?

Lowther's character becomes clearer when examining the four decision points in his career: (1) the mutiny in the Gambia, (2) the choice to turn pirate, (3) the epiphany on Blanco Island, and (4) the pursuit of a royal pardon.

MUTINY

The totality of his life shows that George Lowther was not born a scofflaw but came to sea robbery reluctantly—though deliberately. He and his shipmates on the *Gambia Castle* faced disease and death while performing very disagreeable duty in service to the Royal African Company. It is no wonder they wanted to get out of Africa, but their situation was no worse than what numerous other slave ships endured. Two developments provided the impetus for Lowther to launch a mutiny aboard the *Gambia Castle*. First, his prior discussions with John Massey offered Lowther the means for a successful mutiny. With the army captain's cooperation, he could capture both ship and fort. Once they had control of Fort James, the mutineers could empty the warehouses to provision the ship for the voyage out of African waters. The second development, the confrontation with Captain Russell, provided the necessary spark for Lowther to turn his thoughts into action. The moment the crew intervened to prevent his confinement, Lowther knew that he had the support of his shipmates and that failing to act would lead to his confinement and likely death at Fort James. Self-preservation mixed with his compassion for a distressed crew proved enough for Lowther to instigate the mutiny.

PIRACY

What he and John Massey planned together was a mutiny. However, Lowther, a clear-thinking planner, could see that committing a capital crime was no solution by itself. He certainly reasoned that taking the *Gambia Castle* might get him out of the Gambia, but where could he go after that? Massey's idea of sailing back to Britain to put their case before the king was a fool's errand. Turning pirate and living on the account had to be part of his overall scheme. Lowther succeeded in duping Massey and some of the soldiers at Fort James into joining the mutiny before they realized that becoming buccaneers came as a consequence. His original motives, as extolled by Massey in the rambling petition to the king, may have had an admirable purpose, but Lowther knew he was stepping into an outlaw life as the price of getting out of Africa.

Even if he turned to piracy grudgingly, Lowther fully embraced his role as captain of a sea-roving company. Success in sea banditry meant casting off moral restraints and half measures. The skills that made him a good sailor and leader stayed with him as he plotted the course of his ship and crew into the dark waters of piracy. Merchant vessels were seized with an eye to sustain the company on the sea, not to strike out against the world. Nevertheless, he did what was needed to collect food, drink, ammunition, naval stores, and forced men from innocent merchantmen. Besides robbery, Lowther presided over beatings of men and the burning of their ships, activities consistent with maintaining his criminal enterprise. He usually eschewed the wanton cruelty exhibited by his protégé, Ned Low, but that is faint praise. His pirate company lived and sometimes prospered while disregarding the personal misery and economic damage they inflicted on honest seafarers.

Lowther's story speaks to the enticement of the eighteenth-century buccaneering lifestyle. Pirates shed the strict shipboard discipline that had constrained them to hardship in the navy or merchant marine. As they grew into their lives as sea bandits, they relished the freedom that came with throwing off all vestiges of higher civic, legal, and moral authority. They reveled in their newfound liberation, embracing leisure, laziness, excessive drinking, and lack of concern for the future. The ease of stealing wealth rather than earning it blinded them to their poor long-term prospects. When lowly cabin boys could strut in silken waistcoats stolen from a merchant captain's wardrobe, it was easy to think of themselves as lords of their fates, even if their outcomes likely would come at the end of a rope. Lowther himself fell into piracy's moral sinkhole, flouting religious conviction and disparaging the eventual repercussions of his criminal acts.

Mesmerized by their ill-gotten gains and befuddled with intoxication, corsairs gave no thought to the self-destructive and counterproductive nature of their careless way of life. They failed to appreciate that the discipline and order they disdained were needed to perpetuate themselves at sea. Their ships and rigging gradually deteriorated from inattention, whereas contemporaneous logs of navy ships recorded daily cleaning and mending of sails, spars, lines, etc. Pirate crews preferred to leave it to their forced men to keep their ships seaworthy. Lowther, one of the more attentive buccaneer captains, spent years cruising the worm-infested Caribbean but careened his flagship on only four occasions, usually when he happened to have a forced carpenter on board. Two of those occasions had calamitous results. Pirates shrugged off the deteriorating conditions of their vessels, figuring that if their ships became crank, they could always seize a better one. Such logic ignored the importance of being ready when a crisis struck. Sea robbers had a similar disregard for combat readiness. They liked to think of themselves as fearsome men-at-arms but seldom trained on the fighting skills they would need when challenged by an able opponent. Bartholomew Roberts and Charles Harris met their demise when their inebriated crews failed against the methodical gunnery of Chaloner Ogle's and Peter Solgard's crews. Lowther's men fared no better, winning a few minor skirmishes against undermanned merchants but taking a thrashing from John Gwatkin's brig outside Charlestown. Addicted to ease and intemperance, pirates doomed themselves when difficult circumstances and the authorities pressed them. That's why George Lowther's plan to sustain himself roving on the seas eventually became unworkable.

Epiphany

Marooned on Blanco Island after Walter Moore had taken his sloop, Lowther was forced to confront his own shortsightedness. Left with nothing, not even a canvas sail to shelter under, the pirate captain had plenty of time to reflect on his situation and the poor decisions that had left him helpless. He rediscovered his spirituality and moral compass as he stared a miserable, lonely death in the face, as did many buccaneers who expressed their regrets on the gallows. At this nadir, he likely prayed, begging for salvation. Then, somehow, he managed to escape the island or was rescued by a passing vessel. His miraculous deliverance must have struck him as divine intervention, since he returned to an upright and honorable life for the rest of his days.

Pardon

When war came to the West Indies, Lowther had a family, property, and steady income, everything he needed for a contented life—except a clear conscience. The sudden appearance of a British fleet at Porto Bello, led by someone he knew and who knew him, must have seemed a second miracle to Lowther, an act of grace meant to offer him a chance to rehabilitate himself. He accepted a huge risk to trade obscurity for atonement. His bold offer to come forward and serve the king earned him a pardon, but his subsequent actions suggest he yearned for more. No junior officer in the West Indies worked harder or exerted more influence on events than George Lowther. He put his heart and soul into capturing part of the Spanish West Indies, with an eye to erasing the blot of piracy from his name. Through no fault of his own, he fell frustratingly short of achieving victory for Britain and redemption for himself. This tragic shortfall explains why the name of George Lowther conjures only memories of an infamous pirate rather than an honorable mariner.

History gives us different perspectives on the life of George Lowther. He was at one time a vile pirate who dodged the consequences of his criminal conduct. People can feel rightfully angry that he was never held to account for his piratical acts: the one who got away. He was also a penitent sinner who found his lost faith and returned to an honorable way of life, a real-life Jean Valjean. Those with forgiving natures can feel contentment that a lost soul was restored to righteous living. One can also have a touch of sympathy for Lowther as a man driven to efface a black mark against his name who was not quite able to achieve the legacy he hoped for. Those who see his whole life story will sense many contradictory emotions about George Lowther, a far more complex man than the sea rover known from pirate lore.

Appendix

Known Members of Lowther's Company

Name	Date Joined	Joined as	Outcome
Atwell, Christopher	January 10, 1722[1]	forced man	unknown
Austins, Pelham	June 12, 1721[2]	mutineer	unknown
Badger, Richard	June 12, 1721	mutineer	unknown
Bobons, Thomas	June 12, 1721	mutineer	unknown
Bonny, William	June 12, 1721	mutineer	unknown
Broun (Brown), John	June 12, 1721	mutineer	hanged
Broun (Brown), William	June 12, 1721	mutineer	unknown
Cairn, George	June 12, 1721	mutineer	unknown

Cander, Ralph[3]	unknown	unknown	hanged
Churchill, John	unknown	unknown	hanged
Churchill, William	September 15, 1723[4]	volunteer	unknown
Corp, Robert	September 15, 1723	volunteer	hanged
Crane, Abraham	September 15, 1723	volunteer	unknown
Deloe, Jonathan	June 18, 1723[5]	forced man	acquitted
England, Thomas	June 12, 1721	mutineer	unknown
Evartet, Mathew	June 12, 1721	mutineer	unknown
Follott, Peter	June 12, 1721	mutineer	unknown
Fowler, Benjamin	June 12, 1721	mutineer	unknown
Freebarne, Matthew	unknown	unknown	hanged
Gibbons, Dennis	June 12, 1721	mutineer	unknown
Gibbons, William	September 15, 1723	forced man	freed
Gordon, William	June 12, 1721	mutineer	unknown
Grace, James	June 12, 1721	mutineer	unknown
Grange, Roger	unknown	unknown	hanged
Hankins, James	June 12, 1721	mutineer	unknown
Hardwell, Richard	September 15, 1723	volunteer	unknown
Harper, John	June 12, 1721	mutineer	unknown
Harris, Charles	January 10, 1722	forced man	hanged
Hugett, Thomas	June 12, 1721	mutineer	hanged
Hunter, Andrew	June 18, 1723	forced man	acquitted
Hunter, Henry	June 18, 1723	forced man	unknown
Huston, Andrew	June 12, 1721	mutineer	unknown
Jones, Moris	June 12, 1721	mutineer	unknown
Kendale, Ralph	July 5, 1723[6]	forced man	unknown

Kidman, William	June 12, 1721	mutineer	unknown
Kinnion, John	June 12, 1721	mutineer	unknown
Lavalles, Baptist	June 12, 1721	mutineer	unknown
Levercot, Samuel	unknown	unknown	hanged
Levieux, Andrew	June 1723	forced man	released
Lewis, Nicholas	unknown	unknown	hanged
Linch (Lynch), James	June 12, 1721	mutineer	unknown
Lindsey, David	January 10, 1722	forced man	unknown
Long, William	June 12, 1721	mutineer	unknown
Low, Edward	December 1721	volunteer	unknown
Lowther, George	June 12, 1721	mutineer	pardoned
Luya, John	June 12, 1721	mutineer	unknown
Massey, John	June 12, 1721	mutineer	hanged
McDonald, Edward	unknown	unknown	hanged
McDonald, John	June 12, 1721	mutineer	unknown
McLean, Robert	June 12, 1721	mutineer	unknown
Mersow, Jeremiah	June 12, 1721	mutineer	unknown
Newman, William	June 12, 1721	mutineer	unknown
Parrey, George	June 12, 1721	mutineer	unknown
Pattisons, Robert	June 12, 1721	mutineer	unknown
Pettman, Thomas	June 12, 1721	mutineer	unknown
Powell, Thomas[7]	January 1722	forced man	hanged
Provin, William	June 12, 1721	mutineer	unknown
Reed, William	June 12, 1721	mutineer	hanged
Rich, Richard	May 28, 1722[8]	forced man	unknown
Richardson, John	June 12, 1721	mutineer	unknown
Scowen, William	June 12, 1721	mutineer	unknown

Sedgwick, James	September 15, 1723	forced man	freed
Shaw, John	unknown	unknown	hanged
Silvil, Antonio	June 12, 1721	mutineer	unknown
Sinclar (Sinclair), John	June 12, 1721	mutineer	unknown
Smith, Henry	January 10, 1722	forced man	unknown
Smith, William	June 12, 1721	mutineer	unknown
Sownd (Sound), James	June 12, 1721	mutineer	unknown
Spriggs, Francis	June 12, 1721	mutineer	unknown
Steel, Thomas	June 12, 1721	mutineer	unknown
Sweetser, Joseph	May 28, 1722	forced man	acquitted
Sympson (Simpson), James	June 12, 1721	mutineer	unknown
Thompson, Alexander	June 12, 1721	mutineer	pardoned
Toms, Humphrey	June 12, 1721	mutineer	unknown
Toob, George	June 12, 1721	mutineer	unknown
Tucker, Thomas	June 12, 1721	mutineer	unknown
Watson, Henry	July 5, 1723	forced man	freed
West, Richard	June 12, 1721	mutineer	hanged
White, Robert	unknown	unknown	hanged
Willis, Joseph	January 10, 1722	forced man	unknown
Willis, Robert	May 28, 1722	forced man	acquitted
Wynn, Henry	September 15, 1723	volunteer	freed
Young, John	June 12, 1721	mutineer	unknown
Young, Robert	June 12, 1721	mutineer	unknown

GLOSSARY

abeam:	Sailing with the wind perpendicular to the direction of movement.
alcalde:	Spanish local magistrate, mayor.
anchor:	Metal device fashioned with flukes and attached to a cable to hold a vessel to the seafloor; and a cask capable of holding 10 gallons.
asiento:	Treaty provision allowing foreign merchants to sell slaves in Spanish colonies.
athwart:	Crossing the direction of the wind or another ship.
bend, unbend:	Fastening a sail to its yard or stay, removing a sail.
bitts:	Stout, upright posts to secure anchor cables when a ship is moored.
boot topping:	Expedient method to clean a portion of the hull when a full careen is not practical.
bowline:	Rope secured to the vertical edge of a sail and used to keep it from flapping, especially when sailing close-hauled against the wind.
brace:	Rope attached to a yardarm, used to change the orientation of a sail.
bream:	Procedure for cleaning seaweed, barnacles, and filth from the hull by applying flame to the accretions.
brigantine:	Two-masted merchant ship with a square-rigged foremast and a combination of square- and aft-rigged sails on the main mast.
broad reach:	Sailing with the wind coming from the port or starboard aft quarter.
buntline:	Rope fastened to the bottom of a sail used to lift it up to the yard.
burthen:	Cargo capacity of a ship, usually measured in tons.
cannon:	Type of large-caliber gun capable of firing 32-, 42-, or 60-pound shot and weighing 2–3 tons.
careen:	Procedure to heel a ship onto its side to clean its hull.
cathead:	Beam extended from either side of the forward bulkhead to suspend the anchor cable away from the side of the ship.
charterparty:	Contractual agreement between a ship's captain and its owner stipulating the terms of a voyage.
clapped on a wind:	Term for steering into a headwind.
clew line:	Rope attached to the corner of a square sail and used to roll it up to the yard.
close-hauled:	Sailing as close as six points (60°–70°) against a headwind.

course:	Large square sail hung from the lowest yard.
culverin:	Gun capable of firing a 9- or 18-pound shot.
dashee:	Bribe or gift given to an African lord.
firkin:	Cask capable of holding 9 gallons.
fore-and-aft rigged:	Arrangement of sails and rigging that attaches the sails vertically to the masts in line with the hull.
frigate:	Warship with three square-rigged masts and twenty-eight to forty guns mounted on a single gun deck.
gaff:	Boom along the top edge of an aft-rigged sail to extend its width.
gallant:	Square sail set above a topsail.
grog:	Rum drink diluted with water and flavored with sugar, created by Admiral Vernon.
grometta:	Slave kept by local traders in Africa.
guardacosta:	Spanish coast guard, privateer licensed to seize foreign merchant vessels sailing near Spanish West Indies colonies.
gun deck:	One or more levels of a ship lined with guns.
hawse, harse:	General term referring to the space in front of the forward bulkhead where the anchor cables pass through a "hawse" hole and extend to anchors on the seafloor.
heave to, hove to:	Procedure to halt a ship's movement by turning its sails to counteract each other.
heel:	Tilting of a ship toward its port or starboard side.
hogshead:	Cask capable of holding 63 gallons.
horses:	Ropes extended along a yard for sailors to stand on while working the sails.
hove-in:	Expression implying use of force to pass into or through.
hove to:	*See* heave to.
impressment:	Forcible recruitment of merchant seamen into the Royal Navy.
jib:	Triangular sail attached to the foremast and extending to the bowsprit.
kilderkin:	Cask capable of holding 18 gallons.
king's letter-boy:	Underage son of a well-to-do family sent to sea to learn how to become a naval officer and favored by a letter of introduction from the king.
lift:	Rope and tackle extending from the masthead to the ends of the yardarm to support or raise the end of the yard.
lords justices:	Noblemen and government leaders who rule on behalf of the monarch during his absence.
lubber:	Pejorative term for someone unfamiliar with service on a ship.
lying to:	*See* heave to.
matross:	Gunner's mate on a naval gun crew who handles the swabbing and ramming of the gun's barrel.
minion:	Small gun capable of firing a 3–4-pound shot.
navio permiso:	British permission ship entitled by the asiento to deliver foreign goods and slaves to Spanish colonial ports.

neat wages:	Sailors' net pay after deductions for charitable contributions and personal expenses incurred on board.
ordinary:	Classification for a ship that is serviceable but held in port without a crew or armaments.
parliament heel:	Expedient method of partially heeling a ship to expose some of its hull normally underwater.
periagua, piragua, pirogue:	Large, shallow draft canoe capable of sailing on the ocean.
peruke:	Long, flowing wig.
pipe:	Cask capable of holding 172 gallons.
press:	*See* impressment.
quarterdeck:	Top surface of the aft superstructure above the weather deck.
reef, unreef:	Furling of sails onto the yard and securing the folds with ties, undoing ties, and unfurling.
rigging pay:	Reduced wages paid while a ship is preparing for sea duty.
run:	Sailing with a following wind.
saker:	Gun capable of firing a 6-pound shot.
schooner:	Vessel with two or more masts rigged with fore-and-aft sails.
sea pay:	Classification for a ship that is manned and operational.
sheet anchor:	Spare anchor used to secure a ship in an emergency.
ship of the line:	Large warship with multiple gun decks holding fifty or more naval guns.
ship-rigged:	Arrangement of sails and lines that attaches square sails horizontally to the masts athwart the hull.
shrouds:	Sets of horizontal and vertical ropes attaching the mastheads to the sides of the ship to provide structural support.
sloop:	Vessel commonly rigged with one raked mast supporting an aft-rigged mainsail and a square-rigged course.
slop clothes:	Garments purchased by sailors from purser's mate while aboard ship.
stay:	Ropes extended from mastheads forward to the bowsprit or forward part of the ship to provide support.
tack:	Technique of sailing a vessel against the wind on alternating close-hauled courses to port and starboard.
tar:	Slang term for British sailors, attributed to their tar-stained clothes.
top armor:	Platform midway up the main and foremasts, used for scouting and firing small arms at opposing ships.
topsail:	Square sail attached to a yard extended across a topmast.
warp:	Procedure to move a ship inside a harbor by pulling on a rope secured to a kedge anchor, buoy, or fixed object on the shore.
weather deck:	Topmost deck running the length of the ship.
yard, yardarm:	Horizontal spar suspended on a mast that holds a square sail.

ENDNOTES

Chapter 1: A Life at Sea

1. Woodward, "The Seaman's Monitor," in Baer, *British Piracy*, 4:224.

2. Admiralty Records [ADM], 8/14, 33/300, and 51/69, National Archives [NA], Kew; Earle, *Sailors*, 34–35; and Rediker, *Deep Blue Sea*, 162–63.

3. Dow and Edmonds, *Pirates of the New England Coast*, 212.

4. Earle, *Sailors*, 17–18.

5. Winfield, *British Warships*, 295; Lavery, *Ship of the Line*, 1:168; Schomberg, *Naval Chronology*, 4:14; and ADM 39/150, NA, Kew.

6. Laughton, "Vernon, Edward (1684–1757)," in *Dictionary of National Biography*, 58:257–72.

7. Kemp, *British Sailor*, 61–62; Vernon to Admiralty, 17 July 1719, in ADM 106/730, f. 302, NA, Kew; Vernon, *Vernon Papers*, 417; and Vernon to Admiralty, 26 March 1715, in ADM 106/701, f. 336, NA, Kew.

8. See Vernon's comments in Vernon to Wager, 5 April 1740, in Vernon, *Vernon Papers*, 82; and Kemp, *British Sailor*, 71.

9. Rediker, *Deep Blue Sea*, 14; ADM 51/69, NA, Kew; and Breverton, *Pirate Handbook*, 287.

10. ADM 8/14, 33/300 and 51/69, NA, Kew; Earle, *Sailors*, 32; and Rodger, *Command of the Ocean*, 622–24.

11. ADM 51/69, 52/128 and 33/300, NA, Kew; and Rediker, *Deep Blue Sea*, 88.

12. ADM 51/69 and 52/128, NA, Kew; and Commissioners of the Admiralty, *Manual of Seamanship*, 130–32.

13. ADM 8/14 and 51/69, NA, Kew.

14. The following paragraphs are drawn from Clifford, *Expedition Wydah*, 136–40; Woodard, *Republic of Pirates*, 124–34; and *Calendar of State Papers*, 29: 240 i, 308 i–ii, and 411 i.

15. Melville, *Lady Mary Wortley Montagu*, chaps. 8 and 9.

16. ADM 8/14 and 51/69, NA, Kew.

17. ADM 51/4118, NA, Kew.

18. ADM 51/4118, NA, Kew; and Melville, *Lady Mary Wortley Montagu*, chap. 9.

19. ADM 51/4118, NA, Kew.

20. ADM 8/14 and 33/300, NA, Kew.

Chapter 2: The Royal African Company

1. Azurara, *Discovery and Conquest of Guinea*, 1:39–51.

2. Azurara, *Discovery and Conquest of Guinea*, 1:81–83; and Atkins, *Voyage to Guinea*, 61–62.

3. Davies, *Royal African Company*, 9, 122, and 152; Bertrand, "Downfall," 1–7 and 20; Pettigrew, *Freedom's Debt*, 37–39 and 153; and Atkins, *Voyage to Guinea*, 153–56.

4. *Post Boy*, May 28, 1720; *Daily Post*, July 21 and August 3, 1720; Bertrand, "Downfall," 33; and *London Journal*, September 17, 1720.

5. *Daily Courant*, June 8 and September 17, 1720; and Sanborn, *History of New Hampshire*, 115.

6. Cremer, *Ramblin' Jack*, 31–32.

7. Records of the Royal African Company, Lists of Ships and Their Voyages, Treasury [T] 70/1225, f. 8, NA, Kew; and Gibbs, "John Massey and George Lowther," 461–79.

8. *Applebee's Original Weekly Journal*, November 5, 1720.

9. Depositions in *Daily Post*, November 22, 1720.

10. *Applebee's Original Weekly Journal*, November 5, 1720; and *Daily Post*, November 4, 19, and 22, 1720.

11. *Applebee's Original Weekly Journal*, November 5, 1720; *Daily Post*, November 19, 1720; and *Weekly Packet*, November 19, 1720.

12. *Daily Post*, November 19 and 29, 1720; and Colonial Society of Massachusetts, *Publications*, 34:255–73.

13. *Weekly Journal or British Gazetteer*, December 3, 1720; RAC to Whitney, 1 December 1720, in T 70/55, NA, Kew, also in Gray, *Gambia*, 161; and *Applebee's Original Weekly Journal*, January 28, 1721.

14. T 70/1225, f. 8. NA, Kew.

15. Lynn to Burchett, 4 January 1721, in ADM 1/3810; T 70/1225, f. 8, NA, Kew; and *Daily Post*, November 10, 1720.

16. *Applebee's Original Weekly Journal*, December 3, 1720; and *Daily Post*, November 10, 1720. The rank of captain-lieutenant was held by the officer commanding a headquarters company in the place of the regimental colonel.

17. Anonymous, *Convicts*, 271.

18. Anonymous, *Convicts*, 271; Cannon, *Thirty-Fourth Regiment*, 20; and War Office Records [WO], 64/3, f. 57, NA, Kew, in Gibbs, "John Massey and George Lowther," 465.

19. Anonymous, *Convicts*, 271; Hayward, *Remarkable Criminals*, 125; and Cannon, *Thirty-Fourth Regiment*, 21–22.

20. Gibbs, "John Massey and George Lowther," 465-66.

21. *London Journal*, December 31, 1720; *Weekly Journal or Saturday's Post*, December 31, 1720; *Daily Post*, January 6, 1721; and Petition, EXT 1/261, f. 3, NA, Kew, also in Fox, *Pirates*, 126–35. Although HMS *Swallow* did not stop at the Gambia, Lowther and Massey's petition explicitly states that Colonel Whitney sailed on *Swallow*, at least until the convoy split at Cape Verde.

22. Selcraig, "Robinson Crusoe," 82.

23. Atkins, *Voyage to Guinea*, 32.

Chapter 3: Voyage to the Gambia

1. US Naval Oceanographic Office, *Sailing Directions*, 17–32 and 41–2.

2. *Post Boy*, February 7, 1721; and Atkins, *Voyage to Guinea*, 2.

3. Petition, EXT 1/261, f. 3, and T 70/1225, f. 8, NA, Kew.

4. Bertrand, "Downfall," 22.

5. Petition, EXT 1/261, f. 3, NA, Kew.

6. Charles Johnson, *History of the Pyrates*, 1:347; and *Post Boy*, March 5, 1721.

7. Rediker, *Deep Blue Sea*, 47, 93–94, and 218–22; Sanders, *If a Pirate*, 4; Falconbridge, *Slave Trade*, iii; Cordingly, *Black Flag*, 133–34; and Earle, *Sailors*, 8–9 and 130.

8. Gibbs, "John Massey and George Lowther," 471.

9. Atkins, *Voyage to Guinea*, 57; ADM 51/1057, NA, Kew; and Gray, *Gambia*, 163.

10. Atkins, *Voyage to Guinea*, 57; Gray, *History of the Gambia*, 158–59 and 163–64; Royal African Company, *Particular Evaluation*; and Johnson, *History of the Pyrates*, 181–84.

11. Atkins, *Voyage to Guinea*, 39–40.

12. Bertrand, "Downfall," 4–5, 12–13, and 117.

13. Gibbs, "John Massey and George Lowther," 467–68; and Bertrand, "Downfall," 4–5 and 22.

14. Anonymous, *Convicts*, 272. In his September petition, Massey would claim that his men landed in perfect health.

15. T 70/1225, f. 8, and State Papers [SP] 35/44, ff. 72–73, NA, Kew; Gibbs, "John Massey and George Lowther," 468; Southron, "The Gambia," 533–34; and Smith, *Drafts of Guinea*, plate 5.

16. Petition, EXT 1/261, f. 3, NA, Kew; and Gray, *History of the Gambia*, 164.

17. Petition, EXT 1/261, f. 3, NA, Kew; and Anonymous, *Convicts*, 272.

18. Petition, EXT 1/261, f. 3, NA, Kew; and Johnson, *History of the Pyrates*, 348.

19. Johnson, *History of the Pyrates*, 348.

20. Petition, EXT 1/261, f. 3, NA, Kew; and Anonymous, *Convicts*, 272.

21. Petition, EXT 1/261, f. 3, NA, Kew; and *Daily Courant*, September 17, 1720.

22. Lloyd and Coulter, *Medicine and the Navy*, 103.

23. Anonymous, *Convicts*, 272.

24. Petition, EXT 1/261, f. 3, NA, Kew; Gray, *History of the Gambia*, 166–67; and Rediker, *Deep Blue Sea*, 49n85.

25. Davies, *Royal African Company*, 197; and Petition, EXT 1/261, f. 3, NA, Kew.

26. SP 35/44, ff. 72–73, NA, Kew.

27. Johnson, *History of the Pyrates*, 349.

Chapter 4: Mutiny

1. Johnson, *A General History of the Pyrates*, 349; and Petition, EXT 1/261, f. 3, NA, Kew.

2. Johnson, *A General History of the Pyrates*, 349; Rediker, *Between the Devil and the Deep Blue Sea*, 308–9; Sanders, *If a Pirate*, 22; Atkins, *Voyage to Guinea*, 92–93; Petition, EXT 1/261, f. 3, NA, Kew; and Anonymous, *Convicts*, 273.

3. Bertrand, "Downfall," 27; and Johnson, *History of the Pyrates*, 349–50.

4. SP 35/44, ff. 71–73, NA, Kew.

5. Johnson, *History of the Pyrates*, 349–50.

6. Johnson, *History of the Pyrates*, 350; and Thompson Deposition, High Court of the Admiralty [HCA], 1/55, ff. 23–24, NA, Kew.

7. SP 35/44, ff. 71–73, NA, Kew.

8. Johnson, *History of the Pyrates*, 350; Thompson Deposition, HCA, 1/55, ff. 23–4, and T 70/1446, ff. 23–24, NA, Kew; and Gray, *History of the Gambia*, 168.

9. Johnson, *History of the Pyrates*, 350.

10. Gray, *History of the Gambia*, 165–66.

11. Johnson, *History of the Pyrates*, 350; Leach, *Map of the River Gambra*; Petition, EXT 1/261, f. 3, NA, Kew; and Thompson Deposition, HCA, 1/55, ff. 23–24, NA, Kew.

12. Petition, EXT 1/261, f. 3, NA, Kew.

13. Thompson Deposition, HCA, 1/55, ff. 23–24, NA, Kew; and Petition, EXT 1/261, f. 3,

NA, Kew. According to *A General History of the Pyrates*, the mutineers took eleven pipes of wine.

14. Petition, EXT 1/261, f. 3, NA, Kew; and Gibbs, "John Massey and George Lowther," 471.

15. List of Living and Dead, T 70/1446, NA, Kew; and Gray, *History of the Gambia*, 164 and 170.

16. Petition, EXT 1/261, f. 3, NA, Kew.

17. Johnson, *History of the Pyrates*, 350; and Sanders, *If a Pirate*, 192.

18. Johnson, *History of the Pyrates*, 350–1; and Petition, EXT 1/261, f. 3, NA, Kew. The sources do not provide a precise order of events, but the most logical time for the start of this engagement would be after the governor's son had been brought off the ship.

19. Johnson, *History of the Pyrates*, 350–51.

20. Johnson, *History of the Pyrates*, 350–1; Penrice to Lords Justices, 9 July 1723, in SP 35/44, ff. 55–57, NA, Kew; and Gray, *History of the Gambia*, 169.

21. Petition, EXT 1/261, f. 3, and T 70/1446, ff. 23–24, NA, Kew.

Chapter 5: Turning Pirate

1. Johnson, *History of the Pyrates*, 351.

2. Little, *Sea Rover's Practice*, 23; Sanders, *If a Pirate*, 104, 117, and 119; and Johnson, *History of the Pyrates*, 351.

3. Johnson, *History of the Pyrates*, 352; and Thompson Deposition, HCA, 1/55, ff. 23–24, NA, Kew.

4. Kemp, *British Sailor*, 51–52.

5. Johnson, *History of the Pyrates*, 351; Thompson Deposition, HCA, 1/55, ff. 23–24, NA, Kew; and Cordingly, *Black Flag*, 17; See also Sanders, *If a Pirate*, 36–37. The ship was sometimes called the *Happy Delivery*. For simplicity, the name *Delivery* will be used.

6. Earle, *Sailors*, 74.

7. Rediker, *Deep Blue Sea*, 107–08.

8. For comments on ship sightings, see Little, *Sea Rover's Practice*, 105; and Breverton, *Pirate Handbook*, 217.

9. Johnson, *History of the Pyrates*, 352–53; Thompson Deposition, HCA, 1/55, ff. 23–24, NA, Kew; *Applebee's Original Weekly Journal*, September 23, 1721; *Boston News-Letter*, September 4, 1721; and Petition, EXT 1/261, f. 3, NA, Kew. The sources differ on the date of the attack, ranging between July 20 and 22. The firsthand accounts also differ. Thompson states the attack began in the dark and lasted two days. Captain Douglas reported his ship was held three days. Massey and Lowther's petition was dated on July 22. The captain of HMS *Hector* recorded the *Charles* arriving in Barbados on July 27.

10. Cordingly, *Black Flag*, 107; *Boston News-Letter*, September 4, 1722; and Johnson, *History of the Pyrates*, 352–53.

11. Thompson Deposition, HCA, 1/55, ff. 23–24, NA, Kew.

12. Petition, EXT 1/261, f. 3, NA, Kew.

13. Johnson, *History of the Pyrates*, 353.

14. Cox to Council of Trade and Plantations, August 23, 1721, in *Calendar of State Papers* 32: no. 621 v; *Applebee's Original Weekly Journal*, September 23, 1721; *Boston News-Letter*, September 4, 1721; and Lieutenant's Logs [ADM/L] ADM/L/F/75 and ADM/L/H/101, National Maritime Museum [NMM], Greenwich.

Chapter 6: Divisions and Departures

1. See a description of Dominica's appearance in Buckley, *British Army in the West Indies*, 31.

2. Blunt, *American Coast Pilot*, 412–13.

3. Thompson Deposition, HCA, 1/55, ff. 23–4, NA, Kew.

4. Blunt, *American Coast Pilot*, 412–13.

5. Thompson Deposition, HCA, 1/55, ff. 23–4, NA, Kew. For common hailing customs, see Little, *Sea Rover's Practice*, 129–31.

6. Johnson, *History of the Pyrates*, 353; Thompson Deposition, HCA, 1/55, ff. 23–4, NA, Kew; and Anonymous, *Convicts*, 273. These three contemporaneous sources provide different details of the seizure that the above description attempts to reconcile.

7. Johnson, *History of the Pyrates*, 353; Thompson Deposition, HCA, 1/55, ff. 23–4, NA, Kew; and Sanders. *If a Pirate*, 10. See Cordingly, *Black Flag*, 107–08, for similar descriptions of the looting process.

8. Hayward, *Remarkable Criminals*, 126.

9. Thompson Deposition, HCA, 1/55, ff. 23–4, NA, Kew.

10. Anonymous, *Convicts*, 273; and Thompson Deposition, HCA, 1/55, ff. 23–4, NA, Kew.

11. Earle, *Sailors*, 67–70 and 74; and Little, *Sea Rover's Practice*, 84.

12. Anonymous, *Convicts*, 273; T 1446, ff. 23–4, NA, Kew; and Johnson, *History of the Pyrates*, 353–54.

13. Johnson, *History of the Pyrates*, 354.

14. Anonymous, *Convicts*, 273.

15. Thompson Deposition, HCA, 1/55, ff. 23–4, NA, Kew; and Johnson, *History of the Pyrates*, 354.

16. Johnson, *History of the Pyrates*, 354–55; and Thompson Deposition, HCA, 1/55, ff. 23–4, NA, Kew.

17. *Daily Courant*, August 29, 1721; and *Weekly Journal or British Gazetteer*, September 2, 1721.

18. Bertrand, "Downfall," 33–35; T 70 1446, NA, Kew; and Gray, *History of the Gambia*, 178.

Chapter 7: Prowling the Greater Antilles

1. Lawes to Council of Trade and Plantations, 29 August 1717 and 21 June 1718, in *Calendar of State Papers* 29: no. 54, and 30: no. 566.

2. Johnson, *History of the Pyrates*, A3–4; Lawes to Council of Trade and Plantations, 21 June 1718 and 31 January 1719, in *Calendar of State Papers* 29: no. 54, and 31: no. 34; and Sanders, *If a Pirate*, 97.

3. Lawes to Council of Trade and Plantations, 28 December 1720 and 20 April 1721, and Vernon to Burchett, 8 March 1720, in *Calendar of State Papers* 32: nos. 340, 459, and 527i.

4. Johnson, *History of the Pyrates*, 355.

5. ADM/L/H/46, NMM, Greenwich; ADM 51/432, NA, Kew.

6. *London Journal*, 30 September 1721; and Court of Assistants to Russell, 22 September 1721, in T 70/64, ff. 66–67, NA, Kew.

7. Stein and Stein, *Silver, Trade, and War*, 181 and 216; Georges Scelle, "Slave-Trade," 614, 653, and 656–57; and Johnson, "Corsairs of Santo Domingo," 9–15 and 26.

8. Johnson, "Corsairs of Santo Domingo," 26; and Pares, *War and Trade*, 22–24.

9. Johnson, *History of the Pyrates*, 357–58.

10. See Flemming, *Point of a Cutlass*, 29–31 and 39–40.

11. Johnson, *History of the Pyrates*, 358.

12. Johnson, *History of the Pyrates*, 358; and Hope to Carteret, 17 January 1724, in *Calendar of State Papers* 34: no. 13.

13. Hope to Council of Trade and Plantations, 1723, in *Calendar of State Papers* 33: no. 444; and Hart to Council of Trade and Plantations, 12 July 1724, in *Calendar of State Papers* 34: no. 260.

14. Sanders, *If a Pirate*, 154–55; and Blunt, *American Coast Pilot*, 393–97.

15. Cordingly, *Black Flag*, 185; Rediker, *Deep Blue Sea*, 146–47; and quote by Edward Ward in Lloyd, *British Seaman*, 110.

16. Rediker, *Deep Blue Sea*, 147–49.

17. United Kingdom, *An Act for the More Effectual Suppressing of Piracy, 1721*, 8 George I.

18. Johnson, *History of the Pyrates*, 358; Sanders, *If a Pirate*, 203–04; and Mather, *Useful Remarks*, 13.

Chapter 8: A Pirate Admiral

1. ADM/L/H/46, NMM, Greenwich; and Hayward, *Remarkable Criminals*, 126.

2. Johnson, *History of the Pyrates*, 355; and Anonymous, *Convicts*, 273–74.

3. Charles Johnson, in his book *A General History of the Pyrates*, claims that Lowther and his band stayed at the careening island until after Christmas, but that timeline makes no sense.

4. Blunt, *American Coast Pilot*, 384–85.

5. Blunt, *American Coast Pilot*, 385; and Craton, *Cayman Islands*, 27–28.

6. Johnson, *History of the Pyrates*, 358.

7. Johnson, *History of the Pyrates*, 366–68; Snow, *Pirates and Buccaneers*, 183–84; Dow and Edmonds, *Pirates of the New England Coast*; Len Travers, *Notorious Edward Low*, 27–32; and Rediker, *Deep Blue Sea*, 139.

8. Council of Trade and Plantations to King George, 25 September 1717, in *Calendar of State Papers* 30: no. 104; and Blunt, *American Coast Pilot*, 494–95.

9. Uring, *Voyages*, 342–43; Blunt, *American Coast Pilot*, 498; and *Map Showing the Gulf of Mexico*, #91683705, Geography and Map Division, Library of Congress, Washington, DC [LOC].

10. Dow and Edmonds, *Pirates of the New England Coast*, 4; and Little, *Sea Rover's Practice*, 106–10.

11. Johnson, *History of the Pyrates*, 358.

12. Ben Edwards, correspondence to author, June 17, 2020.

13. T 70/1446, ff. 24 and 33, NA, Kew.

14. Little, *Sea Rover's Practice*, 137–38; *Boston News-Letter*, April 22 and May 7, 1722; *Post Boy*, July 3, 1722; and Johnson, *History of the Pyrates*, 359.

15. Johnson, *History of the Pyrates*, 359; Dow and Edmonds, *Pirates of the New England Coast*, 289; Cordingly, *Black Flag*, 120–21; *American Weekly Mercury*, March 15, 1722; and *Boston News-Letter*, April 22 and May 7, 1722.

16. Barnard, *Ashton's Memorial*, 4; Flemming, *Point of a Cutlass*, 29–31; Fox, *Pirates in Their Own Words*, 171, 193–95, and 236–37; and Cordingly, *Black Flag*, 122–23.

17. See the testimony of John Fillmore for an example of a forced man at the helm of a pirate ship in Fox, *Pirates in Their Own Words*, 223.

18. Johnson, *History of the Pyrates*, 359; *Boston News-Letter*, May 7, 1722; and *Post Boy*, July 3, 1722.

19. Rediker, *Deep Blue Sea*, 267–68.

20. Dow and Edmonds, *Pirates of the New England Coast*, 289–90; and Johnson, *History of the Pyrates*, 272–73.

Chapter 9: Port Maho

1. Jeffreys, *West-India Atlas*, plate 10; *Map Showing the Gulf of Mexico*, #91683705, and *Draught of the Bay of Honduras*, #72003581, Geography and Map Division, LOC; *Boston News-Letter*, May 7, 1722; and Johnson, *History of the Pyrates*, 359. The *Boston News-Letter* stated that the pirates went to "Port Maho in the Gulph of Montick." Johnson's narrative, probably based on newspaper accounts, gives the location as "Port Mayo in the Gulph of Martique" (Gulf of Amatique). However, eighteenth-century maps identify Port Maho at the current location of Omoa, Honduras.

2. Johnson, *History of the Pyrates*, 359–60; and *Boston News-Letter*, May 7, 1722.

3. Cordingly, *Black Flag*, 95–96; and Falconer, *Dictionary of the Marine*, s.v. "Bream" and "Careen."

4. *Boston News-Letter*, May 7, 1722; and Johnson, *History of the Pyrates*, 359–60.

5. Johnson, *History of the Pyrates*, 360.

6. Johnson, *History of the Pyrates*, 266–70; and Sanders, *If a Pirate*, 213–16.

7. Johnson, *History of the Pyrates*, 270–72; and Sanders, *If a Pirate*, 216–20.

8. Atkins, *Voyage to Guinea*, 192.

9. Sanders, *If a Pirate*, 236–40.

10. Sanders, *If a Pirate*, 246–48.

11. Johnson, *History of the Pyrates*, 355–56.

12. Johnson, *History of the Pyrates*, 356.

13. Johnson, *History of the Pyrates*, 356; *Boston News-Letter*, May 21, 1722; *Daily Post*, February 26, 1722; and Cordingly, *Black Flag*, 188.

14. HCA 1/55, ff. 23–24, and SP 35/41/16, ff. 33–34, NA, Kew.

Chapter 10: Trolling Northern Waters

1. Johnson, *History of the Pyrates*, 360.

2. Evans, "Jamaica Sloop," 69–73; Chappelle, *American Sailing Ships*, 27; and Cordingly, *Black Flag*, 158–61.

3. Johnson, *History of the Pyrates*, 248; Rediker, *Deep Blue Sea*, 261–62; Little, *Sea Rover's Practice*, 5–6; and Uring, *Voyages*, 344.

4. ADM L/G/130, NMM, Greenwich; *Boston News-Letter*, June 18, 1722; Travers, *Notorious Edward Low*, 61–64; and Johnson, *History of the Pyrates*, 38–39.

5. United Kingdom, *An Act for the More Effectual Suppressing of Piracy, 1721*.

6. Little, *Sea Rover's Practice*, 105.

7. Johnson, *History of the Pyrates*, 360.

8. Johnson, *History of the Pyrates*, A4.

9. Atkins, *Voyage to Guinea*, 225; Blunt, *American Coast Pilot*, 2; Breverton, *Pirate Handbook*, 218–19; and National Geospatial-Intelligence Agency, "Pilot Charts of the North Atlantic".

10. Deposition of Smith and Meffon, in *Boston News-Letter*, June 18, 1722; *Daily Courant*, August 8, 1722; and Dow and Edmonds, *Pirates of the New England Coast*, 145–46 and 277.

11. Deposition of Smith and Meffon, in *Boston News-Letter*, June 18, 1722; *Daily Courant*, August 8, 1722; Barnard, *Ashton's Memorial*, 7; and Johnson, *History of the Pyrates*, 361.

12. Blunt, *American Coast Pilot*, 37.

13. *Boston News-Letter*, June 18, 1722; Dow and Edmonds, *Pirates of the New England Coast*, 135; and Johnson, *History of the Pyrates*, 361.

14. Johnson, *History of the Pyrates*, 361.

15. *American Weekly Mercury*, June 28, 1722; and *New England Courant*, June 18, 1722.

16. Cordingly, *Black Flag*, 16–17; and Sanders, *If a Pirate*, 229.

17. Dow and Edmonds, *Pirates of the New England Coast*, 135.

18. *New England Courant*, June 11, 1722; *American Weekly Mercury*, June 21, 1722; *Daily Courant*, August 8, 1722; Flemming, *Point of a Cutlass*, 15–16; and Johnson, *History of the Pyrates*, 368–69.

19. *New England Courant*, June 11, 1722.

20. *Boston News-Letter*, July 2, 1722; Dow and Edmonds, *Pirates of the New England Coast*, 149 and 302; and Gibbs, "Golden Age Piracy Trials," 759.

21. Dow and Edmonds, *Pirates of the New England Coast*, 149–50; Johnson, *History of the Pyrates*, 369–70; *Boston News-Letter*, July 2 and 9, 1722; Flemming, *Point of a Cutlass*, 31–32; and *New England Courant*, June 11, 1722.

22. *Boston News-Letter*, July 2, 1722.

23. Hughson, *Carolina Pirates*, 74–75.

Chapter 11: Disaster in the Carolinas

1. Barnard, *Ashton's Memorial*, 7–8; *American Weekly Mercury*, August 16, 1722; and *Boston News-Letter*, August 6, 1722.

2. For hailing procedures, see Little, *Sea Rover's Practice*, 130.

3. Barnard, *Ashton's Memorial*, 8.

4. Dow and Edmonds, *Pirates of the New England Coast*, 151.

5. *American Weekly Mercury*, July 12 and 26, 1722.

6. *American Weekly Mercury*, July 26, 1722.

7. ADM 8/15, NA, Kew.

8. *Post Boy*, September 18, 1722; Johnson, *History of the Pyrates*, 361–62; and Faden, *Map of Charlestown Harbor*, 1780, LOC. The sources for this pirate battle provide general comments on the action. Coupling these statements with the known topography of Charlestown's harbor provides the basis for this account of where and how the engagement took place.

9. ADM L/B/100, NMM, Greenwich. The entry in Lieutenant Stephens's log records a brigantine leaving Charlestown for England on August 14. It was the only unidentified outbound ship in the three to eight weeks before *Amy* arrived in Britain.

10. Gwatkin Will, Probate Records [PROB] 11/587/16, and ADM 32/80, f. 24, NA, Kew.

11. Johnson, *History of the Pyrates*, 361; Falconer, "LyingTo," in *Dictionary of the Marine*. See also Breverton, *Pirate Handbook*, 126.

12. *Post Boy*, December 18, 1722.

Chapter 12: Slaughter in the Bay

1. Johnson, *History of the Pyrates*, 362.

2. London Metropolitan Archives [LMA], ref: LMSLPS150330105; "John Massey," London Lives 1690 to 1800, https://www.londonlives.org/; and HCA, 1/17, f. 181, NA, Kew.

3. SP 35/44, ff. 71–73, NA, Kew; and Anonymous, *Convicts*, 270.

4. Hayward, *Remarkable Criminals*, 126; and Anonymous, *Convicts*, 270.

5. Melville, *Lady Mary Wortley Montagu*, chap. 9.

6. Johnson, *History of the Pyrates*, 373–74.

7. Barnard, *Ashton's Memorial*, 10.

8. Barnard, *Ashton's Memorial*, 10–11.

9. Johnson, *History of the Pyrates*, 362.

10. There is no firsthand source for the reunion of Low and Lowther. Philip Ashton, the eyewitness with Spriggs and Low, escaped on March 9 without seeing Lowther's sloop with Low's company. Succeeding events show that Lowther and Low were together on March 10.

11. Barnard, *Ashton's Memorial*, 12–13; *American Weekly Mercury*, May 2, 1723; ADM 51/605 and ADM 52/440, NA, Kew; and ADM L/M/170 and ADM L/M/173, NMM, Greenwich. The logs of HMS *Mermaid* do not record the encounter but show they were in the vicinity of Low and Spriggs on that date.

12. Uring, *Voyages*, 246 and 355; and Atkins, *Voyage to Guinea*, 226–28.

13. *American Weekly Mercury*, May 2, 1723; Johnson, *A History of the Pyrates*, 377–79; and Dow and Edmonds, *Pirates of the New England Coast*, 204–05. Dow erroneously identifies Spriggs as the commander of the second pirate sloop.

14. Barnard, *Ashton's Memorial*, 12; and Johnson, *History of the Pyrates*, 378.

15. Johnson, *History of the Pyrates*, 378; *Daily Courant*, July 25, 1723; *Stamford (UK) Mercury*, May 16, 1723; *British Journal*, July 23, 1723; and Dow and Edmonds, *Pirates of the New England Coast*, 204–05 and 300–301.

16. *Daily Courant*, July 25, 1723; and Dow and Edmonds, *Pirates of the New England Coast*, 300.

17. Johnson, *History of the Pyrates*, 378.

18. *American Weekly Mercury*, May 2, 1723; *Boston News-Letter*, May 20, 1723; and Dow and Edmonds, *Pirates of the New England Coast*, 139. Dow and Edmonds identify Lowther's sloop as the *Happy Delivery*, but Johnson does not name Lowther's vessel after the encounter with Gwatkin and the *Amy*. According to CO 152/14, ff. 292–93, NA, Kew, the sloop was called *Fortune's Free Gift* when Lowther's crew was put on trial in 1724.

19. *American Weekly Mercury*, June 13, 1723; and Cremer, *Ramblin' Jack*, 170.

20. *New England Courant*, June 3, 1723.

Chapter 13: A Time for Reckoning

1. *American Weekly Mercury*, June 13, 1723; and Travers, *Notorious Edward Low*, 100–102.

2. *New England Courant*, June 17, 1723; Travers, *Notorious Edward Low*, 102–03; Little, *Sea Rover's Practice*, 113; and Cordingly, *Black Flag*, 114–19.

3. *New England Courant*, June 17, 1723; and *American Weekly Mercury*, June 27, 1723.

4. *New England Courant*, June 17, 1723; Travers, *Notorious Edward Low*, 109–18; and Johnson, *History of the Pyrates*, 381.

5. *New England Courant*, June 17, 1723; and *American Weekly Mercury*, June 27, 1723.

6. *American Weekly Mercury*, June 27, 1723.

7. Blunt, *American Coast Pilot*, 11; Sanders, *If a Pirate*, 108; Dow and Edmonds, *Pirates of the New England Coast*, 137; and Johnson, *History of the Pyrates*, 362.

8. Johnson, *History of the Pyrates*, 362; *New England Courant*, July 29, 1723; *American Weekly Mercury*, August 8, 1723; and *Boston News-Letter*, August 22 and September 19, 1723.

9. SP 35/44, f. 72, NA, Kew; *Daily Post*, July 8, 1723; and *Weekly Journal or British Gazetteer*, July 13, 1723;

10. *Weekly Journal or British Gazetteer*, July 13, 1723; SP 35/44, ff. 71–73, NA, Kew; and Johnson, *History of the Pyrates*, 357.

11. *Weekly Journal or British Gazetteer*, July 13, 1723; SP 35/44, ff. 71–73, NA, Kew; and *Daily Post*, July 8, 1723.

12. SP 35/44, f. 73, NA, Kew; *Daily Post*, July 8, 1723; *Weekly Journal or British Gazetteer*, July 13, 1723; and *Daily Journal*, July 8, 1723.

13. Updike, *Rhode Island Bar*, 260–66; and Baer, ed., *British Piracy*, 3:168–69. One man taken off *Ranger*, Thomas Reeve, did not appear for trial.

14. Updike, *Rhode Island Bar*, 266–92; Baer, *British Piracy*, 3:171–92; and T 70/1446, ff. 23–24, NA, Kew.

15. Updike, *Rhode Island Bar*, 293; Cordingly, *Black Flag*, 223–24; *Boston News-Letter*, July 25 and August 1, 1723; and Dow and Edmonds, *Pirates of the New England Coast*, 308.

16. Job 22:15; and Mather, *Useful Remarks*.

17. Dow and Edmonds, *Pirates of the New England Coast*, 307.

18. *Boston News-Letter*, September 19, 1723; and *New England Courant*, July 29, 1723.

19. *American Weekly Mercury*, October 4, 1723; and *Boston News-Letter*, September 19, 1723.

20. *Boston News-Letter*, August 22, 1723; and Dow and Edmonds, *Pirates of the New England Coast*, 138 and 212.

21. *London Journal*, August 24, 1723. Charles Johnson claims that Low was the pirate who pressured Graves to share a drink. See Johnson, *History of the Pyrates*, 388.

22. Cordingly, *Black Flag*, 224; "Execution Dock," Historic UK, *History Magazine* online, historic-uk.com/; Anonymous, *Convicts*, 275; and Hayward, *Remarkable Criminals*, 127.

23. SP, 36/149, ff. 42–45, NA, Kew. A marriage record exists for a John Massey and Mary Two on December 30, 1722, of St. Andrew Holborn Parish, LMA, Ref: P69/AND2/A/002/MS06668/03.

24. *Weekly Journal or Saturday's Post*, July 27, 1723; and Hayward, *Remarkable Criminals*, 127.

25. Hayward, *Remarkable Criminals*, 127; and *London Journal*, August 3, 1723.

26. *London Journal*, August 3, 1723; Cordingly, *Black Flag*, 224; Hayward, *Remarkable Criminals*, 127; and Anonymous, *Convicts*, 275.

Chapter 14: Blanco Island

1. *American Weekly Mercury*, October 4, 1723; and Johnson, *History of the Pyrates*, 389.

2. Johnson, *History of the Pyrates*, 388–89.

3. *Boston News-Letter*, October 18, 1723.

4. Johnson, *History of the Pyrates*, 389.

5. Johnson, *History of the Pyrates*, 390 and 412; Dow and Edmonds, *Pirates of the New England Coast*, 216–17; and *Daily Courant*, June 19, 1724. Johnson claims that the ship, *Delight*, had been HMS *Squirrel*, but there is a record of an HMS *Delight* that was sold in 1712 that fits the description better.

6. Johnson, *History of the Pyrates*, 363. Sources do not identify where Lowther made landfall, but Dominica is the customary stop for ships coming to the West Indies from Europe.

7. CO 28/18, f. 23, NA, Kew; and Johnson, *History of the Pyrates*, 363.

8. CO 28/18, f. 23, NA, Kew; and Little, *Sea Rover's Practice*, 128.

9. CO 28/18, f. 23, NA, Kew.

10. ADM 8/15 and 51/4251, NA, Kew.

11. *Calendar of State Papers* 33: no. 576.

12. Blunt, *American Coast Pilot*, 450.

13. Johnson, *History of the Pyrates*, 363.

14. Scelle, "Slave-Trade," 653; Stein and Stein, *Silver, Trade, and War*, 181; and Paul, "South Sea Bubble," *European History Online*, ieg-ego.eu.

15. Brown, "Contraband Trade," 667–68; Nelson, "Contraband Trade under the Asiento," 55; and *Daily Courant*, May 27, 1724.

16. CO 152/24, f. 289, NA, Kew.

17. CO 152/14, f. 289, NA, Kew; and *Daily Courant*, June 12, 1724.

Chapter 15: A Pirate's Fate

1. CO 152/14, f. 289, NA, Kew; and Johnson, *History of the Pyrates*, 364.

2. Johnson, *History of the Pyrates*, 415.

3. *Universal Journal*, May 6, 1724; Hart to Board of Trade & Plantations, 25 March 1724, in CO 152/14, ff, 285–87, NA, Kew; and ADM/L/H/101, NMM, Greenwich.

4. CO 152/14, ff. 289–92, NA, Kew.

5. CO 152/14, f. 292, NA, Kew

6. CO 152/14, f. 293, NA, Kew.

7. CO 152/14, f. 287 and 28/18, f. 23, NA, Kew.

8. CO 152/14, ff. 285–87, NA, Kew.

9. Cordingly, *Black Flag*, 224.

10. CO 152/14, ff. 286–87, NA, Kew.

11. Dow and Edmonds, *Pirates of the New England Coast*, 216–17; and *Boston News-Letter*, March 27, 1724, and February 11, 1725.

12. T 70/1446, NA, Kew.

13. Dow and Edmonds, *Pirates of the New England Coast*, 286–87; and *London Journal*, August 3, 1723.

14. Rediker, *Deep Blue Sea*, 256 and 283; Cordingly, *Black Flag*, 203 and 227–28; and Bladen to Townshend, 20 August 1724, in CO 35/51, f. 69, NA, Kew.

15. CO 152/14, ff. 289–90, NA, Kew.

Chapter 16: Porto Bello

1. Garganta, *Relacion de lo acaecido*, Archivo General de Simancas [AGS], Valladolid, Spain.

2. Garganta, *Relacion de lo acaecido*, AGS, Valladolid, Spain; Leslie, *A New History of Jamaica*, 293–95; Cerda Crespo, *Conflictos Coloniales*, 94–95; and *Gentleman's Magazine* 10 (March 1740): 124–25.

3. Vernon, *Vernon Papers*, 35–36.

4. Ford, *Admiral Vernon*, 124; Vernon to Waterhouse, 2 October 1739, in Vernon, *Vernon Papers*, 24–25; and Membrillo Becerra, *La Batalia de Cartagena de Indias*, 88.

5. Vernon to Wager, 5 April 1740, in Vernon, *Vernon Papers*, 82. Some of the events in the following paragraphs can be inferred from the details in Vernon's letter to Admiral Wager.

6. *Original Papers Cuba*, 204 and 210–11; and PROB 11/750/312, ff. 146–47, NA, Kew.

7. ADM 51/936, NA, Kew.

8. Vernon to Wager, 5 April 1740, in Vernon, *Vernon Papers*, 80–81.

9. ADM 51/936, NA, Kew; and Vernon to Wager, 5 April 1740, and Vernon to Knowles, 18 March 1740, in Vernon, *Vernon Papers*, 77 and 82.

10. Vernon to Wager, 5 April 1740, in Vernon, *Vernon Papers*, 82–84 and 87.

11. Vernon to Wager, 5 April 1740, in Vernon, *Vernon Papers*, 82.

12. SP 36/51, ff. 229–30, NA, Kew.

Chapter 17: Cuba

1. Schomberg, *Naval Chronology*, 197–98; ADM 8/21, NA, Kew; Richmond, *Navy in the War of 1739–48*, 1:93–94; Beatson, *Naval and Military Memoirs*, 1:68; Muster, CO 5/42, f. 25, and SP 36/52, f. 130, NA, Kew; and Vernon to Newcastle, 12 January 1741, in Vernon, *Vernon Papers*, 161–62.

2. Vernon to Maynard, 22 January 1741, in Vernon, *Vernon Papers*, 167–68.

3. ADM, L/P/32, NMM, Greenwich; and *Weekly Journal or British Gazetteer*, April 25, 1719.

4. Vernon to Newcastle, 24 February 1741, in Vernon, *Vernon Papers*, 177–80; ADM 51/898, NA, Kew; and ADM/L/S/263, NMM, Greenwich.

5. Vernon to Newcastle, 30 May 1741, in Vernon, *Vernon Papers*; *Original Papers Carthagena*, 139–40; and ADM 51/898, NA, Kew.

6. ADM 51/898, NA, Kew; and Crewe, *Yellow Jack and the Worm*, 12–14.

7. *Original Papers Carthagena*, 139–40; and Anonymous, *Second Genuine Speech*, 16.

8. Vernon to Newcastle, 26 April 1741, in Vernon, *Vernon Papers*, 226–31; Vernon to Wentworth, 22 May 1741, and Vernon to Trelawny, 23 May 1741, in *Original Papers Carthagena*, 126–28.

9. Councils of War, MS 40776, f. 128, British Library [BL], London; and Vernon to Newcastle, 18 June 1741, in *Original Papers Carthagena*, 146–49.

10. Cavelier Statement, in *Original Papers Cuba*, 16–18; and Plano del Castillo del Morro San Pedro delaroca, Santo Domingo, 124, Archivo General de Indias [AGI], Seville, Spain.

11. Vernon, *Vernon Papers*, 228.

12. *Original Papers Cuba*, 16–18; and Plano de la Costa de Santiago de Cuba, Santo Domingo, 417, AGI.

13. Vernon to Wentworth, 12 July 1741, and Drake Statement, 10 July 1741, in *Original Papers Cuba*, 12–16; and Wentworth to Vernon, 12 July 1741, in MS 40829, BL.

14. Trelawny to Wentworth, 24 June 1741, in CO 5/42, ff. 117–18, NA, Kew; and Trelawny to Vernon, 28 June 1741, in MS 40829, BL.

15. CO 5/42, f. 163, NA, Kew.

16. Vernon to Ogle, 18 July 1741, and Vernon to Newcastle, 29 July 1741, in *Original Papers Cuba*, 21–22 and 32–46; and ADM 51/4129, NA, Kew. Captain Washington was the older half-brother of George Washington.

17. Vernon to Wentworth, 19 July 1741, in *Original Papers Cuba*, 22–23.

18. Generals' Resolution, 19 July 1741, and Council of War, 20 July 1741, in CO 5/42, ff. 119–22, and Wentworth to Newcastle, 28 August 1741, in CO 5/42, ff. 68–75, NA, Kew.

19. CO 5/42, ff. 121-22, NA, Kew.

20. Vernon to Sturton, 24 July 1741, in *Original Papers Cuba*, 25–27.

21. Sturton Statement, 4 August 1741, and Vernon to Wentworth, 5 August 1741, and Lowther Statement, 14 August 1741, in *Original Papers Cuba*, 53–54, 193–98, and 210–11.

22. Wentworth to Vernon, 5 August 1741, in CO 5/42, ff. 127–28, NA, Kew; and Vernon to Wentworth, 6, 10, and 12 August 1741, and Caxigal to Guerra, 30 and 31 July and 2 August [NS] 1741, in *Original Papers Cuba*, 54–57, 62–65, and 199–201.

23. CO 5/42, ff. 131–34 and 139–48, NA, Kew.

24. Wentworth to Newcastle, 14 August 1741, CO 5/42, ff. 68–69, NA, Kew; and Vernon to Newcastle, 30 August 1741, and Lowther Report, 30 August 1741, in *Original Papers Cuba*, 80–9 and 211.

25. Historical Manuscripts Commission, *Duke of Buccleuch*, 1:397–98.

26. Towlard Statement, in CO 5/42, ff. 151–52, NA, Kew.

27. ADM 51/4129, NA, Kew; Historical Manuscripts Commission, *Duke of Buccleuch*, 397–98; and Wentworth to Newcastle, 5 October 1741, in CO 5/42, ff. 80–81, NA, Kew.

28. Wentworth to Vernon, 3 November 1741, in MS 40829, ff. 35–36, BL; Malie to Wentworth, 6 November 1741, in CO 5/42, ff. 161–62, NA, Kew; Vernon to Wentworth, 8, 23, and 24 November 1741, and Vernon to Newcastle, 1 and 10 December 1741, in *Original Papers Cuba*, 159–61, 169–73, and 181–86.

Chapter 18: Panama

1. ADM 51/4129, and 33/377, NA, Kew.

2. Newcastle to Vernon, 15 October 1741, in Vernon, *Vernon Papers*, 243–46; Vernon to Wentworth, 23 November 1741, in *Original Papers Cuba*, 169–71.

3. Wentworth to Couraud, 5 February 1742, in CO 5/42, ff. 112–14, NA, Kew; and Woodfine, "Friend to the General," 254–55.

4. Oglesby, "The British and Panama, 1742," 73–74; Towlard Deposition, 21 October 1741, in CO 5/42, ff. 151–52, NA, Kew; Wentworth to Vernon, 29 October 1741, in MS 40829, BL; and Councils, 8 January 1742, and Wentworth to Couraud, 5 February 1742, in CO 5/42, ff. 111–12 and 168–70, NA, Kew.

5. CO 5/42, ff. 168–70, NA, Kew.

6. "Methods Proposed to Every Article," MS 22680, ff. 3–4, BL.

7. The dialogue is paraphrased in CO 5/42, ff. 170–71, NA, Kew.

8. CO 5/42, f. 171, NA, Kew.

9. CO 5/42, ff. 173–77, and Wentworth to Newcastle, 11 February 1742, in CO 5/42, ff. 166–67, NA, Kew. See also Vernon to Wentworth, 12 January 1742, in *Original Papers Panama*, 6–8.

10. CO 5/42, f. 177, and Wentworth to Newcastle, 4 February 1742, in CO 5/42, ff. 164–67, NA, Kew.

11. ADM 51/309, NA, Kew; and Vernon to Dennis, 2 February 1742, in *Original Papers Panama*, 15–16.

12. *Original Papers Panama*, 16–17.

13. ADM 51/309, NA, Kew.

14. The records do not show whether Lowther took *Triton* into Porto Bello's harbor or he traveled the 5 miles overland.

15. ADM 36/1083 and 51/309, NA, Kew.

16. Woodfine, "Friend to the General," 258; and ADM 51/309, NA, Kew.

17. Disposition of Troops, 7 February 1742, and Wentworth to Newcastle, 11 February and 1 March 1742, in CO 5/42. ff. 164–67, 188–89, and 201–2, NA, Kew.

18. *Original Papers Panama*, 58–63; and Woodfine, "Friend to the General," 258.

19. ADM 36/1083 and 51/309, NA, Kew.

20. Woodfine, "Friend to the General," 257–58.

21. Woodfine, "Friend to the General," 258; and Oglesby, "The British and Panama, 1742," 75.

22. Vernon to Ogle, 13 March 1742, and Vernon to Newcastle, 15 March 1742, and Vernon to Wentworth, 25 March 1742, in *Original Papers Panama*, 61–68.

23. ADM 51/4129 and 51/615, NA, Kew.

24. ADM 51/615, NA, Kew.

25. ADM 51/4129, NA, Kew; and *Original Papers Panama*, 69–70.

26. Wentworth to Vernon, 27 March 1742, in CO 5/42, ff. 211–12, NA, Kew.

27. Vernon to Wentworth, 27 March 1742, in *Original Papers Panama*, 71.

28. Woodfine, "Friend to the General," 259–60.

29. ADM 51/309, NA, Kew; and Vernon to Newcastle, 31 March 1742, in *Original Papers Panama*, 74–79.

30. Oglesby, "The British and Panama, 1742," 75–76; Harding, *Amphibious Warfare*, 143; and Beatson, *Naval and Military Memoirs*, 136.

31. ADM 51/4129, NA, Kew; *Original Papers Panama*, 74–79; Oglesby, "The British and Panama, 1742," 76; Woodfine, "Friend to the General," 260; and Harding, *Amphibious Warfare*, 143.

32. Beatson, *Naval and Military Memoirs*, 139.

33. The interaction between Lowther and Vernon can be deduced from Woodfine, "Friend to the General," 260.

34. Resolution, and Wentworth to Newcastle, 31 March 1742, in CO 5/42, ff. 207–10, NA, Kew; and Woodfine, "Friend to the General," 261–62.

35. Vernon to Dennis and Vernon to Lowther, 13 April 1742, in *Original Papers Panama*, 91–93; and ADM 51/309, and 51/4129, NA, Kew.

Chapter 19: Return to Britain

1. ADM 51/309, NA, Kew.

2. ADM 51/309, NA, Kew; and Vernon to Dennis, 6 July 1742, in *Original Papers Panama*, 118–19.

3. ADM 51/309, NA, Kew; and Vernon to Newcastle, 19 May 1742, in *Original Papers Panama*, 101–03.

4. CO 5/42, ff. 237–38, NA, Kew.

5. CO 5/42, f. 238, NA, Kew; and Vernon to Newcastle, 30 June 1742, and Vernon to Dennis, 3 July 1742, in *Original Papers Panama*, 112–18.

6. Vernon to Newcastle, 27 April 1742, in *Original Papers Panama*, 94–100; and Wentworth to Couraud, 9 August 1742, in CO 5/42, ff. 270–1, NA, Kew.

7. ADM 51/309, NA, Kew.

8. ADM 51/4129, NA, Kew; and Harding, *Amphibious Warfare*, 148.

9. ADM 33/378 and ADM 36/653, NA, Kew; Lowther Journal, ADM L/C/255, NMM, Greenwich; and Wentworth to Newcastle, 7 January 1743, in CO 5/42, ff. 287–88, NA, Kew.

10. Navy Board Replies [ADM B]/123, f. 197, and ADM B/124, f. 210, NMM, Greenwich; Rodger, *Command of the Ocean*, 622–24; and Will of George Lowther, PROB 11/750/312, ff. 146–47, NA, Kew.

11. ADM L/C/255, NMM, Greenwich.

12. ADM 1/233, Ogle Part 2, ff. 260–63, 267–70, and 287, NA, Kew.

13. ADM 33/378 and 33/401, and ADM 1/233, Davers, 5 August 1745, ff. 655–59, and ADM 51/742, NA, Kew.

14. ADM 8/14 and 51/742, NA, Kew.

15. ADM B/142, f. 172, NMM, Greenwich.

16. Laughton, "Vernon, Edward (1684–1757)," in *Dictionary of National Biography*.

17. Will of George Lowther, PROB 11/750/312, ff. 146–47, NA, Kew.

18. Church of England, Baptisms, Marriages, and Burials, 1538–1812, ref no. P87/JS/004, LMA. Online, Ancestry.com.

Appendix

1. *Boston News Letter*, April 22 and May 7, 1722.

2. T 70/1446, NA, Kew.

3. CO 152/14, NA, Kew.

4. CO 28/18, NA, Kew.

5. Dow and Edmonds, *Pirates of the New England Coast*, 137.

6. *Boston News-Letter*, August 22 and September 19, 1723.

7. Gibbs, *On the Account*, 161.

8. *Boston News-Letter*, June 18, 1722; and *Daily Courant*, August 8, 1722.

BIBLIOGRAPHY

Archival sources

Archivo General de Indias, Seville, Spain [AGI]: Santo Domingo.

Archivo General de Simancas, Valladolid, Spain [AGS]: Estado, Marina:

> Garganta, Juan Francisco. *Relacion de lo acaecido desde el día 26 de noviembre de 1739 hasta 4 de diciembre.*

British Library, London [BL]: Journal of Sir John Norris; Councils of War.

Library of Congress, Washington, DC [LOC]: Geography & Map Division.

London Metropolitan Archives [LMA].

National Archives, Kew, London [NA]:

> National Archives, Kew, London [NA]:
>
>> Admiralty Records [ADM]: List Books, Pay, Muster, Captains' Logs, Journals.
>>
>> Colonial Office Papers [CO]: Expedition to Carthagena [5/42], Barbados [28], Leeward Islands [152], Petition of Lowther and Massey, 22 July 1721, EXT 1/261, f. 3.
>>
>> High Court of the Admiralty [HCA]: Deposition of Alexander Thompson, 2March 1722, HCA 1/55, ff. 23–24..
>
> Probate Records [PROB]:
>
>> Will of Peter Grahame, PROB 11/604/239; Will of Johannis Gwatkin, PROB 11/587/76; Will of George Lowther, PROB 11/750/312, ff. 146–47; Will of Thomas Whitney, PROB 11/628/11.
>
> Treasury [T]: Royal African Company Records.
>
> State Papers [SP]: Domestic, Letters and Papers, Naval.
>
> War Office Records [WO].

National Maritime Museum, Greenwich, UK [NMM]:

> Lieutenants' Logs [ADM L].
>
> Navy Board Replies [ADM B].

Theses and dissertations

Bertrand, Alicia Marie. "The Downfall of the Royal African Company on the African Atlantic Coast in the 1720s." Master's thesis, Trent University, October 2011.

Evans, Amanda Michelle. "Institutionalized Piracy and the Development of the Jamaica Sloop, 1630–1743." Master's thesis, Florida State University, 2005.

Johnson, Victoria Stapells. "Corsairs of Santo Domingo: A Socio-economic Study, 1718–1779." Master's thesis, University of Ottawa, 1985.

Books

Atkins, John. *A Voyage to Guinea, Brasil, and the West-Indies; in His Majesty's Ships, the Swallow and Weymouth*. London: Ward and Chandler, 1737.

Azurara, Gomes Eannes de. *The Chronicle of the Discovery and Conquest of Guinea*. Translated by Charles Raymond Beazley and Edgar Prestage. Vol. 1. New York: Burt Franklin, ca. 1966.

Baer, Joel H., ed. *British Piracy in the Golden Age: History and Interpretation, 1660–1730*. 4 vols. London: Pickering & Chatto, 2007.

Barnard, John. *Ashton's Memorial*. Boston: Samuel Gerrish, 1725.

Beatson, Robert. *Naval and Military Memoirs of Great Britain from 1727 to 1783*. Vol. 1. London: Longman Hurst, 1804.

Blunt, Edward M. *The American Coast Pilot*. New York: E. & G. W. Blunt, 1850.

Breverton, Terry. *The Pirate Handbook: A Dictionary of Pirate Terms and Places*. St. Athan, UK: Wales Books, 2004.

Calendar of State Papers: Colonial, America and West Indies. 45 vols. London, 1934.

Cannon, Richard. *Historical Record of the Thirty-Fourth, or the Cumberland Regiment of Foot*. London: Parker, Furnivall & Parker, 1844.

Cerda Crespo, Jorge. *Conflictos Coloniales: La Guerra de los Nueve Años, 1739–1748*. San Vicente del Raspeig, Spain: Publicaciones Universidad de Alicante, 2010.

Chapman, Craig S. *Disaster on the Spanish Main: The Tragic British-American Expedition to the West Indies during the War of Jenkins' Ear*. Lincoln, NE: Potomac Books, 2021.

Chappelle, Howard I. *The History of American Sailing Ships*. New York: Bonanza Books, 1935.

Clifford, Barry, and Paul Perry. *Expedition Whydah*. New York: HarperCollins, 1999.

Colledge, J. J., and Ben Warlow. *Ships of the Royal Navy*. London: Chatham, 2006.

Colonial Society of Massachusetts. *Publications*. Vol. 34. Boston: Merrymount, 1943.

Commissioners of the Admiralty. *Manual of Seamanship*. Vol. 1. London: Eyre & Spottiswoode, 1915.

Cordingly, David. *Under the Black Flag: The Romance and the Reality of Life among the Pirates*. New York: Random House, 2006.

Craton, Michael. *Founded upon the Seas: A History of the Cayman Islands and Their People*. Kingston, Jamaica: Ian Randle, 2003.

Cremer, John. *Ramblin' Jack: The Journal of Captain John Cremer (1700–1774)*. Edited by R. Reynell Bellamy. London: Jonathan Cape, 1939.

Davies, K. G. *The Royal African Company*. London: Longmans Green, 1957.

Dolin, Eric Jay. *Black Flags, Blue Waters: The Epic History of America's Most Notorious Pirates*. New York: Liveright, 2018.

Donnithorne, Christopher, ed. *Warrant Officers of the Royal Navy, 1695 to 1751*. Vol. 2. Kew, UK: List and Index Society, 2013.

Dow, George Francis, and John Henry Edmonds. *The Pirates of the New England Coast, 1630–1730*. Salem, MA: Marine Research Society, 1923.

Downey, Christopher Byrd. *Charleston and the Golden Age of Piracy*. Charleston, SC: History Press, 2013.

Earle, Peter. *Sailors: English Merchant Seamen, 1650–1775*. London: Methuen, 1998.

Falconbridge, Alexander. *An Account of the Slave Trade on the Coast of Africa*. London: J. Phillips & George Yard, 1788.

Falconer, William. *An Universal Dictionary of the Marine*. London: Cadell, 1869. Online at www.gutenberg.org/files/57705/57705-0.txt.

Finamore, Daniel. "A Mariner's Utopia: Pirates and Logwood in the Bay of Honduras." In *X Marks the Spot: The Archaeology of Piracy*. Edited by Russell K. Skowronek and Charles R. Ewen. Gainesville: University Press of Florida, 2006.

Flemming, Gregory N. *At the Point of a Cutlass: The Pirate Capture, Bold Escape & Lonely Exile of Philip Ashton*. Lebanon, NH: ForeEdge, 2014.

Ford, Douglas. *Admiral Vernon and the Navy: A Memoir and Vindication*. London: Fisher, 1907.

Fox, E. T., ed. *Pirates in Their Own Words*. Fox Historical, 2014.

Gibbs, Joseph. *On the Account in the "Golden Age": Piracy and the Americas, 1670–1726*. Portland, OR: Sussex Academic, 2014.

Gray, J. M. *A History of the Gambia*. New York: Barnes & Noble, 1966.

Harding, Richard. *Amphibious Warfare in the Eighteenth Century: The British Expedition to the West Indies, 1740–1742*. Woodbridge, UK: Royal Historical Society and Boydell, 1991.

Hayward, Arthur L., ed. *Lives of the Most Remarkable Criminals*. New York: Dodd Mead, 1927.

Historical Manuscripts Commission. *Report on the Manuscripts of the Duke of Buccleuch and Queensbury Preserved at Montagu House, Whitehall*. Vol. 1. London: Eyre and Spottiswoode, 1899.

Hughson, Shirley Carter. *The Carolina Pirates and Colonial Commerce*. Baltimore: Johns Hopkins University Press, 1894.

Jeffreys, Thomas. *The West-India Atlas*. London: Robert Sayer and John Bennett, 1775.

Johnson, Charles. *A General History of the Pyrates*. Vol. 1. London: T. Woodward, 1726.

Kemp, Peter. *The British Sailor: A Social History of the Lower Deck*. London: J. M. Dent & Sons, 1970.

Konstam, Angus. *The Pirate Ship, 1630–1730*. New York: Osprey, 2003.

Laughton, John Knox. "Vernon, Edward (1684–1757)." In *Dictionary of National Biography*. Vol. 58, 257–72. London: Smith & Elder, 1899.

Lavery, Brian. *The Ship of the Line*. 2 vols. Annapolis, MD: Naval Institute Press, 1983.

Leach, John. *Map of the River Gambra from Its Mouth to Eropina*. 1732.

Leslie, Charles. *A New History of Jamaica, from the Earliest Accounts to the Taking of Porto Bello by Vice-Admiral Vernon*. London: J. Hodges, 1740.

Little, Benerson. *The Sea Rover's Practice: Pirate Tactics and Techniques, 1630–1730*. Dulles, VA: Potomac Books, 2005.

Lloyd, Christopher. *The British Seaman, 1200–1860: A Social Survey*. Rutherford, NJ: Fairleigh Dickinson University Press, 1970.

Lloyd, Christopher, and Jack L. S. Coulter. *Medicine and the Navy, 1200–1900*. Vol. 3, *1714–1815*. London: E. & S. Livingstone, 1961.

Mather, Cotton. *Useful Remarks: An Essay upon Remarkables in the Way of Wicked Men*. New London, CT: T. Green, 1723.

McBride, J. David. "Contraband Traders, Lawless Vagabonds, and the British Settlement and Occupation of Roatan, Bay Islands, Honduras." In *X Marks the Spot: The Archaeology of Piracy*. Edited by Russell K. Skowronek and Charles R. Ewen. Gainesville: University Press of Florida, 2006.

Melville, Lewis. *Lady Mary Wortley Montagu: Her Life and Letters (1689–1762)*. Boston: Houghton Mifflin, 1925. Online at www.gutenberg. org/cache/epub/10590/pg10590-images.

Membrillo Becerra, Francisco Javier. *La Batalla de Cartagena de Indias*. Seville, Spain: Caligrama, 2017.

Original Papers Relating to the Expedition to Carthagena. London: M. Cooper, 1744.

Original Papers Relating to the Expedition to Panama. London: M. Cooper, 1744.

Original Papers Relating to the Expedition to the Island of Cuba. London: M. Cooper, 1744.

Padfield, Peter. *Guns at Sea*. London: Hugh Evelyn, 1973.

Pappalardo, Bruno. *Royal Navy Lieutenants' Passing Certificates (1691–1902)*. Part 2 (K–Z). Kew, UK: List and Index Society, 2001.

Pares, Richard. *War and Trade in the West Indies: 1739–1763*. London: Frank Cass, 1963.

Pennell, C. R., ed. *Bandits at Sea: A Pirates Reader*. New York: New York University Press, 2001.

Pettigrew, William A. *Freedom's Debt: The Royal African Company and the Politics of the Atlantic Slave Trade, 1672–1752*. Chapel Hill: University of North Carolina Press, 2013.

Rediker, Marcus. *Between the Devil and the Deep Blue Sea: Merchant Seamen, Pirates, and the Anglo-American Maritime World, 1700–1750*. New York: Cambridge University Press, 1987.

Richmond, Herbert W. *The Navy in the War of 1739–48*. Vol. 1. Aldershot, UK: Gregg Revivals, 1993.

Rodger, N. A. M. *The Command of the Ocean: A Naval History of Britain, 1649–1815*. London: Penguin, 2004.

Royal African Company. *A Particular Evaluation of the Company's Forts, Castles, and Factories in Africa. As the Same Was Made Out in 1713*. N.p., n.d.

Sanborn, Edwin D. *History of New Hampshire, from Its First Discovery to the Year 1830*. Manchester, NH: Clarke, 1875.

Sanders, Richard. *If a Pirate I Must Be . . . The True Story of "Black Bart," King of the Caribbean Pirates*. New York: Fall River, 2007.

Schomberg, Isaac. *Naval Chronology*. Vol. 4. London: T. Edgerton, 1802.

A Second Genuine Speech, Deliver'd by Adm . . . l V . . . n, on Board the Carolina, to the Officers of the Navy, Immediately after the Salley from Fort St. Lazara. London: T. Cooper, 1741.

A Select and Impartial Account of the Lives, Behavior and Dying Words, of the Most Remarkable Convicts. Vol. 1. London: J. Applebee, 1760.

Skowronek, Russell K., and Charles R. Ewen, eds. *X Marks the Spot: The Archaeology of Piracy*. Gainesville: University Press of Florida, 2006.

Smith, William. *Thirty Different Drafts of Guinea*. London, 1727.

Snow, Edward Rowe. *Pirates and Buccaneers of the Atlantic Coast*. Boston: Yankee, 1944.

Starkey, David J., E. S. van Eyck van Heslinga, and J. A. de Moor, eds. *Pirates and Privateers: New Perspectives on the War on Trade in the Eighteenth and Nineteenth Centuries*. Exeter, UK: Exeter, 1997.

Stein, Barbara H., and Stanley J. Stein. *Silver, Trade, and War: Spain and America in the Making of Early Modern Europe*. Baltimore: Johns Hopkins University Press, 2000.

Syrett, David, and R. L. DiNardo, eds. *The Commissioned Sea Officers of the Royal Navy, 1660–1815*. Aldershot, UK: Navy Records Society, 1994.

Travers, Len. *The Notorious Edward Low: Pursuing the Last Great Villain of Piracy's Golden Age*. Yardley, PA: Westholme, 2023.

Tucker, Spencer. *Arming the Fleet: US Navy Ordnance in the Muzzle-Loading Era*. Annapolis, MD: Naval Institute Press, 1989.

United Kingdom. *An Act for the More Effectual Suppressing of Piracy, 1721*. 8 George I, chap. 24. London: Baskett, 1722.

US Naval Oceanographic Office. *Sailing Directions for the South Coast of England*. Washington, DC: US Government Printing Office, 1952.

Updike, Wilkins. *Memoirs of the Rhode Island Bar*. Boston: Thomas H. Webb, 1842.

Uring, Nathaniel. *A History of the Voyages and Travels of Capt. Nathaniel Uring, with a New Draught of the Bay of Honduras*. London: Clarke, 1749.

Vernon, Edward. *The Vernon Papers*. Edited by B. McL. Ranft. Aldershot, UK: Navy Records Society, 1958.

Winfield, Rif. *British Warships in the Age of Sail, 1603–1704: Design, Construction, Careers and Fates*. Barnsley, UK: Seaforth, 2009.

Woodard, Colin. *The Republic of Pirates*. New York: Mariner Books, 2015.

Woodward, Joshua. "The Seaman's Monitor." In *British Piracy in the Golden Age: History and Interpretation, 1660–1730*. Vol. 4. Edited by Joel H. Baer. London: Pickering & Chatto, 2007.

Newspapers

American Weekly Mercury (Philadelphia).

Applebee's Original Weekly Journal (London).

Boston News-Letter.

British Journal (London).

Caledonian Mercury (Edinburgh).

Daily Courant (London).

Daily Journal (London).

Daily Post (London).

Gentleman's Magazine (1731–43).

London Journal.

New England Courant (Boston).

Post Boy (London).

Stamford Mercury (Stamford, UK).

Universal Journal (London).

Weekly Journal or British Gazetteer (London).

Weekly Journal or Saturday's Post (London).

Weekly Packet (London).

Periodicals

Brown, Vera Lee. "The South Sea Company and Contraband Trade." *American Historical Review* 31, no. 4 (July 1926): 661–78.

Gibbs, Joseph. "The Brevity and Severity of 'Golden Age' Piracy Trials." *International Journal of Maritime History* 31, no. 4 (November 2019): 729–86.

———. "John Massey, George Lowther, and the Taking of the *Gambia Castle*, 1721." *International Journal of Maritime History* 28, no. 3 (August 2016): 461–79.

Nelson, George H. "Contraband Trade under the Asiento, 1730–1739." *American Historical Review* 50, no. 1 (October 1945): 55–67.

Oglesby, J. C. M. "The British and Panama, 1742." *Mariner's Mirror* 58 (1972): 71–79.

Scelle, Georges. "The Slave-Trade in the Spanish Colonies of America: The Asiento." *American Journal of International Law* 4, no. 3 (July 1910): 612–61.

Selcraig, Bruce. "The Real Robinson Crusoe." *Smithsonian* 36, no. 4 (July 2005): 82.

Southorn, Thomas. "The Gambia: The Earliest British Settlement in West Africa." *Journal of the Royal Society of Arts* 91, no. 4647 (September 1943): 529–39.

Woodfine, Philip. "A Friend to the General: Extracts from the Journal of Major George Lestanquet, September 14th, 1741, to April 14th 1742." *Journal of the Society for Army Historical Research* 71, nos. 285, 286, and 288 (1993): 26–41, 127–32, and 253–65.

Online sources

Espenak, Fred. "Six Millennium Catalog of Phases of the Moon." September 5, 2020. astropixels.com/ephemeris/phasescat/phasescat.

Historic UK, *History Magazine* online. www.historic-uk.com/HistoryUK.

"London Lives 1690 to 1800: Crime, Poverty and Social Policy in the Metropolis." www.londonlives.org/.

National Geospatial-Intelligence Agency. "Pilot Charts of the North Atlantic." May 31, 2018. msi.nga.mil/Publications/APC.

Paul, Helen J. "The 'South Sea Bubble,' 1720." *European History Online*, July 1, 2022. ieg-ego.eu/en/threads/european-media/europeanmedia-events/helen-j-paul-the-south-sea-bubble-1720.

INDEX

Index